FIRE
AND
ROSES

SUNY Series,
Postmodern Culture

Joseph Natoli, Editor

FIRE
AND
ROSES

Postmodernity and the Thought of the Body

Carl A. Raschke

STATE UNIVERSITY OF NEW YORK PRESS

Production by Ruth Fisher
Marketing by Fran Keneston

Published by
State University of New York Press, Albany

© 1996 State University of New York

For information, address the State University of New York Press, State University Plaza, Albany, NY 12246

Library of Congress Cataloging-in-Publication Data
Raschke, Carl A.
  Fire and roses : postmodernity and the thought of the body / Carl A. Raschke.
    p. cm. — (SUNY series, postmodern culture)
  Includes bibliographical references and index.
  ISBN 0-7914-2729-3. — ISBN 0-7914-2730-7 (pbk.)
  1. Postmodernism. 2. Postmodernism—Religious aspects. 3. Body, Human. 4. Body, Human—Religious aspects. 1. Title. II. Series: SUNY series in postmodern culture.
B831.2.R37 1996
128—dc20   95-4242
                                                                   CIP

10 9 8 7 6 5 4 3 2 1

CONTENTS

PREFACE

Condorcet, as a victim of the Terror awaiting the guillotine, experienced the meaning of the "Age of Reason" that he formalized into his now famous prophecy of modernity. The reality of the rational, he pronounced in *The Progress of the Human Mind,* resides in "the history of man" as "an uninterrupted chain of facts and observations," in a word, as a nexus of unbroken signification that retrogresses endlessly away from the phenomenal sensation of the present—the transcendental unity of "aesthesis"—toward the epochal representation of collective memory itself. The Enlightenment project commences with the imagination of a fantastic totality just prior to a beheading, a Cartesian glimpse into the unity of all consciousness and everything "historical" as the metaphysical condition of one's own death. If we had not already been exposed to the wintry critiques of Nietzsche, it would be possible to construe the birth of modernism as comical. In the case of Condorcet, we acquire instead a profound feeling for what Nietzsche himself regarded as the genius of the philosophical; that is, the tragical.

It is not that both philosophical and theological thinking today has forgotten to think the body. One can never forget what one has never committed to memory. Modernism, which may be called *the romance of the subject,* remains intelligible only if we can empathize with Condorcet, if we can visualize him in his fetid and fear-scoured prison cell on the eve of his demise. The expansion of the *cogito* into the Hegelian "concept" has its genesis in the confrontation between the body in its deniable self-existence and the scene where the sound of the falling blade augurs the immensity of human finitude itself. Thus, the discourse of the "postmodern" suggests a realization of such an irresolvable lesion, the illumined and "tragic" inference that philosophical speculation is routinely conditioned by the footfalls of the executioner in the corridor. Postmodernity, in contradistinction to modernism, is immanently *inscribed in the thought of the body.* One can never, of course, name the "unthought" within the spectral architectonic of historical reason, even if its very "unthinkability" is predicated upon the invisibility of embodiment. The thought of the body raises the heftier possibility of a postrepresentational analytic of signifying praxis itself, of the "infrahistorical" chain of sign-actions and undecoded intentions that we know as *will* and *desire*.

In that sense we are on the threshold of a "theological think-ing" that comprehends the sort of postmodern religiosity that has been dogmatically disseminated and popularized as "archetypal psychology," as the symbolism of the underworld, of satyrs below and gods within. Such a psychology contains within itself a strange sort of demonism that seeks to sacralize the inherently elusive and fragmented. The illusion of "wholeness" is a dangerous, modernist myth that masks the dynamism of the inchoate it rages to total-ize. In that sense all "gods of the New Age" must remain crazed and caged beasts. But a theological thinking that, like Nietzsche's Zarathustra, must give up its light and "go under" understands the shades of the nether realm for what they precisely are—move-ments of signifying presence that are "somatically" coded in such a way that they can be reflected into the richer semiology of Godhead.

Theological thinking is always an exegesis of the Johannine prologue. Postmodernity takes us beyond the "metaphysical" only because it immerses us in the signs of "physis," which is signifi-cation at its origin. The Cross is a signature of brokenness only because it points to the full flowering of the unascetic beauty of the body in its artistic coming to presence—the disclosure of the rose, the eschaton. The so-called rosy cross has for too long been an occult symbol that has never been uncovered for what it actu-ally means, the linking of two substances, one historical, the other the "end of history." The unity of the fire and the rose is the unity of both "religious thought" and thought itself, which cannot be separated from *re-ligio,* a "linking back" to an unrecoverable, and hence "transcendent," moment of embarkation.

This work is not for the prosaic, nor for the lethal pragmatists and "clarifiers" of sentences. The body is incapable of clarifica-tion—hence, the faith in its resurrection. It marks not only the "end of theology," but the end of something that could never claim legitimacy as a "discipline" and a "method," not even as a genealogy in the Nietzschean sense. We are talking, of course, about the "study of religion," religious studies, an addiction to the representational systems of sacred desire without any comprehen-sion of their Dionysian genealogy. It is no longer possible to "study" religion. We must bring it to presence in the same way that Nietzsche himself saw the madman's prophecy of God's death as the way to overcoming nihilism. We must embrace it, and dance arm in arm with it.

Let us call what we have in mind *The Faustian Project*. It should be added that, if one understands Goethe correctly, Faust is the last of the great Christian heroes, the sign of overcoming, the sentinel of the *parousia*.

In completing this book I am indebted to friends, loved ones, and students. I would like to thank the University of Denver for giving me a sabbatical to finish the last chapters of the manuscript, to Diane Macdonald whose feminist and "transgressive" readings of the many of the same materials always challenged me to explore new pathways, to John "Leo" Meeks for the final editing, to Dwight Smith for some provocative suggestions, to Pam Morrow for some reflections on the rhythms of the dancer, to Erik for the thought of overcoming, to Susan for the vision of the rose and who, in fact, did "tell me about the fire."

We conclude with a line from Goethe: *es bildet ein Talent sich in der stille, sich ein Charakter in dem Strom der Welt.*

ACKNOWLEDGMENTS

The entirety of chapter 1 first appeared as "Fire and Roses: Toward Authentic Post-Modern Religious Thinking" in the winter 1991 edition of the *Journal of the American Academy of Religion*.

A version of chapter 4 first appeared as "Jacques Lacan and the Magic of Desire: A Post-Structuralist Subscript" in Edith Wyschogrod, David, Crownfield, and Carl Raschke, *Lacan and Theological Discourse* (Albany NY: State University of New York Press, 1989).

A version of chapter 6 first appeared as the article "The Deconstructive Imagination: A Response to Mark Taylor"—in the winter 1988 edition of *Religion in Intellectual Life*.

Section I

The Body Erotic

If we were to make completely explicit the architecture of the human body, its ontological framework and how it sees itself, we would see that the structure of its mute world is such that all possibilities of language are already given in it. . . .

Maurice Merleau-Ponty, *The Visible and the Invisible*

Chapter 1

Fire and Roses

Down the passage we did not take
Toward the door we never opened
Into the rose-garden . . .

T. S. Eliot, "Burnt Norton"

At the conclusion of Umberto Eco's *The Name of the Rose*—considered by many critics one of the greatest of the so-called postmodern novels—what has proceeded all along as a murder mystery suddenly turns into a revelation concerning workings of language and the adventure of signs.

The "discovery" of the perpetrator of a string of baffling, and heinous, crimes inside a late Medieval abbey becomes the occasion for what today might be termed a "deconstructive" literary covert operation, indeed, the deconstruction of the literary itself. The murders in the monastery turn out to be the artifice of a fanatical friar, Jorge, who has connived and conspired to protect a mysterious book in the secret chambers of the abbey. The "book", of course, is Aristotle's legendary "lost" treatise on laughter.

Jorge defends his crimes by arguing that the opening of such a book to the learned would transvalue all the values of classical learning and Christian civilization. It would unleash the spirit of levity. In addition, reading the book would initiate the process of destruction for the entire metaphysical architectonic upon which holy "faith" has been erected as the capstone. "I have been the hand of God," protests Jorge to his inquisitor William of Baskerville. Jorge insists that the hand of God must conceal, and that "there are boundaries beyond which" the probe of language "is not

1

permitted to go." But William replies: "God created the monsters, too. And you. And He wants everything to be spoken of."[1]

Saying the unsaid, reaching toward the unreachable, naming the unnamed name—all signified by the rose—is literally "the end of the book." *The Name of the Rose* concludes with a fire immolating the monastery and its expansive library. We may read into the fire an eschatological event—the apocalyptic capsizing of a metaphysical era in which God's secrets have remained closeted in forbidden books. The ghastly spectacle of David Koresh's Ranch Apocalypse engulfed in flames in Waco, Texas, during the spring of 1993—now etched in the public imagination as a kind of grandiose bonfire of the vanities charring "secular" theories of religion—has provided some recent media panache to such "archtypal" drama. From a philosophical point of view, "naming" the rose is at the same time its dissolution; a semantic displacement of the signified by the act of signification. Signification is disruption, a violation of context, a transgression.

The term *postmodern* itself has come to serve of late as a kind of clandestine intrusion into the kingdom of signification. The word concomitantly baffles, bedazzles, and enrages—principally because it neither denotes nor intimates anything other than an incursion across the borderland of sensibility. The postmodern is everything that cannot be compressed in the term *modern*. Heidegger is generally regarded as the first postmodern thinker because of his declarations about "overcoming" metaphysics and the "end" of philosophy. At the "semiotic" level—that is, in the distinctive space where language performs no longer as code or syntax but as a skein of tracings, as the movement of complex and ephemeral modules of signification that cannot be repeated or circumscribed—so-called postmodernity means much more than some ill-defined historical periodization.

Postmodernity amounts to a redescription of logic as "aesthetics," of message as medium, of communication as dramatics, of truth as embodiment. Postmodernity is the transcendence, "overcoming," of all archaic or "legendary" orders of significance that have underwritten cultural discourse. Understood superficially, the postmodern represents a transition from the highly formalized, "modern," understanding of things to the "carnival" of popular culture. But this defection is less a revolution in taste than a reappropriation of the theory of meaning itself. The idea rebounds upon what Eco in one of his semiotic treatises refers to as *carnivalization*. The study of carnivals—Brazil's *escloa de samba*, New Orleans *Mardi Gras*, the ancient Roman *saturnalia*—offers a glimpse into the origin of language itself as an assault upon the hegemony of silence. "Carnival," says Eco, "can exist only as *authorized* transgression."[2] With its ornate pageantry of music and sensual dancing, the exhibition of costume and color, the exposure of bodies, the enactment of folk drama, "carnival" creates a "scene" in which the achievement of the "signifier" no longer depends on language as social interaction, but emerges through the very distention of the grammar of culture. The inquiry into popular culture—at least from the standpoint of formal semantics—has always been a "dangerous liaison."

The term *postmodernism* has burgeoned, crowded, and suffused academic conversation during the last decade like so much lush, green Carolina Kudzu. Once strange and unfamiliar, if not disarming, locutions like *subtext, discursivity, metanarrative,* and *alterity* have become their own sort of patois within the humanities. It is as though a philosophical irredentism had been set in motion, dislodging the once seemingly immovable sovereignty of Germanic thought in a more than century-long "Franco-Prussian" war of methods, phraseologies, and notions.

Gallic preciosity and rhetorical sportiveness appear to have triumphed over Teutonic global rationality or any probing into what Hegel termed the *depths of Spirit.* The distinction, as well as the antagonism, can be espied in Jurgen Habermas's waspish dismissal of Derrida as a *nicht argumentationsfreudiger Philosoph;* literally, a "philosopher who does not enjoy argumentation."[3] Postmodern works of scholarship, however, have deliberately avoided "argumentation," because they are regalia of a "style" more than a discipline. In this respect postmodern reflection—particularly the philosophical and theological kind—stands in relationship to its earlier twentieth century antecedents as Renaissance humanism compared with earlier religious scholasticism. In the "humanism" of the *quattrocento,* rhetoric supplanted Aristotelian logic, eloquence displaced inference, the performative took precedence over the referential. Indeed, it is the *power of performance* that appears to have emerged as the common denominator among the variegated "postmodernisms" of art, philosophy, theology, textual criticism, and the like.

When Derrida in *Of Grammatology* proclaimed the end of the "age of the sign," he most likely did not intend to claim that the event of signification was now impossible. But Derridean "deconstruction," once shorn of its metonymic excesses and its tropic diffusions, is precisely the philosophical reversal of Roland Barthes's semiotics of the everyday. The point can be easily overlooked, inasmuch as Barthes's recognition that *to signify* means to *disconnect* the token from the object in generation of a sign-system anticipates the "deconstructive" view that textuality is inseparable from temporality, from the self-erasure of language as action. The sometimes maddening penchant of "deconstructionists" for word-games and punning bespeaks an unself-conscious mimesis of the semiotic enterprise. Barthes's semiosis of reading, encapsulated in the slogan the "pleasure of the text," would appear to be the schema for Derrida's "supplement" of writing. Barthes's *jouissance* as a sense of the libidinous freedom and *revelatory* aesthetics of sign-production, nonetheless, is transfigured by Derrida into a "joyless" chain of paralogisms, which turn out to be transgressions without conquests, wounds without healings, lesions without disclosures. The irony is captured in Derrida's own "parapractical" rereading of Heidegger's discussion of the "work of art." Whereas for Heidegger Van Gogh's peasant shoes can be "seen" in terms of an ontological manifestation, a "worlding," through the pen of Derrida they become the utter negativity of difference—the "disparity of the pair," a "separateness" that is "in itself, in the word, in the letter, in the pair."[4]

Derrida himself has failed to intuit his own nihilism, the nihilism of an ongoing textual commentary no longer capable of signification. Instead Derrida has elected to mythify his own "total eclipse" of the power of signs in terms of the chaos mother, the Great Kali, which abrogates even the archetypal form of "female" in the primal and eternal recurrence of darkness. "No woman or trace of woman . . . save the mother, that's understood. . . . Everything comes back to her, beginning with life."[5] But any mythopoesis of life is also a mask for death, as Jean-Francois Lyotard, today's pre-eminent philosopher of *postmodern culture,* has reminded us. The "post-modern" is, he says, "that which searches for new presentations, not in order to enjoy them but in order to impart a stronger sense of the unpresentable."[6] In a later work Lyotard tells us the "unpresentable" is "Auschwitz." It is the "differend" of the silent victims.[7] The differend as the bare negativity of concealed violence constitutes the ultimate limits of a logocentric universe. It is, to employ Edith Wyschogrod's terminology, "spirit in ashes."[8]

The differend is the antonym of the referent; but is also something much more, and far stronger, than what Paul Ricoeur and others have termed the *plurisignificative,* the unlimited semiosis that characterizes fluid and allusive language.[9] The differend is the pure unvocalizable that quivers not only at the boundaries of discourse, but at the fringes of existence. Like the Heideggerian *nihil,* Lyotard's *differend* is both limit and horizon. It is the "line" circumscribing signification beyond which a new and more fundamental occasion for "semiophany" becomes possible. The end of the age of the sign, disclosed in the *differend,* in the silence, is at the same time an overture to what is genuinely postmodern, understood at last as a total presence, an eschatological fullness, a *parousia*—after the fashion of Heidegger—of the very sign-universe.

The problem with the recent stampede into postmodern discourse throughout the study of religion and in religious thought, however, is that its "semiotic" overtones are too often overlooked. The fascination with that which we may broadly call *deconstruction* has led ironically to what might be dubbed an old school or "late" modernist cast of thought that has wrongly been described as postmodern. The expressions *modernism* and *postmodernism* were originally contrived to identify styles and trends in the arts and architecture. *Modernism* refers to a preoccupation with the conditions of aesthetic creativity as well as the problem of composition, contrasting with an interest in artistic content and the methods of representation. The antirepresentationalism and extreme textualism of putative postmodern philosophers and critics amounts, in fact, to a recycling of earlier modernist concerns under the aegis of the humanities, compelled by many of the same attitudes that captivated visual artists in the early years of this century. The "painterly" self-scrutiny of the modern artist—the Fauvist's precision with color, the minimalist's reduction of the worm to shapes and surfaces—is transposed into the grammatology of the text.

Authentic postmodernism, on the other hand, involves a recovery of the richness of "natural" signifiers, if not a return to the naturalism or realism of the late classical era. In art so-called postmodernism has actually meant a "return to content," as Charles Jencks has so aptly put it, along with a rediscovery of "historical continuum and the relation between past and present." This renaissance of classical figuration, proportionality, and stylized elegance has at the same time taken place within the modernist setting of cultural pluralism and representational heterogeneity, so that postmodernism generates narratives without plots as part of world of "divergent significations" compelling "multiple readings" of the familiar.[10] Postmodern style enfolds within itself tradition without bowing before the canon, form without formality, beauty without monumentality, coherence without symmetry. The two most popular and powerful editions of visual postmodernism—pop art and so-called earth art—have been self-cognizant efforts to revive the esthetics of signification, the one through the commercial replication of popular culture icons and the other through an almost magico-ritual expression or earth lines, geometries, and energies. If from a semiotic point of view, there is a deeper lying postmodern principle of interpretation, it is simply that the world glitters with signs, and the signs belong to an encompassing and polyvalent harmony of semantic sighs and whispers.

Unfortunately, postmodernism as a religious, or theological, libretto has all too often been assimilated to what are patently at best modern, and at worse premodern, types of discursivity. The crypto-modernism of what purports to be postmodernism can be inferred from the ideological continuity between deconstructionism and late 1960s death-of-God theology, which in turn derived from the postwar fashions of European religious existentialism.[11]

Another postmodern feint has also been devised for what is prima facie a premodern gnosticism or "perennialism." Huston Smith, as an illustration, has characterized the postmodern mind in almost archaic terms. The genuine postmodernist is the devotee of the "sacred unconscious," he or she is an Oriental adept on the path to an enlightenment, a *jivamukti,* one who "lives in the unvarying presence of the numinous."[12] The same leanings can be glimpsed in the postmodern theological program of David Griffin, which is little more than process thought—a modernist metaphysic—leavened with the politics and eco-mysticism of the aging 1960s counterculture.[13]

More recently, as the word *postmodernism* has come to refer in the literature to poststructuralist kinds of philosophical and literary arguments, Smith has turned his wrath against the concept itself. In a plenary address to the American Academy of Religion at Anaheim, California, in late 1989 Smith dismissed postmodernism as merely a degenerate form of modernism, which arose when science and empiricist epistemology supplanted revelation and what Smith calls "the wisdom of the ages" as the fountainhead of truth. The sin of postmodernism, according to Smith, is its denial of "ontological transcendence," by which he means the hierarchical metaphysics of religious esotericism tracing back to ancient Vedantism and hermeticism. Smith has urged that postmodernist impulses be judiciously dislodged to commence "a return to the truth claims of our field as impounded in the world's great traditions."[14]

The upshot of all of this, however, is that a serious postmodernism has not left its stamp on religious thought. The impasse may have more to do with the poverty of academic theology than with the "theological" promise of postmodernism per se. If theological thinking is not a task but an oeuvre, or a "work" in the Ricoeurian sense, then, to become postmodern, it must become what Eco dubs the "open work." In the open work, according to Eco, "the signs combine like constellations whose structural relationships are not determined univocally, from the start, and in which the ambiguity of the sign does not . . . lead back to reconfirming the distinction between form and background."[15]

The capaciousness of postmodern theological thinking would, like the artwork itself to which Eco applies such a hermeneutic, be both "informal" and "cultural" in a comprehensive sense. It would no longer emanate strictly from arcane conversationalists, who claim to be avant-garde and trend motivated, but who in actuality have contrived a curious, convoluted, and overdetermined scholasticism of the academic Left. It would become "popular" in the sense that pop art, which in many respects launched postmodernism, has served as an aesthetic idiom of mediation between familiar representational systems and the imagism of urban folk culture. Just as the movement over a generation ago from abstraction to "pop" can be construed as a revolt against the discreet nihilism of purely formal painting, so postmodern religious thinking no longer takes as its "texts" the recondite writings of the so-called deconstructionists.

The strategy can be adduced in part from the theory of culture advanced by Jim Collins in his insightful study of what empirically falls under the heading of postmodernism. Collins faults what he terms the *grand hotel theory* concerning mass culture, which has been a whipping boy for choleric Western critics from the Frankfurt School on down through the existentialists. Grand hotel theory is a kind of surrogate canon for those intellectuals who despise the "canonical referentiality" of the classical humanities. It looks down upon the whole of popular culture as crude exploitation and the purveyance of alienation, all the while ignoring the subtle modes of intelligibility inherent in its different functions and genres. As Collins notes: "When the punk rocker tears holes in her jeans and closes them with safety pins, or when the fashion designer adds a mink collar to a purposely faded denim jacket, both construct specific signs with quite divergent ideological values—but in each case, the meaning produced is predicated on the violation of the sign's earlier incarnations."[16]

In other words, the notion of the "popular," according to Collins, suffers from oversimplification. Popular culture, as opposed to the image of the "grand hotel" in which cultural elites dominate over a mass consumer population of untutored kitsch mongers, can be viewed as a multicentered dynamic in which sign manufacturing and semiotic performance have the effect of both expressing and differentiation. Semiotics, therefore, should be understood as a veiled praxis of "liberation," whereby deeper values of freedom can be decoded from the would-be vulgarisms or even the apparent "crass commercialism" of quotidian social representations. In this connection we can begin to understand the hostility of Frankfurt School followers toward the very idea of postmodernism. Postmodernism no longer presumes an "avant-garde" of cultural opposition in much the same way that post-Marxist leftist politics, following the collapse of communism, has dispensed handily with the paradigm of the "party" as the "vanguard" of revolutionary change.

For example, in his influential *Theory of the Avant-Garde* German philosopher of culture Peter Bürger dismisses what we have called postmodernism as "commodity aesthetics" designed to "enthrall" and concoct "a false sublation of art as institution."[17] From the semiotic standpoint the postulate of postmodernism unmasks the hidden, and one might even go so far as to say hypocritical, elitism in the conventional grand hotel reading of the role of cultural elites. A social semiotics need no longer presuppose that signification equals oppression, that it is invariably a vertical imposition of symbol-controllers upon the mass, but that it may also be a kind of *cri de coeur* of the disenfranchised. The horizontal dissemination of sign-performances through a "decentered" popular culture does not necessarily legitimate either their moral or ontological character, but reframes their purpose, primarily in terms of the categories of regimentation, subversion, "ceremonial" articulation, and ideological oscillations. According to the sociologist Erving Goffman, who in his later work coopted the semiotic method, the "commercialism" of so-much popular culture can best be considered a complex set of typifications that are not so far distant from ritualized, everyday language and behavior.[18] Sign-events cluster around "displays," which in turn coalesce around different social coding operations, not to mention *codings of difference,* that may or may not be coordinate with the insignia of class.[19]

In the postmodern context the sign becomes, to use Lyotard's term, more "presentation" than representation. The semiotics of presentation demands the *differend,* which in turn yields a query more than a direct, "metaphysical" statement—even if it be the sort of metaphysics that masquerades as critical sociology. "In the differend," says Lyotard, something 'asks' to be put into phrases, and suffers from the wrong of not being able to be put into phrases in the right way."[20] The differend is, in effect, the Heideggerian "unsaid," or at a deeper, "speculative" level, the "unthought;" it is the speaking of the unspoken that writhes toward articulation in the wilderness of contemporary culture. It is the "semiotic" reminder of social contradiction that reveals itself in the face of the homeless wanderer at the New York Port Authority. It lingers in the midnight offer of the street walker in Guadalajara. It is both Moral Majority and MTV. It is the death of an abused child. It is the "Velvet Revolution" in Prague. It is, also, strangely, Mickey Mouse and Goofy. But it is the crystal draped around the neck of a Sante Fe socialite, and the blood on the back of an Indian *penitente* as he follows the stations of the cross.

The so-called postmodernism of certain contemporary theological writers who have somehow cornered the word, therefore, is but shadow ballet. When someone like Griffin asserts that "postmodern theology rejects the extreme voluntarism of supernaturalistic theism and the atheistic naturalism of modernity, replacing both with a naturalistic form of theism,"[21] he is not brushing oils on the canvas of a genuine postmodernism, but merely hooking on a trendy label to the kind of standard, American "empirical theology" that has been current for many generations. Similarly, in the book of essays by diverse authors entitled *Spirituality and Society: Post-Modern Visions,* postmodernism becomes nothing more than a buzzword for the sort of New Age utopianism spun from the cerebra of many California dreamers during the 1960s—a folio of themes and notions that are almost now a generation outdated.[22]

The contribution of a semiotician like Eco, however, to an authentic postmodern idiom lies in his recognition of the intimate linkage between "theological" reflection and aesthetics. Eco lays the groundwork for his postmodernist, aesthetic "hermeneutic" in an early work entitled *Art and Beauty in the Middle Ages.* It is the task of historical analysis, Eco points out, to scrutinize how a particular epoch "solved for itself aesthetic problems" within the syntax of its own cultural organization.[23] Whereas Medieval thought has often been regarded as inordinately "metaphysical" and obsessed with questions of suprasensible cognition at the expense of intramundate concerns, in inward legacy of the culture itself was always, according to Eco, the search for a plausible "ontology of concrete existence." Such an ontology Eco finds in the Medieval emphasis on the power of color, proportion, and symbol. The grandeur of the Chartres cathedral, the scientific interest in the properties of natural light and the effects of luminosity, the detailing of both the sublime and the grotesque in what have wrongly come to be treated as "fanciful," clerical accounts of both geography and natural history—these "aesthetic" preoccupations were actually the philosophical subcodes for a later grammar of signs and modes of signification that flowered both in Renaissance humanism and the style of artistic expression known as *mannerism*.

The School of Chartres, for example, held that God is essentially an artist and that the world could be conceived as a grand artwork. Intellectual contemplation was compared to aesthetic appreciation. The notion of "beauty" was closely connected to the classical ideal of the "good." In the words of Albert the Great, *non est aliquid de numero existentium actu, quod non participet pulchro et bono* (There is no existing being that does not share in beauty and goodness).[24] For Eco, the aesthetic consciousness is wrapped up with a philosophical grasp of the lability and evanescense of sign-activity. Texts are no longer bare runes to be puzzled over. They are at once an intricate braid of the latent and the manifest, of form and function, of intimation and opacity, of word and image, of grapheme and difference. Indeed, *textuality* and *culture*—regarded in the primitive sense of all that is somehow is indicative—now emerge as reciprocal constructs.

The preeminence of an aesthetic postmodernism is underscored not simply by the origin of the word in contemporary art criticism, but by the striking similarity between the new artistic values and certain strategies of interpretation in the humanities. The so-called conceptual art that flourished in the 1970s disengaged the effort at aesthetic creation from its actual output, much in the same way that authorship and writing were separated within the deconstructionist movement. Postmodern architecture has been characterized in one recent historical account as by its "color, variety and capriciousness" that is not so much decorative as textually light and elusive.[25] If postmodernism as a discursive design is marked in Lyotard's terminology by the "end of grand narratives," then as cultural episode it is what Julia Kristeva has called the *theorie d'ensemble,* an "intertextuality" of heterogeneous, yet *significant,* moments of disclosure.[26] According to David Carroll, postmodernism can be summed up in the German term *Begebenheit, which may be translated as* "givenness," albeit in the dynamic sense. Another rendering is "mere occurrence."[27] Postmodern discourse itself "is concerned with theorizing the historical moment."[28] According to David Levin, postmodernism constitutes the "critical deconstruction of the essence still at work in the modernist." It is a weave of "aesthetic moments," each of which performs as a "critical commentary" on past aesthetic moments.[29] Levin distinguishes between the analytic postmodern and the metaphoric postmodern. The analytic postmodern should be construed as the formalist reappropriation of the antimetaphysical propensities within modernist culture and thought. When, for instance, Stephen Moore brands Mark Taylor as a thoroughgoing "modernist" installed as an apostle of the postmodern because of the latter's undue attention to "horizontality" and "surfaces," he is inadvertently acknowledging that postmodernism itself rests on an interior act of reinscription covering all that has been modern in the most fruitful sense of the word. One problem with Taylor's work, and with the now expiring fashion of deconstructionism in religious writing for that matter, is that it has reached a seemingly insurmountable impasse, so far as the critical task is concerned, largely as a result of its inability to embrace the metaphoric postmodern, which ultimately harks back to the desire of Nietzsche's Zarathustra to *dance*. The metaphoric postmodern rests on a profound postmetaphysical insight—what the Czech novelist Milan Kundera has called the *unbearable lightness of being*. The metaphoric postmodern is Eco's "travels in hyperreality." It is the transcendence of nihilism—a nihilism that is the hidden agenda behind what Derrida calls the *truth in painting*, the emptiness of all frames and representations, including the dysrepresentational entropy of the deconstructive campaign. The end of deconstruction, strangely enough, is not the freedom of the text, but a totalizing twilight, a *Götterdämmerung* in which philosophy and theology no longer paint even a gray on gray, but recede into the ice-entombed, ink-black night of exhaustion. Deconstruction constitutes the universal "closing time" that Heidegger has termed the *end of philosophy*. It is the veritable summa of the analytical postmodern. It is the reduction of the sign to an anonymous exterior, to the unidimensional word-canvas upon which its cracked and discolored oils have left their crepuscular impression.[30]

The metaphoric postmodern, on the other hand, arises phoenixlike to recover the power of signification in an even more radical fashion. The metaphoric postmodern can best be described as a *fundamental ontology of the body*, where metaphysics, now dismembered and disassembled, can be "rewritten" as pure somatology, as the deciphering of the "aesthetic" or sensate markings we know as *world* and as *culture*. As Jencks notes with respect to postmodern architecture that is an aesthetic incorporating "ornaments and mouldings suggestive of the human body" that also "humanizes inanimate form as we naturally project our physiognomy and moods onto it."[31]

Eco's understanding of semiotics as "carnival" in the sense of ribald and "polyform" aesthetic display anticipates such a *hermeneutic* of the metaphoric postmodern. But the same presentation more appropriately can be identified with what Kristeva has spiritedly termed *Giotto's joy,* the dissolution of the space segregating signifier and signified in the painting, or image-texture. The racinatory symbolism of the Medieval Giotto constitutes a *narrative* of the incarnate signifier, of semiology as aesthetic encounter and appreciation. It is also proleptic with respect to the postmodern revelation of the body. Just as Giotto's joy is derived from the holy yearning of the supplicant for immanent fulfillment, so the metaphorical postmodern hinges upon what Kristeva acknowledges as the ontology of "desire" that grounds not just aesthetic discourse but the signifying act itself. Whereas Kristeva's somatology is, unfortunately, still circumscribed within a late psychoanalytic grid-language of paternal wish, displacement, substitution, transgression, and repression, the codings for her own version of a metaphoric, postmodern grammatology of both masculine and feminine are inherent in her own semiotics. Semiotics, for Kristeva, is "polylogue"—where the "speaking subject" is unmasked as body, as "bursts of instinctual drive—rhythm," as "heterogeneous strata . . . that can be multiplied and infinitized."[32]

The concept of "body" in the postmodern context, of course, refers to something more than the mere physical agent. *Body* itself becomes a "metaphor" for the metaphoric postmodern; it connotes both the region of alterity, of the "outlandish" and the *outré,* with respect to the Cartesian, metaphysical subject; it becomes the prediscursive horizon for all possible significations that transcend the logic of linguistic acts and their applications. *Body* is a basal, "aesthetic" metaphor insofar as it correlates with Kristeva's infinity of sign-moments, with mutability, with a kind of "music." *Body* becomes a metaphor for the dance of signification. The "dance" of the metaphoric postmodern—and of the body as infinite sign-ensemble, as "semio-text," as the cipher of culture—surpasses all implicit modernisms to the extent that it belies the privatized substantial self of the old metaphysics and the old aesthetics. The body as metaphor contravenes the totalizing force of ideological belief systems, even the many neo-Marxist and crypto-metaphysical kinds of political romance that employ the rhetoric of the postmodern. It works against the temptation, so prevalent in the contemporary agonism of the "cultural politics" that also calls itself *postmodern*, of "hyperrealizing the social," as Steven Connor has put it.[35] A postmodern somatology would in this sense serve as a genuine, transfinite semiotics that is not simply a rhetorical double for Marxist criticism or for deconstructionist badinage. The language of the body, together with the ontological category of embodiment, tracing the origin of that peculiar polylogistic style of communication that embraces psychology, philosophy, theology, and aesthetics, thus emerges as its own distinctive *lingua franca* for postmodernist conversation.

Ironically, the somatic emphasis in the development of a postmodern, aesthetic sensibility, including what might be described as a distinctive postmodern *religiosity*, brings us into the realm of popular culture. Many recent theoreticians of popular culture have concentrated on what might be described as the different modes of body signification, and the different styles of somatic repression and expression that characterize the *signa populi*.

Popular culture by its very nature is exhibitionist. It seeks to idealize certain iconic representations of the human *figura*—shamans in colorful costume, kings and queens in their finery, popes with their tiaras, rock stars in their outrageous and often half-naked get-ups, the present-day postmillenial Madonna, whose hit song "Like a Prayer" outrages the church because it is concomitantly hierophantic and crudely sensual—and to invoke these presentations as exemplary patterns for identification and enactment. In short, popular culture, as anthropologists have been telling us for generations, is held together by the power of multiple, and often ambiguous, significative functions. Texts and other types of discursive formalities—even the highly sophisticated "metatextual" operations of deconstructionist readers—provide us with only a stylized, and one might even go so far as to say neo-metaphysical, rendering of what persists down through the ages as "book culture."

From this standpoint Derrida's proclamation of the "end of the book" is but a reinscription of the old textual ideology. A true postmodern closure of the book would involve not just an exercise in what has become the weird, new fashion of Derridean scholastics, but a "cultural" or "semiotic" turn to fill out and finalize the earlier "linguistic turn" that overshadowed an earlier era in philosophy and theology. A semiotician is interested, not just in religious thought, but also in the religious context out of which the discursive ensembles of "thought" are crystallized. In the same

way that a Mick Farren can interpret the whole of twentieth century culture through the iconics of the black leather jacket, so a
theological thinker privy to the aesthetics and the poetics of the
postmodern can begin to envision "sacrality," not simply as a
complex of stock theological emblems or representations, but as a
veritable marquee flashing with the evanescent tokens and hints
of religious sentimentality in the twentieth century.[34] The inter-
twining of religious aspiration and popular culture as a peculiar
variant on postmodern aestheticism can be seen in what have
wrongly been termed *new religious movements* or *New Age* religion.
So much would-be "new religiosity"—whether we are talking about
channeling, "satanic rock," crystal madness, or the pop metaphysics of Shirley Maclaine, J. Z. Knight, and Barbara Marx
Hubbard—is nothing new at all. It is simply old-time esotericism,
and in many instances archaic superstitions or dangerous obsessions, repackaged for present day consumer tastes and employing
the semiotic conveyances of popular culture.

New Age religion may in many respects be described as the
commodification of the arcane and obscure, but we must comprehend its "materiality" not with the raw ideological slant that al-
legedly postmodern "political economists" adopt, but as a showing
of embodied sign-contents. Sexuality and popular religion, for
instance—including even the scandals of Jim Bakker and Jimmy
Swaggart—cannot be disentangled from each other because of
their very "carnivality" (in Eco's sense) or "in-carnality" (from a
broader semiotic perspective). The materiality of the postmodern,
aesthetic mode of meaningfulness, therefore, must not be understood according to some subtextual stance of metaphysical dualism in which an "authentic" sacrality stands as a scepter of austere
judgment over its popular formats. Although a responsible "cultural politics" does, in fact, require a self-conscious distinction
between canonical works and the fleeting products of collective
consumption, a postmodern aesthetic hermeneutics of culture—
embracing the various subdisciplines of the study of religion—
must tear down the long-standing, scholarly Maginot lines barring
religious thinking from penetrating the "otherness" of its own
democratic milieu. The Tillichean with its passion for workings of
"Spirit" in the night of *Existenz* must displace the Eliadean with its
historical preservationist bent for dusting off and displaying behind glass the ancient, golden calves. A Tillichean theological
thinking concerning culture comes once more to the forefront.

The postmodern era, no matter what the concept implies
diachronically, can best be understood as the unveiling of a new

epoch in the historicality of Being, as Heidegger would claim. Yet, we must now seriously consider taking several, giant philosophical steps beyond both the Heideggerian program of fundamentally rereading the Western tradition and two-dimensional Derridean wordgrams with their curious, Dadaist messages of inconsequentiality. If, as Ferdinand Saussure (the founder of modern linguistics) and Eco (the progenitor of a comprehensive, cultural semiotics) stress, signs "work" exclusively because they set in motion the play of differences, then deconstruction can be freed from Derrida's hidden modernist semantics of surface.[35] The moment of difference now discloses the transcendental backlighting of immanent everydayness; it is the *signature* of a pure presencing.

The "age of the sign" must no longer be conceived, as Derrida once proposed, as merely theological. Postmodernly speaking, it is also the time of *parousia*. *Parousia* is both the closing time of modernist metaphysics and the final naming of the rose whereby the all that has remained unspoken during the long exile of signifier must at last struggle toward speech. Most recently, Derrida himself has alluded to the end of deconstruction itself with his cryptic discussion of "spirit" as "fire."[36] Or perhaps we must uncover the essential meaning in the ending of T. S. Eliot's *Four Quartets* which some commentators regard as the first postmodern poem of the twentieth century.

Four Quartets is postmodern because it is a sweeping *poesis* disclosing not jewels in the lotus but "sapphires in the mud," a genuine Heideggerian "worlding of the world" through the movements of signification that suddenly appear like a "thousand points of light" (Wordsworth) across the craggy terrain of "mass culture." The closure of the poem, however, is not about the "naming" that takes place through discourse, but about fire. The discourse of the world is set aflame. As we discover at the conclusion of The Name of the Rose, the end of the book is also the end of the world. The representations of the metaphysical eon burn up. For "our God is a consuming fire."

The concluding words of *Four Quartets*, therefore, are more than mildly prophetic:

> We can only live, only suspire
> Consumed either by fire or fire.

and, our task, as Eliot directs us, "will be to know the place for the first time." It shall be, semiotically speaking, "a condition of complete simplicity." *When*

All manner of thing shall be well
When the tongues of flame are in-folded
Into the crowned knot of fire
And the fire and the rose
are one.[37]

The *fire* and the *rose*, therefore, become the master ciphers for the postmodern way of thinking. As the fire smolders and the rose unfolds, the ciphers become lines of force, moments of disclosure, vortices of querying, acts of signification. They are the religious metaphors that become the invitation to locate the site of a true postmodern thinking.

--------------------------------- Notes ---------------------------------

1. Umberto Eco, *The Name of the Rose,* trans. William Weaver (New York: Harcourt Brace Jovanovich, 1980), p. 583.

2. Umberto Eco, "Frames of Comic Freedom," in Umberto Eco, V. V. Ivanov, and Monica Rector, *Carnival!* ed. Thomas A. Sebeok (Amsterdam: Mouton, 1984), p. 6.

3. See "On Leveling the Genre Distinction Between Philosophy and Literature," in *The Philosophical Discourse of Modernity,* trans. Frederick G. Lawrence (Cambridge, Mass.: MIT Press, 1987), p. 193; also of interest is a "reply" by Jacques Derrida, "Afterword" in *Limited INC,* trans. Samuel Weber (Evanston, Ill.: Northwestern University Press, 1988), n. 9, pp. 156–58. See a discussion of the problem Habermas raises in Rodolphe Gasche, "Post-Modernism and Rationality," *Journal of Philosophy* 85 (October): 528–538. See Ulrich Schönherr, "Adorno, Ritter Gluck, and the Tradition of the Post-Modern," *New German Critique* 48 (1989): 135–154; and Sabine Wilke, "Adorno and Derrida as Readers of Husserl: Some Reflections on the Historical Context of Modernism and Post-Modernism," *Boundary* 2: 77–90.

4. Jacques Derrida, *The Truth in Painting,* trans. Geoff Bennington and Ian McLeod (Chicago: University of Chicago Press, 1987), p. 352.

5. Jacques Derrida, *The Ear of the Other: Otobiography, Transference, Translation* (Lincoln: University of Nebraska Press, 1988), p. 38.

6. Jean-Francois Lyotard, *The Postmodern Condition: A Report on Knowledge,* trans. Geoff Bennington and Brian Massumi (Minneapolis: University of Minnesota Press, 1984), p. 81.

7. See "Letter to Thomas Carroll," in *The Postmodern Explained,* trans. Don Barry et al. (Minneapolis: University of Minnesota Press, 1992), pp. 12–16.

8. The similarity between Lyotard's and Wyschogrod's arguments is exemplified in the following quotation: "Just as the sheer existence of language points phantatically to its nonviolent character, the birth of the death event in our time opens up a new phantasmatic meaning borne by the speaker, one that accompanies all discourse." Edith Wyschogrod, *Spirit in Ashes: Hegel, Heidegger, and Man-Made Mass Death* (New Haven, Conn.: Yale University Press, 1985), p. 214. Wyschogrod's brilliant treatment of the origin of postmodern thinking in Hegel and Heidegger, however, is distinguished by her call at the end for a "transactional" communitarian self, which may be described more as a modernist concern than a postmodern one.

9. See Paul Ricoeur "The Phenomenological Approach to the Psychoanalytic Field" in *Freud and Philosophy* (New Haven, Conn.: Yale University Press, 1970), pp. 383–386.

10. Charles Jencks, *Post-modernism: The New Classicism in Art and Architecture* (New York: Rizzoli, 1987), p. 338. Says Eco: "the elements of the signifier are set in a system of oppositions in which, as Saussure explained, there are only differences. The same thing with the signified . . . . The correlation between expression-plane and content-plane is also given by a difference: the sign-function exists by a dialectic of presence and absence, as a mutual exchange between two heterogeneities." *Semiotics and the Philosophy of Language* (Bloomington: Indiana University Press, 1984), p. 23. The enhancement that Eco's philosophical linguistics achieves in relation to Barthes's relatively naive poststructuralism cannot be understated. Eco's notion of semiosis as the revelation of a kind of "unsaidness," in contradistinction to Derrida's detextualizing *differance*, also puts the original aims of deconstruction back on a sounder philosophical, and ontological, footing.

11. For an incursion into deconstruction by a "death-of-God" theologian see Thomas J. J. Altizer, *Total Presence: The Language of Jesus and the Language of Today* (New York: Seabury Press, 1982).

12. Huston Smith, *Beyond the Post-Modern Mind* (New York: Crossroad Publishing, 1982), p. 182.

13. See note 21.

14. Huston Smith, "Post-Modernism's Impact on Religious Studies," plenary address before the American Academy of Religion in Anaheim, California, 1989.

15. Umberto Eco, *The Open Work*, trans. Anna Cancogni (Cambridge: Mass: Harvard University Press, 1989), p. 86.

16. Jim Collins, *Uncommon Cultures: Popular Culture and Post-Modernism* (London and New York: Routledge, 1989), p. 17–18.

17. Peter Bürger, *Theory of the Avant-Garde*, trans. Michael Shaw (Minneapolis: University of Minnesota Press, 1984), p. 54. The argument

is similar the well-known one of Frederic Jameson, who sees postmodernism as a "network of power and control" whereby aesthetical enthrallment replaces surplus value as the instrument of social domination. Postmodernism is essentially the "expansion of capital into hitherto uncommodified areas." *Postmodernism, or the Cultural Logic of Late Capitalism* (Durham N.C.: Duke University Press, 1991), p. 36.

18. Erving Goffman, *Gender Advertisements* (New York: Harper and Row, 1979), p. 84.

19. Heinz-Güter Vester has very insightfully and effectively analyzed Goffman's contribution to postmodern discourse in his article on recent trends in both structuralism and semiotics. "Our understanding of a sign, a sign system, or a text is a developing process of unlimited semiosis." See "Erving Goffman's Sociology as Semiotics of Post-modern Culture," *Semiotica* 76: 191–203. The theory of unlimited semiosis through cultural elaboration, a key element in the framing of a postmodern schema of interpretation, is made possible, according to Vester, through the "playfulness" and "intertextuality" of popular productions, as Goffman analyzes them.

20. Jean-Francois Lyotard, *The Differend: Phrases in Dispute,* trans. Georges Van Den Abbeele (Minneapolis: University of Minnesota Press, 1988), p. 13.

21. David Ray Griffin, *God and Religion in the Post-Modern World* (Albany: State University of New York Press, 1989), p. 132.

22. See David Ray Griffin (ed.), *Spirituality and Society* (Albany: State University of New York Press, 1988).

23. Umberto Eco, *Art and Beauty in the Middle Ages* (New Haven, Conn.: Yale University Press, 1986), p. 2.

24. Quoted in Wladyslaw Tatarkiewicz, *History of Aesthetics,* vol. 2 (The Hague: Mouton, 1970), p. 288.

25. See Bruce Cole and Adelheid Gealt, *Art of the Western World: From Ancient Greece to Post-Modernism* (London: Summit Books, 1989), p. 333.

26. See Lyotard, *The Postmodern Condition,* pp. 37–41; also, Julia Kristeva, "The Bounded Text" in *Desire in Language,* trans. Thomas Gora et al. (New York: Columbia University Press, 1980), pp. 36–41. For a more detailed account of Kristeva's position, see *Theorie d'ensemble* (Paris: Seuil, 1968).

27. See David Carroll, *Paraesthetics: Foucault, Lyotard, Derrida* (New York: Methuen Books, 1987). For other recent philosophical, or theological, attempts to epitomize the postmodern, see George James, "The Post-Modern Context," *Contemporary Philosophy* 22 (1989): 1–5; David

Crownfield, "Post-Modern Perspectives in Theology and Philosophy of Religion," *Contemporary Philosophy* 22 (1989): 6–13; Robert Morris, "Words and Images in Modernism and Post-Modernism," *Critical Inquiry* 15 (1989): 337–347; Paul Jay, "Modernism, Post-Modernism, and Critical Style: The Case of Burke and Derrida," *Genre* 21 (1988): 339–358.

28. Robert Merrill, "Simulations: Politics, TV, History," in Robert Merrill (ed.), *Ethics/Aesthetics: Post-Modern Positions* (Washington, D.C.: Maisonneuve Press, 1988), p. 151.

29. David Levin, "Post-Modernism in Dance: Dance, Discourse, Democracy," in Hugh J. Silverman (ed.), *Post-Modernism—Philosophy and the Arts* (New York and London: Routledge, 1990), p. 21.

30. Stephen Moore, "The 'Post-' Age Stamp: Does it Stick?" *Journal of the American Academy of Religion* 52, no. 3 (1989): 548.

31. Jencks, *Postmodernism,* p. 336.

32. Julia Kristeva, "The Novel as Polylogue," in *Desire in Language,* p. 186.

33. Steven Connor, *Post-Modernist Culture: An Introduction to Theories of the Contemporary* (Oxford: Basil Blackwell, 1989), p. 61.

34. See Mick Farren, *The Black Leather Jacket* (New York: Abbeville Press, 1985).

35. See Ferdinand de Saussure, *Course in General Linguistics,* trans. Roy Harris (La Salle, Ill.: Open Court Press, 1983), pp. 79–98; and Eco, *Semiotics and the Philosophy of Language,* pp. 23–24.

36. See Jacques Derrida, *Of Spirit: Heidegger and the Question,* trans. Geoffrey Bennington and Rachel Bowlby (Chicago: University of Chicago Press, 1990).

37. T. S. Eliot, *Four Quartets* (New York: Harcourt, Brace, Jovanovich, 1971), p. 55.

Chapter 2

The Stranger as Guest:
Toward a Philosophical Site for
Postmodern Thinking

Nihilism stands at the door: whence comes this strangest
of guests?

Friedrich Nietzsche

One of the most critical texts for of Western philosophy, and for
postmodern thinking, is Plato's *Sophist*. The dialogue has been
normally read, in conjunction with Plato's *Theaetetus*, as a hap-
hazard probe into the entanglements of epistemology and ontology; it is also taken as a wry commentary using adept dramatic
techniques on the dangers of a rhetorical culture as well as the
misapprehensions of popular philosophy; that is, "sophistry." For
Heidegger, however, the fulcrum of the text is the series of oblique
disclosures and leading remarks attributable to the Eleatic stranger,
"a comrade of the circle of Parmenides and Zeno, and a man very
much a philosopher."[1] The presence of the stranger suggests a
kind of ongoing, yet covert insinuation of the deeper Eleatic problem into Plato's familiar, contrapuntal play of argument. For, as
the dialogue eventually comes round to show, the issue of the
sophist as philosophical *poseur* and a trickster with language ultimately becomes the basic Platonic question of whether the "real"
is identical with the enduring and whether "that which is" must
come to mean the same as what Heidegger has termed *permanent
presence*. What stands at stake in the altercation among philosophers over "sophistry" is not the criteria of "correct speech," over

21

which the more conventional Socratic interlocuters tend to quibble, but "a kind of gigantomachy on account of their mutual dispute about being."[2] The "gigantomachy" of the *Sophist*, of course, emerges as the great metaphysical aporia which the Heideggerian project of *Überwindung*, the "overcoming" of the multimillennia enclosure of the region in which the thinking of the heretofore unthought is made possible and takes as its place of departure.

For Heidegger, such a place of departure, or site of disclosure, belongs neither to the topology of history—even Hegel's history of philosophy—nor to the "situation" of present discourse. Like the mythical gigantomachy itself, the metaphysical "dispute about being" remains inscribed within a distinctive architecture of first principles, an arche-ology of what the philosophical tradition has referred to as *rationality*. Metaphysical rationality, which in every important respect derives from the "saying" of Parmenides that "Being is," is founded upon the proportion and commensurability, or what in Greek aesthetics was known as *sophrisyne*, between the somatico-sensory and the purely intellectual, between the phenomenal and noumenal, or in postclassical terms between existence and essence, temporality and eternity, the mutable and the truly changeless.[3] Kant's effort to develop a whole, new "architectonic" for metaphysics that weighed out the "critical" relationships between what by the eighteenth century had come to be designated as the *empirical* and the *transcendental*—the longstanding gigantomachy between Locke and Descartes—can be viewed as a next-to-last-minute "archival" search on the part of philosophy in its footnoting of Plato.

All along the Kantian critiques have been but meditations of the "groundwork" laid atop the Eleatic saying; they are the very *archaeology* of reason.[4] The archaeology of the "rational," which unearths its own self-embodiment as the tradition of "metaphysics," concludes therefore in Husserl's reckoning of the real as a peculiar formality belonging to the "thesis of reason," to the "primordial data of consciousness" that upon philosophical self-analysis discloses the immanent correlation between the rationally ordered, or noetic, "ground of experiences" and "real objects."[5] The place at which Heideggerian phenomenology departs from the Husserlian archaeology of the rationally posited real can be described precisely as the not-so-hidden subtext of the stranger's comments in Plato's *Sophist*, where "the things that are" (i.e., the veridical as opposed to the phantasmic) are revealed to be something far more than the merely perdurable. They "are not anything else but power."[6]

The realization that *ta onta*, or those things eminently "real," are the vital parenthesis within the vast sentence of "power" cuts to the quick of Heidegger's philosophy. Furthermore, such an understanding lies behind the Heideggerian attempt to disinhabit philosophical thinking from its bondage to the "grammar" of Greek metaphysics and to disclose the pretheoretic, that is, *poetic,* power of language itself.[7] Metaphysical thought, and by extension the historic constellations of metaphysical reasoning, unfold from the general pattern of predicative logic and categorical discourse that Aristotle characterized as "first philosophy." In Book Gamma and Book Zeta of the *Metaphysics* Aristotle constructs the archway for the cathedral of metaphysics with his well-known "reduction" of ontology to the terrain of definition and distinction. "Being" is not univocal in its extension throughout discourse, but has "various meanings."[8] The "primary" meaning of being is *ousia,* translated into the Latin as "substance." Being as substance, according to Aristotle, connotes first and foremost "not what is said of a subject, but being the subject for whatever is said."[9]

In other words, the "primacy" of the "first science" of metaphysics, which is at the same time the *arch-epistemology* that undergirds all conceivable ventures in knowledge, rests upon the primacy of predication and classification itself. *To be* is to remain the one prior term in the total web of significations that constitute "scientific" parlance. The emptiness of the Aristotelian sense of Being as the Great Unpredictable within an interlocking chain of inferences, as what Derrida has named the *Transcendental Signified,* was of course recognized by Hegel in his reframing of logic as dialectic. Yet this emptiness, which indicates philosophically what Heidegger has always had in mind with his judgments concerning the concealed "nihilism" of the metaphysical, does not point to the illusory, or more precisely the "skeptical," character of Western philosophy once the archaeology of the rational has been completed. The emptiness of first philosophy is laid open at the moment in which the epoch of metaphysics comes to a close, when being masked as predicative communication withdraws and, as Heidegger observes in "The Anaximander Fragment," "the history of Being is gathered in this departure."[10]

The *gathering* refers to "the ultimacy of its destiny," to its *eschatology* or moment of self-limitation. The history of Being as metaphysics, when viewed retrospectively in its entirety at the eschatological moment that is the unveiling of that epoch's nihilism, provides sight of the mysterious boundary stone between what Heidegger calls *the end of philosophy* and the commencement of *the task of thinking.* The twilight space, or "reserve," between the end of philosophy as the eschatology of the West and the beginning of what in its still crypted speech can be known as *philosophical thinking* marks out the radical difference, in Heidegger's idiom the *ontological difference,* between the experience of things as predicative discourse and their disclosure as the-coming-to-be of beings, as an originary "wording." This wording, which amounts to what Heidegger genuinely intends with his expression *the worlding of the world,* is what in the argot of French poststructuralism can be described as an archaeological "pre-text" perhaps even the pre-text of what the Romantics metaphysically named the primary imagination, Freud the unconscious, and Nietzsche the will to power.[11]

Not simply by coincidence, Heidegger dwells upon Nietzsche's "thought" of the will to power as the supreme philosophical construct undertaken at the close of the metaphysical epoch. The will to power is the veil of metaphysical discourse that, when pierced by thinking or "deconstructed" in the most fundamental manner at the disposal of the philosopher, can be seen to hide the authentic nature of "things" as power. Nietzsche, therefore, begins to think what was glimpsed by Plato's stranger, but even more strangely has continued "unthought" at the very margins of 2,500 years of metaphysical thought itself. The strangeness of the thought of the will to power becomes apparent in Heidegger's own project of rereading, and thereby reappropriating, Nietzsche as a *praeparatio* for the task of "thinking at the end of philosophy." The task itself, which Heidegger emphasizes "must sound strange to us" and "can be neither metaphysics nor science," has "concealed itself from philosophy since its very beginning, even in virtue of that beginning, and thus has withdrawn itself continually and increasingly in the time to come."[12] The task of thinking, quite curiously, finds its "forethought" in the problematics of art, which is "the most perspicuous and familiar configuration of will to power."[43] In Nietzsche's work, remarks Heidegger, there is a nonlinear sort of discrepancy between art and philosophy or art and "truth"; it is the "raging discordance" whereby the tragic fatality of life as the will to power and philosophy as the architecture of the "true world" are sundered, even as an allure to madness. The Nietzschean discordance, however, becomes the "eschatological" brink from which the task of thinking does not shy, but steps forward. As Heidegger writes, "[t]hat the question concerning art leads us directly to the one that is preliminary to all questions already suggests that in a distinctive sense it conceals in itself essential relations to the grounding and guiding questions of philosophy."[14]

In what sense is the question concerning art "preliminary" to these most essential other forms of inquiry? The conondrum of thinking at the end of philosophy, as we have noted, is the prospect of nihilism, Nietzsche's "strangest of guests." The prospect of nihilism stems from the "eschatological" realization that philosophy as metaphysics has been stripped bare, that every *prote ousia*, absolute ground, or "subject matter" of discursive reasoning dissolves into the nothingness that encompasses its system of pretexts. The end of philosophy is equivalent to both its fulfillment and its emptying in keeping with the immanent logic of its epoch—an insight Hegel profoundly incurred, but squandered with his Romantic prose, at the finale of *The Phenomenology of Spirit*.[15] Whereas Hegel held that the only possible route for the sublation of the nihilistic momentum of Western culture could be traced through the first figurative, then speculative consciousness penetrating the triunity of art, religion, and philosophy at the return into itself of Absolute Spirit, Nietzsche fell back into the mythopoetic affirmation of creativity itself in Zarathustra's teaching of eternal recurrence, "overman," and the will to power. Nietzsche affirmed art, or primal creativity, as the only conceivable countermovement to the impetus of nihilism, says Heidegger, because the symbology of the aesthetic remains the universal pre-text for the imminent, *philosophical* "transvaluation of all values."[16]

If philosophical thinking in its postmetaphysical context is what is implied by such a transvaluation, that is, by "thinking beyond" the end of philosophy itself, then the relationship between artistic production and the philosophical task must be reincised. The convergence of art and philosophy is signified in the structure of the "work," which brings philosophy back to the thinking of the world as the presencing of "things" in their linguistic unity. For Heidegger, the understanding of the "work of art" belongs within the same originary, and therefore unitary, realm of language as a postmetaphysical philosophy of "thinghood." "Thinghood" and "worldness" are the compass points for the early Heidegger's phenomenology of existence as well as his later interpretation of philosophical thought as "poetizing." The thing as that which shows itself in the primordial moment of openness belongs within the sphere of *poesis* or "prescencing"— the coming-to-be that is veiled by *thoughts about* Being in itself.

In his benchmark essay "The Origin of the Work of Art," Heidegger reminds us that "the nature of truth" in his famous sense of *aletheia*, or unconcealment, can be thought through only by a gaze that goes to the "core of things." The gaze of philosophy, which assembles the thing within the openness of thinking, in a strange way corresponds to the gaze of art. For art, like knowledge, "is real in the art work. . . . Art works universally display a thingly character, albeit in a wholly distinct way."[17] The artwork of the ancient temple is the exhibition of the originary environment by which grain was stored and converted into an "economy" of everyday life and within which gods conversed with men. The *Kunstwerk* is the "working" of an originary scene that manifests in language—whether visual, tactile, auditory, or verbal. Art is the stranger that becomes the guest of thinking. Art is, in Heidegger's phraseology, the coming forth and gathering together of the "things of earth"; it is the revelation of their *dynamis* or power to show themselves, the autochthony of their appearings. "To be a work means to set up a world."[18] The setting up of a world is the building of its architecture. The architectonic of metaphysical rationality is no exception.

The strange implication one might draw, not just from Heidegger but from early Greek philosophy as well, is that the history of the Western philosophical tradition is the history of sophistry. The sophist allows *anything* to be "said," and it is this tendentious saying in the sense of predicating for the many subjects within discourse a multiplicity of wholly factitious word-properties and word-things that makes the vast range of philosophical rumination—ethics, aesthetics, epistemology, logic, metaphysics, social criticism, and so forth—empty at the core. Yet the dialogue that bears the title of *Sophist* is not so much about spurious predication as it is about the intimacy of the philosopher and the "artist." According to Plato, the sophist is not an "artist" but an "imitator."[19] His *mimesis* is an unproductive style of "making," a licentious and dissolute substitute for the poetic. The philosopher, as opposed to the sophist, "makes, by the art of house building, a house itself," whereas the sophist constructs pseudo-works as "the offspring of certain similarities."[20] The philosopher is an artist, or even more grandiose a "templar," insofar as he builds the temple of earth, the cathedral of the world's worlding, the "house of Being," in the thinking of the unthought thought of the end of the epoch of metaphysics. The stranger comes perhaps not really from Elea; he is identified with that place of the beginnings of metaphysics only "in birth." May we say that he is the stranger at the gate who, like Scaramouche, ambushes and steals the apparel of Nietzsche's "strangest of guests" and strides incognito into the great postmodern festival of thinking, clothed but not swathed in the black mysteries of the *nihil*?

What is meant here in the philosophical setting, or discursive scene, by what otherwise has been the rhetorical style of the postmodern? And what are its proper modes of signification? One mode of signification is *omni-temporality*, the engorgement of all representational systems by change, fluctuation, and transition. Another, as we have indicated in the last chapter, is what we might specify as the *somatalogical* or *somatically immanent*—Derrida's "genital recapitulation," Jacques Lacan's and Julia Kristeva's *jouissance*, Maurice Blanchot's Orphic gaze, Ihab Hassan's "literature of silence," Alphonse Lingus's "body plenum," Heidegger's *Dasein*. The radical somaticism inherent in all postmodernist themes, however, is the inevitable outcome of the decay of the uniquely modern metaphysic of subjectivity and can be located distinctively in such earlier movements as medical materialism, psychoanalysis, and existentialism. Both the etiology and the etymology of the term *postmodernism*, nonetheless, entail an aesthetic, as we have argued. Yet the aesthetics of the postmodern, according to Lyotard, is teased out not by such familiar Derridean markers as the closure of the book and the abolition of the author. Postmodernity is the aesthetic of the "unpresentable," of "heteromorphous" language striving not toward the "solace of good forms," modern theories of art measured as the canons of taste, but toward the disporting of full signification. "It is our business," Lyotard contends, "not to supply reality but to invent allusions to the conceivable which cannot be presented."[21] The aesthetic of the unpresentable is contingent on the emptying—the Hegelian *kenosis* of Absolute Spirit—of the philosophical and artistic traditions as orders of *re-presentation*.

The postmodern aesthetic, therefore, is an aesthetic that appears nihilistic only with regard to its stylistic transgressions, while remaining at the same time an overture to the thinking of the deepest and (if Nietzschean hyperbole is apt in this connection) the "most abyssmal" currents of thought. The postmodern carnival of language mirrors Nietzschean eternal recurrence. Even for Derrida, the endless becoming for which the will to power is merely a hyphen, rather than a signature, in its postmodern translation "becomes the question of style as the question of writing, the question of a spurring operation, more powerful than any content, any thesis, any meaning."[22] If deconstruction even on Derrida's terms is the triumph of style, shrewdly supplanting Zarathustra's "Thus I willed it" as a fictive countermovement to nihilism, the amalgamation of artistic and philosophical work is secured with the strongest ballast. Says Lyotard, "A post-modern artist or writer is in the position of a philosopher: the text he writes, the work he produces are not in principle governed by preestablished rules, and they cannot be judged according to a determining judgment, by applying familiar categories to the text or to the work. Those rules and categories are what the work of art itself is looking for."[23] The postmodernist as "poetizer" in the Heideggerian sense brings together the philosophical and the artistic work through the transvaluation of the textures of signification we construe as thinking. The "thought" of a postmodern philosophy thus is really the thinking that "If we were to make completely explicit the architecture of the human body," as Maurice Merleau-Ponty says, "its ontological framework and how it sees itself, we would see that the structure of its mute world is such that all possibilities of language are already given in it..."[24] commences at the end of philosophy. A postmodern philosophy is neither epistemology "downgraded" to aesthetics nor the collapse of rationality into style. The postmodern defies the recognizable reductionisms of the modern. It is not any manner of reductionism whatsoever, but the thinking through of the very lesions, contradictions, disjunctions, and closures by which the representational sign-systems of the metaphysical era have discomfited the ageless "dream of reason." A postmodern philosophy would be *deeply* aesthetic and Nietzschean, according to Lingus's formulation, insofar as it is stylistic theater, as both word-play and *world-play*. A postmodern philosophy would be woven through and through not with referents, but with tropes and metonyms. Its essential "strangeness" would like not only in its rhetorical syntax, but in its gratuitous conveyance of the "unpresentable," in its utter alterity. "There would then be *traces* ... of movements that did not seek recompense, that only wanted to pass, completely, only wanted to discharge themselves, without return."[25]

But the "unpresentability" of the postmodern signifier, which is the same as Heidegger's notion of the unre-presented "presencing" that constitutes "thingness," has a profounder gravamen than any possible ideology of style, or psychoanalytic, would warrant. The return of postmodernist aesthetics from a Derridean "metaphysic" of style to a true "eschatology" of thinking requires both a weaning of oneself from the congenital enchantment with Heidegger's Teutonic catachresis and an avoidance of "deconstructionist" gaddings of prose. At such a pass postmodernism might become *ipso facto* philosophical. Indeed, the thought of a postmodern philosophy engendered from Heidegger has already appeared in the brilliant argument of a recent book by Reiner Schuermann. For Schuermann, Heidegger is in fact our "new Nietzsche," the hitherto unplumbed postmodern philosopher of history and culture. The Heideggerian glance at history and culture affords us something illimitably more than the subversion of the sovereignty of metaphysics. It offers "epochal principles" from which we can start to read history as well as culture in terms of their sign-plays, their theatrics, their revelatory modes, their orders of disclosure, their "economics of presence." The Heideggerian glance is a postmetaphysical venture into the thinking-through of history itself, not just the history of philosophy. That "thinking, for its part, is essentially compliant with the flux of coming-to-presence, with constellations that form and undo themselves."[26] The presencing of presence that "forms" history and culture bespeaks the language of new postmodern ontology, an ontology that rings strange in the philosophical ear only because it has not yet become the guest of thinking. Once the stranger is received as guest, as the unit of thought and art, as the vision of culture, as *philosophia* with the twist that Plato probably meant in the originary meditations of the *Symposium,* the discovery of philosophy as eschatology will make far more sense. In one of his essays, "Language in the Poem," Heidegger quotes the poet Georg Trakl: "Many a man in his wanderings / Comes to the gate by darksome paths."[27] If the postmodern predicament is, as Mark Taylor tell us, a wandering or "errancy,"[28] then a postmodern philosophy must arrive at the gate through which guests are admitted only by tenebrous routes. For Heidegger, however, that discernment of darkness is at the same time the world's lighting.

This discernment of darkness may be the key in many ways to a radical hermeneutics that rethinks Heidegger in such a way that the hermeneutic project of the twentieth century is able to pass beyond the "supplement of origin"—the invocation of writing as that which supplies the deficiency disclosed at the beginning, at the very primacy of speech. We are right in accepting Derrida's criticism of logo-centric readings of tradition, because in contrast to Heidegger's primordialism, there can be no privileging of fundamental truth or meaning, no "god that sends" communiqués to earth from Olympus, no "postal service" by which significatory dispatches are delivered down through the ages, no divine Hermes bearing messages from the past, indeed, no hermeneutics in the classic sense of the word. Radical hermeneutics is the agonistics of languages.[24] All humanistic commentary is ultimately an archaeology of the tragic, a sojourn through the abyss, a song of Orpheus.

Yet Heideggerian "re-collection" *(Andenke)*, as opposed to the strict Derridean "dissemination" of the text in an onanism of the signifying machination, is still able to recover the unseen and unthought in a way that a pure grammatology cannot. Luminosity is snatched even from an epistemology of darkness at the instant of hermeneutic reversal. Euridyce is at last redeemed. And the lute melody of origins, the signifying initiative that may properly be called a hermeneutic of embodiment and desire, is at last allowed to perform in a world-historical sense.

The stranger, who for a time was guest, now becomes the friend. He is at home.

He sits beside the fire. He becomes a thinker. He discovers his desire. He is a lover.

Notes

1. Plato, *Sophist* 216a. The English renderings are taken from Seth Bernardete, *Plato's Sophist* (Chicago: University of Chicago Press, 1986).

2. Ibid, 246a.

3. See Martin Heidegger, "The Task of Destroying the History of Ontology," and "The Phenomenological Method of Investigation," in *Being and Time*, trans. John Macquarrie and Edward Robinson (New York: Harper and Row, 1962), pp. 41–63; also of interest would be Martin Heidegger, "Assertional Truth, the Idea of Truth in General, and Its Relation to the Concept of Being," in *Basic Problems of Phenomenology*, trans. Albert Hofstadter (Bloomington and Indianapolis: University of Indiana Press), especially pp. 222–224.

4. See Martin Heidegger, *Kant and the Problem of Metaphysics*, trans. Richard Taft (Bloomington and Indianapolis: University of Indiana Press, 1990).

5. These remarks about Husserl are a rough overview of the argument occuring in Chapter 12 of *Ideen*, titled "The Phenomenology of Reason." See Edmund Husserl, *Ideas*, trans. W. R. Boyce Gibson (New York: Collier Books, 1962), pp. 350ff.

6. Plato, *Sophist*, 247e.

7. See Martin Heidegger, "Holderlin and the Essence of Poetry," trans. Douglas Scott in *Existence and Being* (Washington, D.C.: Henry Regnary Company, 1988), pp. 280–282.

8. Aristotle, *Metaphysics* 1003b. The English rendering is from Aristotle, *Metaphysics*, trans. Richard Hope (Ann Arbor: University of Michigan Press, 1962).

9. Ibid., 1029a.

10. Martin Heidegger, *Early Greek Thinking,* trans. David Krell and Frank Capuzzi (New York: Harper and Row, 1975), p. 18.

11. See Martin Heidegger, "Involvement and Significance; The Worldhood of the World," in *Being and Time,* pp. 114–123.

12. Martin Heidegger, *On Time and Being,* trans. Joan Stambaugh (New York: Harper and Row, 1972), p. 59.

13. Martin Heidegger, *Nietzsche,* vol. 1, trans. David Krell (New York: Harper and Row, 1979), p. 71.

14. Ibid., p. 142.

15. See G. W. F. Hegel, *The Phenomenology of Spirit,* trans. A. V. Miller (New York and London: Oxford University Press, 1977), section VIII.

16. See Heidegger, *Nietzsche,* vol. 1, pp. 200–220; and, vol. 4, trans. David Farrell Krell (San Francisco: Harper and Row, 1982), pp. 58–68.

17. Martin Heidegger, *Poetry, Language, Thought,* trans. Albert Hofstadter (New York: Harper and Row, 1971), p. 40.

18. Ibid., p. 44.

19. Plato, *Sophist,* 267e.

20. Ibid., 266c.

21. Jean-Francois Lyotard, *The Postmodern Condition: A Report on Knowledge,* trans. Geoff Bennington and Brian Massumi (Minneapolis: University of Minnesota Press) p. 81.

22. Jacques Derrida, "The Question of Style," in David B. Allison (ed.) *The New Nietzsche: Contemporary Styles of Interpretation* (New York: Dell Publishing, 1977. See also Stephen A. Tyler, *The Unspeakable: Discourse, Dialogue, and Rhetoric in the Post-Modern World* (Madison: University of Wisconsin Press, 1987), p. 3; Wilhelm S. Wurzer, "Post-Modernism's Short Letter, Philosophy's Long Farewell . . . ," in Hugh J. Silverman and Donn Welston (eds.), *Post-Modernism and Continental Philosophy* (Albany: State University of New York Press, 1988).

23. Lyotard, *The Postmodern Condition,* p. 81.

24. Maurice Merleau-Ponty, *The Visible and the Invisible,* trans. Alphonso Lingis (Evanston, Ill.: Northwestern University Press, 1968), p. 155.

25. Alphonso Lingus, *Excesses: Eros and Culture* (Albany: State University of New York Press, 1983), p. 146.

26. Reiner Schuermann, *Heidegger on Being and Acting: From Principles to Anarchy* (Bloomington: Indiana University Press, 1987), p. 289.

27. Martin Heidegger, *On the Way to Language,* trans. Peter D. Hertz (New York: Harper and Row, 1971), p. 167.

28. See Mark Taylor, *Erring* (Chicago: University of Chicago Press, 1985), pp. 149–169.

29. Derrida's considerations on the "letter," the "communique," and Hermes are especially to be noted in *Dissemination,* trans. Barbara Johnson (Chicago: University of Chicago Press, 1981) and *Le Carte Postale* (Paris: Aubier-Flammarion, 1980).

Chapter 3

Love's New Body

Hearken, fair boy, to whom I speak. This is the experience
that men term love (eros), but when you hear the gods call
it, you will probably smile at its strangeness.

Plato

The "strangeness" of eros, encountered at the cockcrow of Western
thinking, can be deciphered only in terms of the "friendliness" of
philosophical discourse toward its own genealogical account. The
representational systems of both Western theology and philosophy
imply an archaeology that as yet remains undisclosed. That archaeology lies in the reinscription of the truth of erotic desire. The
erotic is the originary grammar of postmodern religious thinking.
For postmodern thought *in toto* can be incised only as a kind of
recherché, a "retro-searching" for what has remained consistently
concealed and covered over in the interpretive odyssey of textual
readings and their interminable cycle of cultural appropriations.
As Heidegger has reminded us before, to read the Greeks is to
think not in a Greek way, but to think through Greek thought in
a fashion the Greeks never thought.

The notion that eros can be regarded as an "originary grammar" suggests something akin to what Lacan alludes to when he
talks about the "unconscious" as a language in itself.[1] In psychoanalytic terms the semantics of unconscious formations is shaped
by what Freud termed the *double sentence:* a parallel set of "inscriptions" that emerges whenever the self struggles to appear as
subject through the violence of the intelligible.[2] The text of the
unconscious is "written down" as desire, as the ungrounded pulse

33

of proto-consciousness, both opening and seeking to heal the breach between the image and the fulfillment of the wish. The language of the "repressed" is precisely symmetrical with the discourse concerning the "world." In their entirety they constitute, not simply a double sentence, but a double speech. They are correlated as closely as an actual particle and a virtual particle in theoretical physics. Because the "power" of the erotic depends on the moment of *difference* intrinsic to the double sentence, what we mythically know as *eros*—Hesiod's stirring of primal darkness, Plato's daimon with the double life—belongs, therefore, to the unsutured, liminal space separating all thought from its matter or essence.

Here, in fact, we must entertain the possibility of a radical reworking of Heidegger's own project of overcoming metaphysics through poetizing philosophical statements and listening to the voice of Being. If we place ourselves within the poststructural idiom of postmodern reflection, as opposed to Heidegger's archaism, we discover that the "voice " is really the uncovering of the intentionality of desire removed from the oubliette of repression. It is the purely fanciful, what is only darkly longed for, transposed into the symbology of primal communication, into myth.

The erotic thus makes up what I have called *originary grammar;* that is, the Word (whether of God or world or both). The erotic in this most foundational sense points to a "transcendental unity" of both perception and cognition because, as Bataille observes, "man is everlastingly in search of an object *outside* himself but this object answers the *innerness* of desire."[3] The erotic defines the origin of both philosophy and art, as Plato argues in his *Symposium,* because it is that movement of thought toward its universal satisfaction. What fails to come clear in the Platonic account, however, is the dependence not only of desire but of reflective reason itself on the incommensurable difference of the double sentence. Difference is something much more than the leveraging of meaning, as Derrida would have it, through the displacement of one signifier by another. Difference earmarks a poststructural ontology that effaces the atavisms and obscurities of the late Heidegger, as well as Derrida's own ghost dance of pseudo-philosophical, literary criticism. As Gilles Deleuze shows us, even the older, Platonic notion of "idea" or "essence" can be reframed as a disclosure arising from the scissions of the sign-universe. What is an "essence"? asks Deleuze. "It is a difference, the absolute and ultimate Difference. Difference is what constitutes being, what makes us conceive being. That is why art, insofar as it manifests essences, is alone capable of giving us what we sought in vain from life."[4] A similar inference can be drawn from Michel Despland's insightful exegesis of Plato, according to which all education or *paideia,* which separates rational knowledge from poetic license, rests on the differencing of the "higher" and "lower" loves within the economy of the soul.[5] The difference bespeaks an ontology in the measure that it mirrors the double sentence of psychology. The thing itself, the *res vera,* is exhibited by the disjunction of the desire and its emblem. "Truth" springs from what Lacan calls the "deconstruction of the drive." Speaking posttheologically, we may say that the deconstruction of the metaphysical conatus steers us, as the artist Paolo Portoghesi sententiously puts it, "toward Ithaca," in the direction of the unthought anteriority of thought under the auspices of what I have elsewhere named a *bathotheology,* a theological thinking appropriate to Hegel's depths of Spirit.[6]

Finally, such a postheological mode of theological thinking is distinctly postmodern to the extent it comports with the overcoming of the regency of the metaphysical subject. The word *postmodern* is originally a locution of art. The overcoming of the subject corresponds to a revolt against the tyranny of novelty, which has highlighted the "modern" and been the unique fetishism of an epoch that defines reality in terms of singularity. Portoghesi says that the postmodern is in actuality "a refusal, a rupture, a renouncement, much more than a simple change of direction." It is a jacquerie against "the perverse guarantee of perpetual renewal."[7] At the same time, it is on the artistic front a rediscovery of the "archetypal," as contrasted with the functional and episodic. As far as theological thinking is concerned, the postmodern hermeneutics of the destructuring of the world according to eros takes us into the realm of the originary, the unseen and the unspoken that has been lost from view. The theme of a postmodern, posttheological version of the theological aim in itself underscores a rupture, a radical differencing. But it is not differencing as nihilation; it is differencing as manifestation, wherein absence, like the empty tomb, is transposed as final presence, where breakage becomes breakthrough, where the ascent of mind and the "descent: of God" are conjoined, and the bifurcated "loves" of the soul are disclosed as the mummery of the infinite.

The writing of the double sentence that identifies desire, however, would be impossible were it not for the self-disclosure of the body as the postmodernist, pangrammatical play of discourse. The integral relationship between so-called body studies and postmodernist modalities of language is not merely fortuitous, but arises out of both the overt transcriptions and the latent signifying regimes that have accompanied the pure psychologizing of truth that began with Nietzsche and came to a flowering in the early Freud. Freud's neurological description of what hitherto would have been known as the "transcendental world" constituted a boundary marker for the movement of Western metaphysical thought toward its own "ending" and "self-overcoming" within postmodernist rhetoric. Couched as it was in a rather odd and inept Newtonianism of the instincts, Freudian psychoanalysis nonetheless shifted the grounds of discourse itself.[8] Whereas Nietzsche had ultimately tumbled back into his own peculiar, "Aristotelian" metaphysic of the will to power, Freud transgressed the long-surviving protocols of philosophy as the search for the transcendental signified, insofar as he located the concept of "origin" in the utterly concealed and unspeakable, in the hideous wish, in the lie rather than the truth, in the abyss. Even the so-called Freudian metapsychology, which is really nothing more than an effort to orchestrate fully the libretto of primal myth, springs from this entrancement with the much vaunted "unthought," with deep fire and impenetrable darkness.[9] The uttering of the double sentence, therefore, depends upon an irreducible scission within the very act of articulation.

Desire is of the "body" that does not yet know its carnality. Desire is of the "polymorphous perverse" body that has not yet created a signifying discipline for the realization of its doubleness, of its coded alterity. The venture of eros in the Platonic sense is driven by the "madness" of the lover who is at once thinker. Body-soul, in fact, constitutes the great double sentence of all representational—that is, metaphysical—thought in the Western world. The "strangeness" of eros is constituted by the unfamiliarity of the soul with its body, with its own substratification. The venture of eros is toward the "god," toward its own self-representation, its eidetic double: "And so does each lover live after the manner of the god in whose company he once was, honoring him and copying him so far as may be, so long as he remains uncorrupt."[10] As Nietzsche recognized far more astutely than his admirers have understood, the Apollonian is not the counterpoint to the Dionysian—*it is its mask.*[11] Metaphysical thinking has always been based on a differencing that has failed to become self-cognizant of the difference, which is at the same time a *dissemblance,* a sheer taking off and putting on of comparative disguises. Plato's well-known, and perennially misunderstood, attack on writing at the close of the *Phaedrus* can thus be explicated along these lines:

You know, Phaedrus, that's the strange thing about writing, which makes it truly analogous to painting. The painter's products stand before us as though they were alive, but if you question them, they maintain a most majestic silence. It is the same with written words; they would seem to talk with you as though they were intelligent, but if you ask them anything about what they say, from a desire to be instructed, they go on telling you just the same thing forever. And once a thing is put in writing, the composition, whatever it may be, drifts all over the place, getting into the hands not only of those who understand it, but equally of those who have no business with it; it doesn't know how to address the right people, and not address the wrong.[12]

The "drifting" of writing is the dissemination of the sign, the disruption of the pure semiotic unity of voice and its dismembering as response, as reading, as interpretation. Hermes-Thoth is the "god" of writing, which is at once a kind of Hegelian "diremption" of reflective consciousness as the movement of the subject toward what is wholly other, as the magnetism of the signifier for the signified, as the eroticness that drives all explication. In writing, the double sentence that begins with the surge of unspoken desire is etched, once and for all, as the quality of paradox in re-presentation. In writing, the body as the "stranger" that confronts desire is represented as text, as the anatomy of the intelligible. Epistemology becomes somatology in the measure that representation is now structured as the discursivity of desire. Empirical philosophy since its inception has always served as a stand-in for material psychology. But in the postmodern setting the alienation is broken down through what Lacan has called the *deconstruction of the drive*. The *deconstruction of the drive* means simply that desire has been articulated as symbol, the unspeakable as the teleological spoken, the unconscious "will" in the Romantic sense of the word as a self-critical form of syntax. The deconstruction of the drive does not lead, however, to a new subjectivism, which can never—if one truly reads Heidegger—count as an ontology.[13] Nietzsche's assimilation of "willing" to "will to power" was a failed lunge, which regrettably remained enmeshed in its own sort of archaeology, at such a target.

The Platonic "duplicity" of desire, in short, is the origin of what from the postmodern vantage point can be regarded as the etiology of metaphysics itself. Diotima's doctrine, as Plato enunciates it in the *Symposium,* is far more than a rhetorical and highly metaphorical narrative about the transfiguration of the passions. The reason that "love will help our mortal nature more than all the world" and that "every man of us should worship the god of love," as Socrates asserts, is because the erotic ascent commissioned by the figuration of beauty must inevitably lead to the vision of truth.[14] And the representation of truth in itself is secured by the intentionality of the drive. The notion of the "deconstruction of the drive," therefore, functions as something far more telling than is imaginable if we remain wedded to a late Victorian philosophical psychology. It serves as a rule for transposing the familiar, libidinal grammatology of body-thought into conventional epistemology and vice-versa. The great, yet inchoate discovery of postmodernist theory as a whole is that any "transcendental analytic" in the Kantian sense and a transcendental somatics are one in the same. Both, in fact, constitute the groundwork for a totally new "empirical" approach to knowledge.

The rudiments of a true transcendental somatics of perception, if not nonetheless of desire, can be found in the late Merleau-Ponty. What has been called in Merleau-Ponty the *primordial perceptual milieu*—the prethematic extension of corporeal relations as the phenomenological correlate to Kant's spatial intuition—anticipates our more fundamental idea of a somatological *a priori*.[15] This somatological *a priori* replaces the Hegelian, the Sartrean, and indeed the "empirical-theological" standpoint of reflexive consciousness as the point of departure for the theoretical. The shadow of Merleau-Ponty hangs heavily over all postmodern hermeneutics and lingers even amid the crags and crevices of feminist and Foucaultian narratologies of power. But a veritable "post-"postmodern transcendental somatics, from which a still unprojected strategy of theological thinking might arise, must all the same be liberated from every type of "modernist" metaphysic, which has been draped over the diverse, contrapuntal categories of subject and object, repression and power, wish and fulfillment. The deconstruction of the drive requires that knowledge finally be emancipated from knowledge in a manner that Marx or Nietzsche could never have countenanced nor Heidegger understood. The deconstruction of the drive, in the beginning of psychoanalytic transform, can now be disclosed as a cross-disciplinary principle of mediation between the interiority of the aesthetic and the autonomy of the "scientific." If, as Plato declared, philosophy in its classic position begins in wonder, in its postmodern guise it matures in something akin to what Nietzsche termed a *fröhliche Wissenschaft*, which might for our purposes be more precisely, and modestly, rendered as a "sensuous semiosis." The twin-visaged godhead of Dionysus and Apollo, the true "transcendental" signification implied in the Nietzschean "birth of tragedy," is at once the muse of all philosophy. For here we have the Socratic "final revelation" as the philosopher disrobes and enters into the "mysteries of love."[16] The revelation is a strange, identity-in-difference: an unenvisioned nonduality that maintains the morphic peculiarities of the double sentence, the double sentence of desire at work as the Heideggerian "worlding of the world," the deconstruction of the drive as truth in its unconcealment.

A transcendental somatics, on the other hand, must retain as its field of inquiry a conceptual domain that is much vaster than an economy of the instincts. Such a somatics must in itself become a kind of "transcendental" economy of signs and their indices that encompass the multiplicity of differentiations in cultural discourse: gender, sexuality, status, dominance, deference, exchange, imagination, performance, prohibition, pleasure, pain, and political identification. The transcendental economy turns on a novel, definitely postmodern comprehension of the rich connectivity of cultural communication itself. The connectivity is established by a rereading of metaphysical forms of discourse, such as theology and philosophy, as intermeshing sign-universes. A transcendental somatics falls back upon the infinite metaphoricity of the "body" as the basic web of discourse. As Drew Leder so masterfully puts it, "the ontology of the body reaches . . . down into the soil of any organismic vitality where the conscious mind cannot follow. Its branches spread throughout the universe. When I gaze upon the stars, or the face of another, or the symbols of divinity, I transgress my limits. Through the lived body I open to the world. The body is not them simply a mass of matter or an obstructive force. . . . It is a jewel in Indra's net."[17] If, as exponents of classical culture tell us, the body was once seen as conjugate with the cosmos, in the postmodern *mise-en-scene* it can be looked upon as correlative with culture. Hence, somatology becomes the higher-order discourse of both the humanities and the social sciences, which have only recently attained an uneasy, and rather unfaithful, marriage in what has come to be known as cultural studies. Somatology as transcendental somatics would trench visibly upon the theological to the extent that it examined the representationalism of the erotic, broadly defined, in terms of the production of the sacred. Elsewhere we have termed such an enterprise the *bathotheological,* the thinking through of what Hegel referred to as the *depths of spirit.*[18] As classics scholar Walter Burkert has noted, the archaic religious meaning of *theos* in the Greek tradition, whence the term *theology* ultimately derives, is that of a "calling" or "annunciation" of clarity from the depths of darkness and confusion, as in the summoning of the "god" during the Dionysic festival.[19] The production of sacrality in this sense must be construed as a sort of prediscursive, Platonic "love" for that which becomes a pure aesthetic presence. Dionysus was always the "beautiful" one, as is Jesus himself in the very ancient liturgy.

Nevertheless, a genuine transcendental somatics, as is the case also with a transcendental aesthetics, must rest as well on the discernment of the semantic structuring of all "body language" as it embraces the religious, the semiotic, and of course the strictly *cultural*. The traditional doctrine of culture has always been devoid of the somatological, because it is founded on the metaphysical presupposition of beauty and truth as purely "transcendent" entities in the Kantian sense. Implicit in the present rather savage, and usually tendentious, critique of "high culture" is the recognition that the long-enduring metaphysics of the purely formal must be overcome. Modern art and modern aesthetic commentary (for example, "new criticism") was the last dynasty in a regime of cultural metaphysics extending back to Alexandrian times. The problem, however, is that the theoretical criticism of cultural metaphysics has been saturated with a kind of insipid socialism and ideology of resentment *(ressentiment)* that could have been generated only by a clerical class in the crepuscular years of the late twentieth century Western university. In the attempt to name what has hitherto been unnamed, the critique of cultural metaphysics has relied, sometimes almost dogmatically, on its own counterontology of psychological repression, social exploitation, and "liberating praxis." This counterontology remains distinctly modernist inasmuch as it elaborates its own closed nexus of mutually implicative signifiers. Freud's so-called hydraulic model of the psyche was quite necessarily cognate with both the Marxian "metanarrative" of revolutionary awakening and violence and the Nietzschean rhetoric of heroic-artistic struggle. Furthermore, the great nineteenth century "trinity" of inverted rationalists has been played out once again, although not at the level of the *Gesamtkunstwerk* plied by Marx, Freud, and Nietzsche, in a variety of so-called multicultural readings of both past and present. The "return of the repressed" is no longer the uprising of the proletariat or outbreak of Dionysian energies. Rather, "critical" forces are now directed toward the reappropriation of texts in terms of those unarticulated readers or writers who have somehow been "left out" of historical consciousness, the multiplicity of "other voices," the infinity of possible acts of signification that remain embodied within the martyrology of pure, anticapitalist politics.

A counterontology of textual inclusion remains thoroughly modernist because it falls within the chain of endless argumentation and inference. Its redescription of culture is a wholly literary one: the characters who have not yet been given a chance to recite their lines, the representational systems that have been ignored, the countless "readings" to be done. What passes for postmodernism in this sense is nothing more than a late scholastic modernism masquerading as an avant-garde, which long ago left the scene. A postmodernist exposition, on the other hand, recognizes the power of the unspoken not as one more opportunity for further division of textual classification, but as a new comprehension of what counts for signification itself. The alleged "discovery" of woman's voice in the text can now be indicted as the "re-covery" of what "stands for" *woman*. It is no accident that women's studies and body studies have gone hand in hand.

According to Helena Michie, the female body within the context of feminist hermeneutics has become a kind of root metaphor, "a figure for literalness and truth, for a realism that is faithful to women's experience of themselves." Furthermore, "enveloped in meaning, the body has taken on mythic and empowering significance that derives in part from the denial of its own figurative richness." Michie concludes by observing that "full representation of the body" cannot be assimilated within a grammar of "absence and difference." The fragmentation of the body in literature and rhetoric ineluctably results from the dispersal of corporeal signifiers within a cultural architectonic of power relations.[20] The female body is not merely, as feminist writing going back to Simone de Beauvoir has avowed, a mask for undifferentiated alterity. Every *gynesomatology*, the grammatics of the female physique, is implicitly built upon the mapping of "folds" and lacunae within the convoluted, and frequently involuted, syntactics of historical body space. For Michie, the challenge of feminist interpretation consists primarily in the reassembly of a cultural discourse that marginalizes by dismembering, by the permanence of "tropes that entrap women's bodies," generally speaking within a representational nexus that is "patriarchal" because it is made up of subterfuges and semantic inversions by which women wholly "reflect" men and not each other, by which their figurations emerge out of the "absence" of the masculine, the nullity experienced when the phallic signifier is withdrawn. The site of the feminine in any patriarchaeology can be located as where the man is "not": the privacy of the home, the refuge from war, the street of clothing shops, the tea garden. The female body thus is "invisible" to culture, language, and interpretation, chiefly because it is the world-spectrum for a kind of shadow semiotics, the domain of what is always "signifying nothing" amid the formal representational patterns of "metaphysical" argument.

Yet this "displacement" of woman's body from the signifying web of culture and history is at once its transfiguration into a conjugate semiotics of the concealing-revealing. Such a conjugate semiotics, which parallels Heidegger's own "fundamental ontology," is conversation of the postmodern. It is the conjugate semiotics of what Adi Ophir has termed the *hidden signified.* "In postmodern signification, no hidden agent governs the manifestation of the phenomenon by which its is signified. Rather, the order of a series of dispersed, meaningful elements is postulated as its newly signified. Every time an order is postulated it is subject to criticism, which does not look for the existence of a metaphysical foundation or its lack, but seeks theoretical deconstruction and practical transgression of the presumed order."[21] The language is, of course, that of Foucault, and one must investigate why such an analytic has been so instrumental in the development of the discursive postmodernity that informs so much of what has been called *body studies.* Foucault's paradigm of body economies, which in turn has left a deep impression upon contemporary cultural hermeneutics, can be described as a "distributive theory" of desire and repression. Foucault's somatology emanates from his *Discipline and Punish,* first published in France during the mid-1970s, where he sketches a "penal semiotics" that regards the body as a living map of political authority and social constraint. The "sentence" of the criminal, therefore, becomes a semiotic statement that discloses the inscription upon the body of the reigning representations of power. The horrible tortures and punishments meted out to "political" criminals throughout history have usually been a *signing* of the regime's representation of sovereignty, or "authorship," in regard to the people or the body of the victim. The victim's body stands in synecdochal relationship to the body politic. As Foucault puts it, "in the darkest region of the political field the condemned man represents the symmetrical, inverted figure of the king."[22] The body of punishment mirrors the body of authority, a kind of upside-down metonymy. Even though Foucault has been heralded as the philosopher of postmodern sensibility, however, his analytic of the body is discretely modernist.

Modernist descriptors of the body, as is the case with Freud, are derived from both mechanist and naturalist epistemologies. We discover Foucault the modernist in his expansive *History of Sexuality*. Foucault's "method" of treating the body derives from his critical psychology, which focuses on the cultural formation and discursive generation of insanity. Foucault has called madness an *ironic sign*,[23] meaning that it shows the liminality of all truth codes. The madman is both pariah and wise man; in certain cultures he is the "holy fool," displaying both his abandonment and prestige, his absent presence. The distribution of madness in a particular epoch coincides with the curvature of power and authority. As "hegemony" is disseminated by means of the democratization of modern culture, madness becomes more prevalent, more easily defined or "diagnosed" by the rhetoric of professional expertise, more present by virtue of the absence of phallic centralization. Foucault's metaphor for both modern psychiatry and modern political economy is the "panopticon," the watchtower from which constant surveillance, gentle vigilance, and preemptive care is always possible. Modern regimes of power do not subject; they encircle.[24] Madness is whatever remains outside the circle, or creeps somehow inside the perimeter of surveillance, but in a sense, it is always present as the design of disruptive intentions within a loose-knit, or technically free, weave of benevolent, but totalizing, legitimization. Hence, madness is a constant possibility and must be always reconfigured, psychiatrically and philosophically. The use of "psychiatric justice" in modern totalitarian regimes is no accident of the times, if we pursue Foucault's path of inquiry. It gives origin to the totalizing leverage of "humanized" discourse with regard to pleasure and pain, affect and representation, instinct and permission, innovation and conformity.

The same is true of sexuality, which signifies the interconnectivity of bodies. The semiotics of sexuality in the Foucaultian mode overcomes eroticism as a natural attribute, as David Halperin remarks, and unveils it as a "cultural production" that "represents the appropriation of the human body and of its physiological capacities by an ideological discourse."[25] The concept that bodies can be "appropriated" by ideology is irrefragably Foucault's. Indeed, bodies are "en-gendered" ideologically, as Foucault has proposed and most feminists presuppose.

Yet the thought of an en-gendered somatics, descended from a political analytic of the circulation of power, still does not correspond to the postmodern ontology of the body erotic. The body erotic differs fundamentally from the Foucaultian body politic insofar as it constitutes a decompressed somatology, where the hydraulics of power and repression have metamorphosed into the coruscating infinity of the "word made flesh." If sexuality *per se* signifies a surrender of "sovereignty over one's body,"[26] then the true teleology of an en-gendered somatics is not the will to power, as Foucault implies, but in-carnation. Earlier we have discussed the isomorphism between the "theological" notion of in-carnation and the semiological sense of "carnivality." But what is missing in both constructions is the contrapuntal diction of en-gendering, that which "produces" through duplicity, which discloses through the inscription of the double sentence. It is not, as Freud surmised, that "anatomy is destiny." But it is appropriate to say by way perhaps of *double entendre* that *gender is eschatology.*

It is here that Foucault and feminism must depart from each other. For the Foucaultian analytic of power-knowledge as the superscript of the body economy rests on a modernist understanding of self-consciousness. Foucault's analytic of the body as the distributive factor in any more fundamental erotology springs out of his social inquiry into sexuality, which in turn depends on the classical ideal of the *cura sui,* the care and formation of the self. According to Foucault, the ethics of sexuality is "governed by relations of force—the force against which one must struggle and over which the subject is expected to establish his domination."[27] The history of sexuality rides upon the shifting constellations of force and corporeal identification that reflect the structures of social dominion.

Feminist readings of the history of sexuality, however, have tended to emphasize the ways in which woman's body serves as a chiasmus, articulated through a dysrepresentation of the dominant discourse. "Reading woman," as Mary Jacobus argues, is an act of textual transgression, a movement that "at once discloses and discomposes itself, endless displacing the fixity of gender identity by the play of difference and division which simultaneously creates and uncreates gender, identity, and meaning."[28]

The semiotics of the female body is founded not on the discipline and dispersal of the *soma,* as Foucault would have it, but on coded intimations of the inarticulable and unspoken. A feminist "ethics," as Julia Kristeva tells us, must move in this direction, for it can no longer be a "rationalist" economy of desire and inhibition, but a field of pure metonymous signification that reveals "incarnate" meaning, or *jouissance.* It is what Kristeva describes as a "herethics that is *a-mort, amour.*"[29] The "linguistic structures" of *jouissance* are "musical" inasmuch as they are cast from a rhythmic contextuality that functions as a sort of mimetic double to woman's somatic history. *Jouissance* is a "heterogeneous economy," an unbounded signifying process that forms a temporary totality, but that can be best described in terms of what Plato termed *chora*—"an essentially mobile and extremely provisional articulation constituted by movements and their ephemeral stases."[30]

The heterogeneous economy of the female *soma* in Kristeva's sense seems to render the body erotic as something countervalent to culture as a whole. The category of *jouissance* implies a reality that is somehow translocal, syntactically global, even *Dionysian*. It is, of course, possible to read the Kristevan phenomenology of the female body as correlative to Nietzsche's primal, tragic dithyramb, as an ecstatic, purely "musical" language. Just as Nietzsche saw the "Dionysian" as "the eternal and original power of art" that serves to "call into being the entire world of phenomena"[31] so Kristeva seems to regard *jouissance* as the "maternal" power of all thought and expression, as the poetic fire that congeals for an instant into the representational monuments of discourse. Even though there are noticeable similarities between Kristeva and Nietzsche—and perhaps we might even say the whole of the Western Romantic tradition—on this score, there is also a fateful disjunctivity that constitutes the boundary state between poststructuralist semantics and vitalist metaphysics. The Kristevan body erotic is not identical, for example, with Norman O. Brown's "love's body," in which the end of all repression is coextensive with a Freudian, polymorphous sensuality.[32] Kristevan feminist theory has little to do with an "ethics" of sexual liberation. It has much in common, on the other hand, with a radical somatology that regrounds feminism and philosophy, if not perhaps theology, in an en-gendering ontology of signification. This en-gendering ontology mirrors an understanding of sexuality that is nonideological and refuses to be victimized by the crypto-patriarchal sociology of knowledge suffused within Foucault's writings. Its en-gendering ontology lingers in the borderlands between desire and speech, between the primitive somatic and the play of signifiers we call the *semiotic*.

It is here, then, that we can begin to appreciate far more deeply and extensively than has been previously possible why the thought of a postmodern style of religious thinking requires, on the one hand, a return to an aesthetic self-awareness and, on the other hand, a conversation with popular culture. Ironically, this rather discomforting linkage can be found in the classic texts themselves, in particular Aristotle's *Poetics*. The difference between poetics (i.e., "productive science") and metaphysics is that the former relies on a mimetic duplication of action in the form of *drama*, whereas the latter merely offers an account of the causes (*aitia*) of action.[33] In a word, poetics is "productive" of a second-order language, a "double sentence," that allows desire to "stand for" itself as the form of the beautiful. That is what Aristotle has in mind when he writes, somewhat cryptically, later in the treatise that the poet speaks not of "incidents which have come to be," but of "incidents which might come to be."[34] In the poetic arts, which are identified by aesthetic inscription, desire is fulfilled by its own representational sign-enactment. Signification demands the subjunctive, which in turn transforms desire itself from something ephemeral into an eternal object. At the same time, the aesthetic inscription that can be called *dramatic* in Aristotle's sense is not a metaphysical singularity that transcends the everydayness of speech and phenomena. Poetics derives the "imitation" of what is for the most part episodic. Its "first things" are not the "first causes" of Aristotelian metaphysics, but entities that are wholly immanent and, as Heidegger would say, "ready to hand," that are indeed *kata physin*, "according to nature."[35] If the "handiness" of the world on the phenomenological model can be reinscribed as the artifactual, then poetic "first things" are necessarily the tokens of popular culture.

The relationship between popular culture and a postmodern erotology of the body—Kristevan, neo-feminist, semiological, or what have you—may lie in that most "handy" prosthesis of the soma, that is, clothing. Clothing is, in truth, the poetics of the body. The idea that clothing could be a proper, if not a profound, topic for phenomenological research and philosophical or theological reflection grates on the mind. The study of clothing belongs to what has derogatorily been termed *handicrafts*.

However, as we have seen, the "handiness" of the craft of *techne* in the Greek meaning, bespeaks its own ontology. Through clothing, Elizabeth Wilson notes, woman has incessantly engaged in the work of "turning herself into something else." Although men wear clothing and have revealed their bodies historically through their attire, it has been the work of female clothing designers deliberately to hide or disclose the "erotic."[36] Women's clothing is inherently "utopian," according to Wilson, to the degree that it idealizes for women the fantasies of the body. Many feminists have wrongly interpreted the cultural fact of fashion as a patriarchal regimenting of the female form for the sake of masculine surveillance, but the demographics of women's magazines and the historiography of costuming indicate the opposite. Fashion design is the "body language" of femininity. Clothing as fashion is the "double sentence" of popular culture.

Popular culture is a rich lode for semiotic inquiry because it is full of what the theory of signification terms the *multimessage.* Multimessages are not simply "anthropological" constructs. Multimessages are the complex, and unrepeatable, processes of signification that surpass, and in many cases trespass upon, the universal and excessively *repeatable* codes that we know as "academic" discourse. The fluidity and inventiveness of semiotic analysis arises from these ephemeral codings. The significatory acts of popular culture are not in any sense "finished discourse, achieved, closed residues from which the creators have left in self-satisfaction, but rather as individual recitals, stories of will sparking with the effort not to repeat its prior work."[37] Postmodern discourse, and by extension postmodern religious discourse, is the mimetic restatement of popular culture's multimessaging. The movement toward popular culture by postmodern critics is not some arbitrary, and perhaps perverse, choice of subject matter, a retreat from the classics in light of either ignorance or *ennui.* An authentic postmodernism, in fact, must be superimposed upon the appropriation of classic texts. The movement is spawned by the rules Aristotle outlined in the *Poetics;* it is a reproduction of what is apophantic and immediate. It is the "drama" of the body. Or, as Merleau-Ponty says, "things have an internal equivalent in me; they arouse in me a carnal formula of their presence."[38]

The "carnal formula" is the principle of representation and exhibition that makes up the iconography of popular culture. In modern painting the female nude, for whatever reasons, is the visual metanarrative of "high culture," as recent art historians have maintained.[39] In Marxist, materialist hermeneutics the female nude can be viewed as the commodified gaze of patriarchal praxis. As in Manet's famous nineteenth century painting *Dejeuneur sur l'herbe,* in which a naked woman sits idly and without indicative gesture amid two fully clothed men embroiled in conversation, the nude represents the alterity of informed speech, the pure "pleasure" of the text that is monopolized by men. In non-Marxist terms the "ideality" of the nude, however, can also be articulated as a coded, erotic transgression of the formal and "naturalistic" scaffolding of signification that makes up so much of eighteenth and nineteenth century painting. The epiphany of the body without comment divulges the substratum of conventional art itself, as

Toulouse Lautrec's prostitutes in a different idiom manifest the social underside of its familiar subject matter. Manet's nude is a kind of "theological" statement, inasmuch as it discloses the insouciannce of the "divine" female, as Bataille has shown. Manet strips the nude of the Greek "goddess" myth that lurks in the background and influenced the Renaissance prototypes from which is own painting was elaborated. His *Dejeuneur* discloses the body straightaway as body, but also as eschatology, as the coming forth by light of what has been most deeply incarcerated. In Manet's nudes, according to Bataille, the aesthetic preoccupation with "beauty," as engrafted into the rules of the academic arts, is raised to the level of ontological "first things." In Manet's nudes "modern painting was born," says Bataille. But we add that the great, "postmodern" insight was retrieved from the metaphysics of art itself. "Thus was majesty retrieved by the suppression of its outward blandishments—a majesty for everyone and no one, for everything and nothing, belonging simply to what *is by reason of its* being, and brought home by the power of painting."[40]

The visual metaphors of high culture depend on the presentation of signs that are transcendental and enduring, that supply a regime of unambiguous representations around which stable, social knowledge and activity could be authorized. In pre-Impressionist art the metaphors were largely monumental and reminiscent of classical truth values. But in so-called modern aesthetic theory, the metaphors reveal the space of art itself. As Fauvist and Expressionist canvases a few generations later laid bare the material facticity of the artwork itself, so Manet's nude "woman" on the grass becomes the utter self-signification of desire in an Edenic setting. The woman is not "looked upon" by men in the picture, as standard feminist-Marxist doctrines of critical voyeurism would have it. She is simply "there," present within the intricate, semiotic web as the "unsaid" and, from the standpoint of Victorian "ethics," *unsayable* because she is the embodiment of Kristevan *jouissance.*

Manet's nude, which bespeaks the function of the body in all forms of postmodern narrative, sketches the horizon of what we have called *popular culture* within the thorough, signifying praxis of high culture. Her "unclothed" character is more than a "displacement" in the grammatological sense. She is transgressive, although toward an end. She is the presence of woman not in some kind of Greek disguise, as *eidos* or *theos,* but as the familiarity of the flesh itself without any grand Freudian economy of longing, inhibition, and projection. She is not "commodified" because she has no use-value. She is, however, an effigy of what we have called *handiness*. The men do not reach for her; they seek neither to ogle, seduce, or violate her. They seem to accept her pure presence-at-hand. In that regard Manet's infamous painting contains all the "strangeness" of eros, because his nude is neither a sensual type nor a lure for the libido of the viewer. Manet's nude is a-sexual, but that is her power. She is woman's body as the ontology behind the entire painting's symbology. She is both abstraction and condensation. To her belongs the sheer sign *W*—for woman.

The sheer sign, however, which both "deconstructs" and decodes the totality of high culture, serves largely to disclose within the galaxy of signification we describe as "popular." Strangely, one may compare Manet's nude with the fully clothed, yet equally diaphanous, Cheryl Ladd on the cover of the March 30, 1991, edition of *TV Guide*. The picture shows the attractive Ladd in a tight-fitting red dress with straps and cleavage twirling a basketball on her finger tips. The cover entices the reader to peer inside for a preview of the battle for TV ratings surrounding the NCAA basketball championship. The headline of the story runs, "It's Heartthrobs vs. Hoops Mania." It offers a "choice" to the readers between "a bunch of tall guys running around in shorts while they try to put a 21-ounce ball through a 10-foot-high-hoop" and "a romantic story about a beautiful TV reporter who has to choose between her glamorous, fast-lane job in New York and her love for a handsome heart surgeon on the West Coast." The deeper coding can be found in the body image of the actress herself on the cover of the great, voyeuristic tabloid for television voyeurs themselves. Ladd is the pop iconic counterpart to Manet's nude, because her presence and her clothing harbors the message that the masculine video text of texts with its apocalyptic "playoff," or "network," of signifers has all at once been decanted into its bare, silver-screen essentiality—frivolity and entertainment. The "serious" code of sports suddenly is undraped as the laughing, taunting "lady in red." As Cheryl says about her shadow role to the "tall men" who sink "thirty-footers" every half-minute to a frenzied crowd at a true, Bacchic froth of intensity, "I'm going to have a real hoot." Perhaps it is the hoot of the pop cultural owl of Minerva that takes flight whenever the spring fashion magazines paint their grape in grape. To enjoy the postmodernist feast of unleavened bread in this instance, and to comprehend how a transcendental triviality becomes revelatory, we must say with the Marxists of a generation ago, "the yeast is red."

Cheryl Ladd is the sheer signified, the apparition of *W,* but that is the subject for another essay. The aporia of "hearts vs. hoops" unveils the erotology of popular culture, which is the absolute "sublimation" of desire into commercial sign, the signification of a choice that is not really a serious choice at all. This sublimation, however, is not a commodification; it is rather a "comedification" of the flesh. Just as the ancient "birth of comedy," which Nietzsche did not analyze, came about through the transport and display of the phallic signifier as ritual flesh "deconstructed" for the enjoyment of the whole community to behold, so the birth of postmodernity occurs with the redescription of eros as entertainment, as electronic *jouissance,* as the body erotic that is at the same time pure costume and dis-play.

Perhaps we can now begin to see that the relationship between so-called high culture and popular culture is not one of privilege or priority. It is instead the measure of multimessaging. It is the secret of the double sentence. The double sentence as the protoinscription of metaphysical discourse not only has its correlate in what has been literalistically dubbed the *soul/body* dualism, but also in a heteronomy of signification that has counted all along as the notion of the "end" in the Western tradition. This heteronomy has been masked throughout the two-millennia-old epoch of Graeco-Christian "metaphysics" by different styles of symbolics that have created the framework for so-called eschatology: the representation of the "last things." The concept of the last things is, however, not really a representational complex but a final and irretrievable dissociating of signifactory operations, a scission in the fabric of discursive relations that reveals what has been implicit, but indecipherable, all along in the metaphysical code itself. The "eschaton" is the yawning chasm that opens amid the seemingly impenetrable riddle of mythic and philosophical sign-linkages. Not at all surprising, the eschatology of the West is founded on a radical reinterpretation of the destiny of the body.

The eschatology of the West has always been derived from variant codings of the double sentence: the liberation of the "soul" from its somatic bondage and what in the Christian faith has been known as the "resurrection of the body." These variant readings, in turn, have materialized as divergent texts. One text we call the *metaphysical* tradition, which has been reengraved in the modern era as the "psychological." The other we shall refer to as the *eschatological.* The first text has been read many times over. The book is closed. The rose has been revealed. The fire is burning. The second text amounts to what we may refer to, tropically, as the "opening of the book ... of life." The eschatological text has for the most part remained unthought within the onto-theological framework of Western interrogation and reflection. The eschatological text is not captioned by the immortality of the soul, but by the physical resurrection. As Margaret Miles has emphasized in her study of the Augustinian tradition concerning the body, the eschatological signifiers of Western theology ultimately point beyond the metaphysical postulate of psychic emancipation in the direction of a somatic spirituality, a "miraculous combination of an immaterial with a material substance,"[41] as it is described in the *Civitas Dei*. In Augustine the mythological anticipation of the body's resurrection, which traces back to Persian sources, is transformed into a root theological metaphor: a *coenesthesis* or the full, incarnate dwelling of the transcendental within the sensual, what in the New Testament was known as *parousia* or "total presence" of the divine at the "end" of time.

The text that we know as the eschatology of the West, therefore, is no longer the Dionysian body that has been repressed, tortured, and condensed—Foucault's body politic or Brown's unbounded body of desire. We do not have to say with Brown that "the unspoken meaning is always sexual."[42] That is the Freudian "deep reading," which is inherently symbolized as "forbidden sapiential, silent. For Freudian sexuality is inherently symbolized as "forbidden fruit," the surplus of discursive meaning, the black violence of the twisted signifier. The Freudian deep reading is the call to "revenge" against time in Zarathustra's sense, the refusal of "overcoming." The second coming of chaos. It is, after all, our "beginning," not our ending. The eschatology of the West is founded on a "final reading" that uncovers the en-gendering of the fundamental text itself. The text discloses the body that has not yet been inscribed, that is not yet the transcendental signified. It is the text that unfolds with the opening of the "second book," the book that has not yet been coded as grammar. It is the hierogamy in the new "heaven." It is the "book of life."

Notes

1. See Jacques Lacan, *Ecrits: A Selection*, trans. Alan Sheridan (New York: W. W. Norton, 1977).

2. See Sigmund Freud, *Introductory Lectures in Psychoanalysis*, trans. James Strachey (New York: W. W. Norton, 1966), p. 87.

3. Georges Bataille, *Death and Sensuality: A Study of Eroticism and the Taboo* (New York: Walker and Company, 1962), p. 29.

4. Giles Deleuze, *Proust and Signs,* trans. Richard Howard (New York: George Braziller, 1972), p. 41.

5. See Michel Despland, *The Education of Desire: Plato and the Philosophy of Religion* (Toronto: University of Toronto Press, 1985), pp. 85ff.

6. See my *Theological Thinking: An In-quiry* (Atlanta, Ga: Scholars Press, 1988), pp. 105–116.

7. Paolo Portoghesi, *Postmodern: The Architecture of the Postindustrial Society* (New York: Rizzoli International Publications, 1983), p. 7.

8. Perhaps the text where Freud genuinely struggles with the question of the transgression of what I have termed his *Newtonianism* is in *Beyond the Pleasure Principle,* trans. James Strachey (New York: W. W. Norton, 1966).

9. This most forcefully comes to the surface in Freud with the feeling of dread or fear that accompanies the "return of the repressed"; that is, the fear of the father's retribution. See Sigmund Freud, *Totem and Taboo,* trans. A. A. Brill (New York: W. W. Norton, 1950), pp. 3–25.

10. Plato, *Phaedrus,* 252d.

11. See Frederich Nietzsche, *The Genealogy of Morals,* trans. Francis Golffing (New York and London: Ancor Books, 1956), especially sections 21, 24, and 25.

12. Plato, *Phaedrus, 275d–275e.*

13. See Jacques Lacan, *The Four Fundamental Concepts of Psychoanalysis,* trans. Alan Sheridan (New York, W. W. Norton, 1977).

14. Plato, *Symposium,* 212b.

15. For an extended discussion of the relation between the body and perception, see Maurice Merleau-Ponty, *Phenomenology of Perception,* trans. C. Smith (London and New York: Routledge and Kegan Paul, 1962), pp. 203–345.

16. Plato, *Symposium,* 210e.

17. Drew Leder, *The Absent Body* (Chicago: University of Chicago Press, 1990), p. 173.

18. See, again, my *Theological Thinking.*

19. See Walter Burkert, *Greek Religion,* trans. John Raffan (Cambridge, Mass.: Harvard University Press, 1985), p. 271.

20. Helena Michie, *The Flesh Made Word: Female Figures and Women's Bodies* (New York: Oxford University Press, 1987), p. 149.

21. Adi Ophir, "Michel Foucault and the Semiotics of the Phenomenal," *Dialogue* (1988): 412.

22. Michel Foucault, *Discipline and Punish: The Birth of the Prison,* trans. Alan Sheridan (New York: Random House, 1979).

23. See Michel Foucault, *Madness and Civilization: A History of Insanity in the Age of Reason,* trans. Richard Howard (New York: Random House, 1965), p. 37.

24. See Foucault, *Discipline and Punish,* pp. 104–131 and 195–228.

25. David M. Halperin, "Is There a History of Sexuality?" *History and Theory* (1989): 258. For application of the Foucaultian body hermeneutics to the study of the female body, see Christine Buci-Glucksmann, "Catastrophe Utopia: The Feminine as Allegory of the Modern," in Catherine Gallagher and Thomas Laquer (eds.), *The Making of the Modern Body: Sexuality and Society in the Nineteenth Century* (Berkeley: University of California Press, 1987). See also Alison M. Jaggar and Susan Bordono (eds.), *Gender/Body/Knowledge* (New Brunswick, N.J.: Rutgers University Press, 1989) Consider the deeply Foucaultian remark of Martha Reineke in her study of women mystics from the standpoint of religious historiography: "a power claimed over a body is a power asserted in the social sphere, a threat issued against the social body is a thread registered by a human body. Moreover, the organic metaphor underscores the fact that power does not seize human minds and consciousness. Rather, as Foucault has claimed, power seizes bodies." "Abjection, Anorexia, and Women Mystics," *Journal of the American Academy of Religion* (Summer 1990): 247–248.

26. See Paul Gregory, "Eroticism and Love." *American Philosophical Quarterly* (October 1988): 342.

27. Michel Foucault, *The Care of the Self* (New York: Pantheon Books, 1986), p. 67.

28. Mary Jacobus, *Reading Women: Essays in Feminist Criticism* (New York: Columbia University Press, 1986), p. 24

29. Julia Kristeva, "Stabat Mater," in Susan Rubin Suleiman (ed.), *The Female Body in Western Culture* (Cambridge, Mass.: Harvard University Press, 1986), p. 118.

30. Julia Kristeva, *Revolution in Poetic Language,* trans. Margaret Waller (New York: Columbia University Press, 1984).

31. See Frederich Nietzsche, *The Birth of Tragedy,* trans. Francis Golffing (Garden City, N.Y.: Doubleday, 1956), aphorism XXV.

32. "To pass from the temple to the body is to perceive the body as the new temple, as the true temple. The house is a woman, and the woman is a house or palace. . . . The land is a woman, the virgin land;

and the woman is a land, my America, my Newfoundland." See Norman O. Brown, *Love's Body* (New York: Random House, 1966), p. 225; also of interest would be the final section of *Life Against Death* (Middletown, Conn.: Wesleyan University Press, 1959), pp. 307–322.

33. Aristotle, *Poetics,* 1448a.

34. Ibid., 1451a.

35. See Martin Heidegger, *Being and Time,* trans. by John MacQuarrie and Edward Robinson (London: SCM Press, 1962), pp. 482–483, and 500–501, n. xxx.

36. Elizabeth Wilson, *Adorned in Dreams: Fashion and Modernity* (Berkeley: University of California Press, 1985), p. 125.

37. Marshall Blonsky, "The Agony of Semiotics: Reassessing the Discipline," in Blonsky (ed.), *On Signs* (Baltimore: Johns Hopkins University Press, 1985), p. xix.

38. Maurice Merleau-Ponty, *The Primacy of Perception* (Evanston, Ill.: Northwestern University Press, 1964), p. 164.

39. See, for example, Marcia Pointon, *Naked Authority: The Body in Western Painting 1830–1908* (Cambridge, Mass.: Cambridge University Press, 1990). See also Jane Root, *Pictures of Women* (Boston: Pandora Press 1984).

40. Georges Bataille, *Manet,* trans. Austryn Wainhouse and James Emmons (New York: Skira, 1955), p. 75.

41. Margaret Miles, *Augustine on the Body* (Missoula, Mont.: Scholars Press, 1979), p. 125.

42. Brown, *Love's Body,* p. 265.

Chapter 4

The Magic of Desire

Tell me, enigmatical man, whom do you love best, your
  father your mother, your sister or your brother?
I have neither father, nor mother, nor sister, nor brother.
Your friends?
Now you use a word whose meaning I have never known.
Your country?
I do not know in what latitude it lies.
Beauty?
I could indeed love her, Goddess and Immortal.
Gold?
I hate it as you hate God.
Then, what do you love, extraordinary stranger?
I love the clouds . . . the clouds that pass . . . up there . . . up
  there . . . the wonderful clouds!

Charles Baudelaire

"What we have learned from Saussure," according to Merleau-
Ponty, "is that, taken singly, signs do not signify anything, and
that each one of them does not so much express a meaning as
mark a divergence of meaning between itself and other signs."[1]
The age of desire commences with the death of the signified. This is
perhaps what we really have in mind when we prate about the
"postmodern."[2] The morning star of modernism, of course, has
always been the Cartesian *cogito*, the interiorization of the previous two millennia of metaphysical thought that at last resulted in
the summation and closure of the book of Christian theology.
From the advent of Cartesian "speculation," the discovery of

speculatio or "self-mirroring," the moment of transcendental reflexivity, springs the passion of modern inquiry and modern criticism. Modernity has enshrined the power of the sign in the same
way that postmodernism has applied the didactic strategy of difference. The power of the sign derives from the projection toward
the infinite of a historically constituted literacy, and by extension
a textuality, that has been severed from any "natural" systematics
of reflection and representations, as Foucault has described it.[3]
The epoch of the sign coincides with the ideology of the "human,"
the immortalizing of the collective capacity for self-representation,
so that classical epistemology is inverted as psychology. Yet the
psychology of the modern can stray only so far. The operation of
the sign as a deratiocinated style of apostolic authority, as a post-
Medieval simulacrum for heavenly charisma, degrades into the
existentialist pathos of defiance, the *Wille zur Macht* of Romantic
subjectivism.

It is here amid a culture where the Cartesian *cogito* has become in effect an "image of the beast," a duplicate of the divine,
a virtual apparition of the transcendental signified, that a
metacriticism from the "psychological" standpoint gains credence.
We find such a metacriticism in the work of Jacques Lacan. Modernity has "postulated" the subject in much the same fashion
that the Kantian architectonic of reason was compelled to postulate the Deity. The subject must both inhere and subsist, or so
Descartes realized, as a stolid requirement of philosophical argument and construction. It is the Archimedean point at which the
entire structure of what we might call the *discourse of experiment* is
balanced and held intact. In the modern idiom the Cartesian
subject operates as the unifying principle of all inference and
conceptual innovation. This necessity was grasped immediately
by German idealism, and it soon became the founding insight for
Hegel's reconstitution of "science" as a dialectical synthesis of
thinking and experience.

Yet Lacan's premise subverts the subject's metaphysical
suzerainty at its very own hallowed site. The "deconstruction" of the
subject in the Lacanian mode arises from the revelation that subjectivity itself is not an "object" that all speech denotes, but an
introjective consequence of the mimetic structure of language itself.
As Lacan notes, "the subject is subject only from being subjected to
the field of the Other."[4] The power that the Other enjoys to define
and configure knowledge through wielding syntactical regularities
rebounds upon the formation of all "self-conscious" representations
and thus creates the subject as God, authors the world.

At the same time, the unmasking of the subject is its primordial dis-closure, the removal of the reification, or closure, of the interplay of signifiers within the space of cognition. The disclosure of the subject is the unrestraining of the energy of desire. Again, in Lacan's delphic formulation: "The truth, in this sense, is that which runs after truth—and that is where I am running, where I am taking you, like Actaeon's hounds, after me. When I find the goddess's hiding place, I will no doubt be changed into a stag, and you can devour me."[5] The location of the subject in the "goddess" lair betokens a kind of primitive reunion between the discourse of the Other and the moment in which the subject is formed from what Lacan terms the *deconstruction of the drive.* The language of the analyst in this sense performs as the hermetic trickster, luring the client toward the abyss of self-revelation where the mediations or "constructions" of the analysand dissolve into the enchantments of the "it" (Freud's id).

The liminal representations of "subjectivity" at this point emerge as the charter language of the hidden "constitution" for multiple modes of discourse posing as a weave of signifiers. The act of signification springs out of what we might term the *dark intentionality* of desire itself, although the very logos of desire, a silent erotology, cannot be deciphered alone, but must be read as a companion volume to the virtual structure of meaning and presence that constitutes the "logic" of the text. The syntactics of the "soul," the so-called humanities, thus are built upon this dark intentionality. As Hamann first glimpsed and Freud later detailed through the methodology of regression, the proto-structure of conversation is myth. Myth itself, as Levi-Strauss has discerned, turns upon the logic of opposition. But the opposition is not so much a social contradiction or a cognitive conundrum. The Oedipus myth, for instance, is not primarily a struggle against the belief in autochthony. Instead it can be comprehended as a mimetic response to the lesion of "consciousness" etched by the inauguration of discourse. The Lacanian *Spaltung,* "the split . . . which the subject undergoes by virtue of being a subject only in so far as he speaks," stands forth as the scene of primal repression and as the power of re-presentation.[6]

Here language commences, not as a lucid exercise in symbol manufacture, but as a veritable division of the darkness, a groping toward functional clarity in contest with the restiveness of unarticulated desire. The Lacanian framework of language, viewed primordially and hence poststructurally, is the same as the Heraclitean logos, which has always been expressed mythically. It is the originary production of measured strife or counterpoint that resides in the "psyche," which forever presses into the light of day yet remains "strange" to those who seek to discern its working.[7] The "truth" of Heraclitus lingers in singular obscurity; it is recovered through the exposure of the duplicity of the phenomenal, corresponding in psychological terms to the saying of the archtetypally unsaid, the step backward into what remains prior to the chain of signification. The "splitting" of desire is tantamount of the founding of the unconscious, which is not so much a topology as a reverse projection, a projection of discourse that remains charged with the numinosity of its own overwhelming self-presence. The carnival of representation perpetrated through the historicizing and codifying of discourse must ultimately be summarized as the deflection of the drive into language.

Language is the palingenesis of desire. Structuralism all along has assumed, falsely, that it is a pathogenesis. But this palingenesis, which transpires amid the agitation of writing and the elaboration of textual markers, is subject to its own deconstitution, its analysis in the strict sense. The ages of discourse are a kind of yellow-brick road wending toward to the site of disenchantment. The disenchantment of discourse comes with the discovery that each signification is a mystification, that the production of referents is but high magic.

The alleged "structure" of the unconscious, therefore, is commensurate with a magical semantics. But what do we mean by *magic*? The field of the magical, and by extension its intricate pathology, has been a cause of avoidance not only for philosophy and theology but for just about all orthodox modes of hermeneutic investigation. The category of the magical does not belong within its organon of inference. Why not? Because whatever is "magic" presupposes a secrecy that by definition cannot be either contemplated or made a predicate. Its occultation suffices as its primacy, as its power. The secret force of the magical subject distends the chain of signifiers. The magical subject, which constitutes the subject in terminus, is the discursive instrumentality of desire. What in Freud's mechanico-metaphysical schema of pushes and pulls has been known, quite tendentiously, as cathexis is changed through the Lacanian series of conceptual transgressions into the discontinuity of the wish. Lacan understands, of course, that Freud's so-called "hydraulics" of the unconscious was but an expansive metaphor for the displacement of desire in the direction of a diguised desideratum. Lacan notes that in the parapraxis, in the riddle of dream life, in the myth, hovers "the sense of impedi-

ment." The impediment is not a task, but a secret mode of signification, what Derrida has called the supplement.[8] The infrastruc-
ture of the text is not revealed by the linkage of signifiers but by
their unraveling and erasure. Repression both hides and unveils
simultaneously.

Thus, analysis constitutes a return to the scene, not to where
the subject is to be found, but to where is was perpetrated. The
subject has been perpetrated in the breach, the breach imparted
by desire. The illumination of the unconscious shows nothing, for
the unconscious is not to be found. "We have," says Lacan, "in
Eurydice twice lost, the most potent image we can find of the
relation between Orpheus the analyst and the unconscious."[9]
Eurydice is a magical entity, because she exists as an erotic phos-
phorescence, as pure heterogeneity, as a representation that flick-
ers forth from the ancient division of names. She is "metonymic,"
as Lacan would argue. In other words, the "meaning" of the
unconscious is the strategy of self-concealment. The language of
the unconscious is the language of feints, diversions, and masks.
It is the vocabulary of the magus.

The psychology of magic, as contrasted with its semantics,
depends on the harboring, through anticipation rather than enun-
ciation, of the forgotten name of the "god." A calculated confes-
sion of the workings of this psychology can be found in the writings
of Aleister Crowley, the notorious Meistersinger for the magical
theater of the twentieth century. It is incumbent upon the magician, Crowley tells us, to seek the "Lost Word," whose "pronuncia-
tion is synonymous with the accomplishment of the Great Work."[10]
The "lost word," the logos that does not speak, is the supreme
magical cipher, because its power seeps from its very inarticulation.
The great work, the magnum opus, the transformation of the
inchoate into a vast, intelligible content turns upon the saying of
the aboriginal unsaid, the presyntactic. "An idea is perpetuated
because it must never be mentioned."[11] The refusal to speak, the
veiling of what remains so difficult to utter, defines the magician's
hegemony within the court of symbols. The magician controls
the energy of the god, because he "knows" it as the mystery of the
cleft, as the message of the vestige, as the manifestation of
the trace. Indeed, the magician is greater than the god, insofar as
he reserves the prerogative of commanding what wavers in the
darkness of the unimagined into the realm of voice. Magic requires both silence and renunciation.

The preference of the magician for the pre-discursive perhaps
helps us understand one of the long-persisting curiosities in the

history of philosophy: Plato's disdain for the use of writing. Writing is amnesia, according to Plato. Plato recounts the king of Egypt's rebuttal to, Theuth, inventor of the graphic and computative skills, who vows that writing will improve the art of memory. But the king protests: "If men learn this, it will implant forgetfulness in their souls; they will cease to exercise memory because they rely on that which is written, calling things to remembrance no longer from within themselves, but by means of external marks."[12] The king, whose views are also Plato's, fears writing as a kind of artifice, a magical substitute for authentic recollection. The king well understands that writing involves repression, that the resort to a mnemonic technology of signs and codes must lead to the uncoupling of meaning from its source along with the creation of a metaphoric web of dissemblances. Plato's own metaphysics of representation was in many ways a sentimental gesture toward retrieving the arcana of the soul that have been left disinherited by the rise of philosophical argument. Socrates himself laments several lines later about the perfidy of "written" *logoi:* "they seem to talk to you as though they were intelligent, but if you ask them anything about what they say, from a desire to be instructed, they go on telling you just the same thing forever. And once a thing is put in writing, the composition, whatever it may be, drifts all over the place, getting into the hands not only of those who understand it, but equally of those who have no business with it; it doesn't know how to address the right people, and not address the wrong. And when it is ill-treated and unfairly abused it always needs its parent to come to its help."[13]

Writing results, as Derrida has told us, in the erasure of presence and the dissemination of significance through the temporality of the text.[14] But this erasure, which amounts to a repression of the "face" *(eidos)* of the original "divinity," produces a force or tension that is now distributed throughout the whole genealogy of the text. The lattice of signifiers is anchored not in a founding signification, but in the contretempts of forgetfulness. The first inscription, or proto-writing, is therefore a mode of magical pseudo-memory. It consists of what the ancients termed *hierogrammatica* ("hieroglyphs"), a picture-script that evokes by representation the sense of what is hidden or forbidden. The hieroglyph eventually becomes the model for the hermetic cosmology of magical correspondences, which was employed as an aid to memory in classical rhetoric. The rules of memory, evoking magical images of things invisible, were indispensible to the art of truth speaking and persuading an audience to the truth.[15] From the psychoanalytic perspective, we may say that the theory of magical correspondences as the pretext of discourse mirrors the relationship between desire and representation, between meaning and metonymy. Magic is not an aberration of reason so much as it constitutes an intermediate "logic" between the formations of the unconscious and the discipline of expression, which depends upon the "grammatology" endemic to all linguistic architectures. Magic flourishes when words are not allowed entirely to have their say. Magic is the effort to build a system of manipulable representations during the twilight hour when the "god" has vanished and its absence has not yet been consecrated as discourse.

The magical, therefore, constitutes the misplaced signifier that the sort of structuralism Lacan has borrowed from Saussure can entirely assimilate. The magical is less than what Lacan terms the *symbolic;* it is certainly something more than the "imaginary." The magical is the logos that makes possible the "return of the repressed." In Lacan's words, it is the plan of investigation that fortifies the subject "in his encounter with the filth that may support him." Whereas the goal of Platonic anamnesis was self-purification, the outcome of Lacanian regression is to generate a countertext to the perjured testimony of the *cogito.* This countertext becomes its own argot. Lacan writes: "Take Socrates. The inflexible purity of Socrates and his atopia are correlative. Intervening, at every moment, there is the demonic voice."[16] Psychoanalysis acts as the scribe for this countertext, the "demonic voice" of the subject who is constrained to speak of his or her passion, but can disclose its intention only through the supplementarity that characterizes the stitch of signifiers. The Socratic demon is not the augur, but the taunt of philosophy. The demon is the "it" that holds forth, that converses in a strange way, as what Lacan terms a *colophon* to the Cartesian meditation, to the discourse of subjectivity. The colophon, however, belongs to the text in the sense that it simultaneously marks and deciphers it. *I* and *it* are coimplicative. The magician tends to the vocalization of that which is unintelligible within the idiom of the subject. The magician possesses the "lost word," the revelation of desire that paradoxically can never be laid bare, because it is the shade of the Other, the shudder of the real.

The Freudian project was to eliminate the illusion of a magic world through the disclosure of desire. The Lacanian enterprise is to show that desire cannot be disclosed, because it is the root of language, the thing in itself, the loom behind the weave of signifiers. For "desire is that which is manifested in the interval

that demands within itself, in as much as the subject, in articulating the signifying chain, brings to light the want-to-be, together
with the appeal to receive the complement from the Other, if the
Other, the locus of speech, is also the locus of this want, or lack."[17]
Because in Lacanian linguistics the signifiers ultimately signify
nothing, the world of representation can be construed as the
ritualization of magic. And magic conjures up a sense of presence
where, in actuality, there is only the repressed.

The psychic mechanism of the surrogate presence was first
examined in a brief essay of Freud's, "The 'Uncanny'," written in
1919. Freud's speculations, although maddeningly tentative and a
bit too casual, do indicate the fruitful hermeneutical possibilities
inherent in the psychoanalytic method, once leave has been taken
from its more "dogmatic" strictures. Freud sets about to examine
the meaning of the expression *unheimlich* ("uncanny" or "unfamiliar") as it pertains to the feeling of the supernatural or haunted,
particularly as conveyed in horror literature. Freud asks what is
truly signified by the fictive construct of the "alien" presence. The
mood of uncanniness is inextricably bound up with the phenomenon of repression, according to Freud. But it is not due simply to
repression of the specific wish-object. The uncanny arises when an
entire psychic range of orientation—primary narcissism, for instance, which first found cultural legitimacy in primitive, animis-
tic thought formations—invades the ego system, disrupting its
capacity for critical discrimination. "An uncanny effect," Freud
observes, "is often and easily produced by effacing the distinction
between imagination and reality, such as . . . when a symbol takes
over the full functions and significance of the thing it symbolizes. . . . It is this element which contributes not a little to the uncanny effect attaching to magical practices."[18] The domination of
the object by the symbol, or more precisely the token by the force
of desire, depends on a superimposition of significatory complexes,
or grammars. The uncanny emerges with the unthrottling of discursive operations or, in Lacan's terms, with the "splitting" of the subject from its innermost self, the production of the subject through
independent, symbolical activity. Whereas Freud understood the
uncanny as the atavism of some discarded habit of cognition, the
Lacanian view permits us to regard it as the penumbra of self-
discursiveness. The uncanny is the revelation of the "unconscious"
as a totalized sector of discourse, as a conjugate semantics to the
"rational" order of both personal and cultural reflection.

The uncanny is "strange" or "not at home" because it represents the magical presence of a mobile desire that cannot settle

down in ordinary language. The uncanny is the reminder not merely of the "unconscious" in its antediluvian mystery, but of the very arche-language that is not language in the formal sense but makes language possible. The Lacanian deconstruction of the totalized logic of significatory systems, therefore, aims at a new kind of postmodern transcendentalism. It is neither the transcendental metaphysics of Kant nor the illuminist subjectivism of the Romantics. It is a provisional sort of poststructuralist transcendentalism, an exceptionally incisive *via negativa* that pursues (in Derrida's wording) the "archaeology of the frivolous." The frivolous, in this instance, is the inessential, the wholly sensible or phenomenal, the myriad modalities of chatter. The discourse of the uncanny is the "structure" of magic.

The category of magic in this respect helps us to comprehend what structuralist thought has mistakenly interpreted as the eternal, transformational agency of the "unconscious." For example, in Levi-Strauss the unconscious operates as a timeless source of representational patterns that supplies the "mythic" format for narrative, ritual, and individual experience. The "vocabulary" of the imaginative performance, argues Levi-Strauss, "matters less than the structure," which is "atemporal" and "limited in its laws."[19] In typical Kantian fashion, Levi-Strauss stresses the genesis of symbol configurations from an aprioristic universal mind. But while structuralism has grasped what might be called the *transpersonal dimensions* of mythico-symbolic reflection in relation to the empirical grammars of culture and language, it has failed to develop a useful account of the alleged semantic conversions that take place in the transition from the deeper unconscious to social cognition. The evident shortcomings of the structuralist program at this level ought best to be explained as a telltale flaw in the methodology itself. Only when the supposed structural transforms have been "destructured" in the measure that they now function as transpositional keys, rather than as underlying registers of meaning, can many apparent "solutions" to the enigma of human creativity be carried out. The transpositions between regular discourse and the subtext of the "unconscious" can now be seen as relative shifts in interpretation, not as perennial and inviolable norms.

Both structural anthropology and analytical psychology in the twentieth century have stoked the illusion that somehow the puzzles of the "irrational" could be described as a sophisticated kind of encryption, which a proper metaphysics of the imagination might dispel. Even the more recent discovery of the primacy of desire, so far as it undercuts the ideological posturing of every formal hermeneutics, has been bent toward reestablishing the structuralist myth of myths. The allusion here, of course, is to the work of Jameson, who seeks to introduce the (Marxian) construct of social mediation as the horizon of both the historical and the textual, as a curious strategy of cooptation for the philosophical moment in which signification is deconstituted as writing, or *ecriture*. Marxism, for Jameson, permits not simply a fundamental interpretation of synchronous codes according to certain "naturalistic" processes embedded in collective symbol making, but more important, the retelling of history, a vaster narrative that unfolds "within the unity of a single great collective story."[20] Can the concept of social mediation suffice for the rule of "difference" in the deconstruction of textual artifacts? Not really. Jameson merely dusts off the metalanguage of structuralist semiotics and gives it a somewhat chic, Marxist polish.

But the substance of the two hermeneutical approaches is identical. Jameson substitutes for Levi-Strauss's keyword *myth* semanteme known as "history." History is transmuted from cultural text to social narrative. The dominion of desire is now pacified in a strange, convoluted ideological move as "the experience of Necessity," which Jameson insists must forestall the reification of historical interpretation. Jameson remarks that "history is what hurts, it is what refuses desire and sets inexorable limits to individual as well as collective praxis." That is "indeed the ultimate sense in which History as ground and untranscendable horizon needs no particular theoretical justification."[21] In a very odd manner Jameson himself actually exposes both the conceit and the deceit of the Marxist valorization of time. For desire is unconditionally bounded, and therefore nullified, by a perverse kind of *ananke,* which Jameson claims as a principle of transcendence. Marxian transcendence is actually the closure of history, the qualification of desire in terms of the *puissance* of the collective, the sham deconstruction of the ideological scaffolding of interpretation only for the sake of a final totalization, or reification, of culture—the "great beast," the human. Marxism thus elaborates its own code of magic.

Despite Jameson's critique of what he terms the *magical narratives* of the modern epoch enforced by a bourgeois schizophrenia afflicting both symbols and work, Marxism retains its own magical syntax. Jameson comes close to making such an admission when he talks about the requirement to "rewrite certain religious concepts," including "the pretheological systems of primitive magic" as "anticipatory foreshadowings of historical materialsm."[22] The magical codings of Marxist rhetoric and analysis are exhibited in its readings of the revolution as, to borrow Jameson's phraseology, "utopian" consummations of the dominion of desire. In the would-be consummation lies the great "construction," or history as representation, that robs the function of desire of its dissimulative task. Social mediation, or the megaform of "society" itself, is not only the glyph for the unriddling of Marxian "theology," it also becomes the sounding device for its dark history. The dominion of desire can never be a metaphor for the human collective. It can only serve as the shadow of the utopian presumption, as a torment, like Ozymandias's mocking inscription, to the structuralist ideality.

In consequence, the Lacanian analytic rushes in where Marxian metahistory fears to tread. The Lacanian analytic understands desire as the truly unreifiable, not the sign of signs, but the moving signature. From desire the sanctuary of intelligibility is first built, and then torn down. As Lacan puts it, "*[d]esidero* is the Freudian *cogito*."[23] Desire is kindled alongside the discourse of the Other; it is the precise momentum of the charged reflex called *consciousness* that spins about the axes of subjectivity and alterity. If we take Lacan quite seriously, we understand far more than the "metonymic" truth that the recital of his name enters into the history of thought a lacuna, a hiatus, a "desideratum." We understand that the utterance of the *nom de pere,* the "name of the father," is an accession to the founding, "deconstructive" moment when Oedipus has at last been banished, when the totalizing magic of the unconscious and all its narcissistic, romantic, and utopian fugues of overdetermined instinctuality have been obliterated in the judgment of language. The Lacanian lacuna, therefore, is the great crack in the ramparts of late modernism. It is the demystification of the demystifiers. It is truly the "end" of ideology and the closing of the book of Sigils.

But the magic of desire is intelligible to itself only through the significatory productions or the self-representative "intentions" of eros itself. The power of eros is not only discernible in the semiotics of the religious imagination, it is also puissant in the generation of the artifacts of popular culture. It is most evident within the semiosis that depends on the constant revealing-concealing of the body. It is, quite strangely, contained within the rhetoric of clothing, in the language of fashion.

———————————————— Notes ————————————————

1. Maurice Merleau-Ponty, *Signs,* trans. Richard C. McCleary (Evanston, Ill.: Northwestern University Press, 1964).

2. For a provocative meditation along these lines, see Marian Hobson, "History Traces," in Derek Attridge, Geoff Bennington, and Robert Young (eds.), *Post-Structuralism and the Question of History* (Cambridge: Cambridge University Press, 1987), pp. 101–115. For a general overview of the background of Lacan and the poststructuralist movement, see Edith Kurzweil, *The Age of Structuralism: Levi-Strauss to Foucault* (New York: Columbia University Press, 1980).

3. See Michel Foucault, *The Order of Things: An Archaeology of the Human Sciences* (New York: Pantheon Books, 1971).

4. Jacques Lacan, *The Four Fundamental Concepts of Psycho-Analysis,* trans. Alan Sheridan (New York: Norton, 1978), p. 188.

5. Ibid., p. 188.

6. Jacques Lacan, *Ecrits: A Selection,* trans. Alan Sheridan (New York: Norton, 1977), p. 269.

7. For a structuralist exposition of the Heraclitean fragments, see Raymond Adolph Prier, *Archaic Logic: Symbol and Structure in Parmenides, and Empedocles* (The Hague: Mouton, 1976), pp. 57f.

8. See Jacques Derrida, *Dissemination,* trans. Barbara Johnson (Chicago: Chicago University Press, 1981), pp. 156–171; and *Of Grammatology,* trans. Gayatarri Chakravorty Spivak (Baltimore: Johns Hopkins University Press, 1972), pp. 141–164.

9. Lacan, *Four Fundamental Concepts,* p. 25.

10. Aleister Crowley, *Magick in Theory and Practice* (New York: Dover Books, 1976), p. 71.

11. Ibid., p. 71.

12. Plato, *Phaedrus,* 275a.

13. Ibid., 275d–275e.

14. See Jacques Derrida, *"Ousia* and *Gramme:* Note on a Note from *Being and Time,"* in *Margins of Philosophy,* trans. Alan Bass (Chicago: University of Chicago Press, 1982), especially pp. 65–67.

15. For a discussion of the ancient theory of correspondences and its effect on Western thought, see Liselotte Dieckmann, *Hieroglyphics: The History of a Literary Symbol* (St. Louis: Washington University Press, 1970; and Francis Yates, *The Art of Memory* (Chicago: University of Chicago Press, 1966).

16. Lacan, *Four Fundamental Concepts*, p. 258. It should be noted that Freud also understood the "dream work" undertaken by the unconscious as due to a "demonic element." See Sigmund Freud, *On Dreams*, trans. James Strachey (New York: W. W. Norton, 1952), p. 95.

17. Lacan, *Ecrits*, p. 263.

18. Sigmund Freud, *Studies in Parapsychology* (New York: Collier Books, 1963), p. 50.

19. Claude Levi-Strauss, *Structural Anthropology*, trans. C. Jacobson and B. G. Schoepf (Garden City, N.Y.: Doubleday Books, 1967), p. 199.

20. Frederic Jameson, *The Political Unconscious: Narrative as a Socially Symbolic Act* (Ithaca, N.Y.: Cornell University Press, 1981), p. 19.

21. Ibid., p. 102.

22. Ibid., p. 285.

23. Lacan, *Four Fundamental Concepts*, p. 154. A similar interpretation is offered by Rene Girard, who sees desire as the hidden metaphysics behind all action and representation in modern literature. See *Deceit, Desire, and the Novel*, trans. Yvonne Freccero (Baltimore: Johns Hopkins University Press, 1965).

Chapter 5

The Intentions of Eros:
Popular Cults of Beauty and
the Signs of Fashion

"No one has uncovered my veil."

—Inscription in ancient times at site of the Great Goddess

In her brilliant and erudite historico-cultural survey of female iconography over the millenia Marina Warner concludes with the following, succinct observation: "The female form metamorphoses from one sign into another, and this flux of signs, each succeeding generation's variations on the ancient topic, is accepted as a sequence of statements of the truth. The body is still the map on which we mark our meanings; it is chief among metaphors used to see and present ourselves, and in the contemporary profusion of imagery, from news photography to advertising to fanzines to pornography, the female body recurs more frequently than any other . . ."[1]

At one level, Warner is merely asserting the obvious—popular images of women belong to the ever-roiling repertoire of male-contoured culture with its demand for titillation and prohibited pleasure, for spectacle, for satyrism. Woman as public icon becomes the dramatic sign that discloses the uncharted abyss of repression, fantasy, and desire. The public reproduction and dissemination, however, of the mute syntax of female flesh through the art memoria of the past and the mass media of this century—all the way from the Gibson girl to Marilyn Monroe to such contemporary "supermodels" as Claudia Schiffer—underscores the common, feminist argument that women, as Warner herself argues, "attest the identity and value of someone or something else, and the beholder's reaction is necessary to complete their meaning."[2] Woman, as John Berger has put it, is always the "seen" and not the "seer," because she is somehow a simple form of materiality; like so much of Western "art" itself, her display for others renders her the property of the beholder.[3]

This "speculative" theory of female figuration—the presumption that woman is a *speculum,* or "mirror," of culture as well as a sophisticated article of ownership and exchange—has been enlarged over the past century by Marxist criticism into a staple of political assessment. In certain academic circles it has become an article of unshakable faith. The creed states that woman is not only "objectified," she is also *commodified.* The intentions of male eroticism overreach themselves along the tuberlike networks of "capitalist" expropriation, consumption, and propaganda to bring forth an ethereal hologram of feminine beauty that is at once supremely unreal, but completely "retailable."

The corollary to this dictum is, curiously, that all conventions of female culture are ultimately high-stepping styles of prostitution: nothing about woman is substantial; all their artifacts and accomplishments, in effect, have "made in the male mind" stamped on their underside as well as a red, tawdry "for sale" tag dangling before all eyes. The political prejudice that women's values and aspirations are nothing more than a sort of coin of the realm for an immutable, plunderous patriarchy comes largely from the thinking of the "eminent Victorians" of the nineteenth century. It can be detected in Marx, reaches a sort of misogynous, semi-climax in Nietzsche, and is most conspicuous in the work of Thorsten Veblen. The little joke today is that a particular polemic, originally deployed by radical reformers to keep women themselves buffaloed and malleable in what later came to be called the *Movement,* has now been seized savagely by some feminist academics themselves to bombard and rain ruin on women's popular culture.

In his *Theory of the Leisure Class,* a book that is understood better as semiotics than as either sociology or satire, Veblen recurrently characterizes the protocols of female domesticity as legitimating the functions of idle leisure and "conspicuous consumption." Veblen acidly remarks that in respect to the "amenities of life, the housewife's efforts are under the guidance of traditions that have been shaped by the law of conspicuously wasteful expenditure of time and substance."[4] In *The Communist Manifesto,* Marx had sized up the degradation of women in the nineteenth century as one incident of the global expropriation of labor, including the "unpaid" services of wives and children, by industrial capitalism. Veblen, nonetheless, as the first political economist to offer an authentic analysis of the culture of consumption, looked upon female taste and the new "aesthetics" of middle class living as the outcome of a purely "pecuniary" system of social prestige and psychological motivation. As far as Veblen was concerned, the feminine definition of the "beautiful" was but a by-product of the decadence of late capitalism. It had become a cipher for self-indulgence, greed, pretension, luxury, inutility, feckless economic activity, and various undemocratic additions to hierarchy. Excessive "accumulation" of wealth had created, in turn, the paradigm of woman as voluptuous archetype of banality and as extravagant trafficker and coemptor of useless stock.

Although still not respected for his achievements, Veblen was really the first political "feminist" in today's sense of the word. In his ruthless unmasking of the so-called leisure class, Veblen narrowed what today we would call *women's issues* to a relentless attack on the preoccupations of the prosperous. He transposed a fledgling appreciation for the complexities of popular culture, which almost as much then as now was largely "female" culture, into a relentless, neo-Puritan cannonade against the vanities of the rising middle class. Like so many of today's scholarly commentators on "mass consumption," he saw woman in her salt-of-the-earth incarnations—devotee of lacquered fingernails and designer labels, habitue of "beauty parlors," and irrepressible reader of the "fashion mags"—as something slightly less than satanic and only a bit more than totally depraved.

The Veblenesque jeremiad against the futility of women and their complicity in popular "cults of beauty" persists, and with no less rancor or stridency, even today. The assumption lingers that woman is somehow a willing, but more or less unconscious, victim of the never-flagging, patriarchal-capitalist conspiracy to rob her of soul and indenture her to the high priesthood of glamor and the merchants of commodity personality. Veblen, of course, was more puzzled than he realized by the tendency of the unlettered, and *unleisurely,* populace to toss its incense on behalf of the leisure class's own cults of beauty. To explain away, without really explaining at all, the phenomenon, he gave currency to the word *emulation.* What Veblen did not realize, and what few practitioners of the new "cultural studies" that seeks to compass even "lowbrow" symbologies that can be found at grocery store checkout lines and on MTV have come to recognize, is that actually certain abiding, "aesthetic" standards may be operative in popular taste.

The same critics of "elitist" canons in art and literature are just as quick to dismiss, usually with a ferocious wag of the sociological finger, the enthusiasms of nonelite women. The truism that most mass representations of feminine desirability are based on the "selling" of beauty products, apparel, and accessories—not to mention "attractive" sexual personae—can be offset by the less obvious insight that the more sophisticated emporia of exchange have themselves been made necessary by basic kinds of aesthetic concerns and preferences.

Art, even "fine art," for example, has always been commissioned, bought, and sold. Veblen was, and oddly remains outside an esoteric group of "materialist" historians of high culture, the single serious examiner of the means by which beautiful, or spiritual, objects require their own "pecuniary" instruments of circulation and methods of distribution and comparison. Veblen's concluding chapter of *The Theory of the Leisure Class,* in which he takes to task higher education in general and the arts and humanities in particular, cannot still be confronted easily by today's "knowledge class"—the broadly dispersed, intellectual mandarinate that parodies in its displays of useless research and unintelligible journal articles the infamous 100-dollar-bill burnings and the dog birthday parties of the Vanderbilts and the Morgans. Commercial transactions and the adoration of the sacred have gone hand-in-hand throughout history, as the juxtaposition of the Medieval cathedral with the market square of the village indicates. And it is hardly true of necessity, Marxist "historical materialism" notwithstanding, that the latter always occasions the former.

The modern, reductionist tendency to regard popular cults of beauty, which to a certain degree are always religious in character, as nothing more than weapons of economic and gender oppression betrays the hidden bigotry within academia toward the working classes, an observation Veblen made over and over in a somewhat more oblique manner. Beautiful bodies are ritually mocked or condemned by the knowledge classes with their own pretensions to leisurely inutility, because such aesthetic ravishments constitute fatal competition with their own ecclesial mystifications of the undecipherable word. The exception to this rule, of course, is classical statuary and Renaissance painting, which the great unwashed are allowed to gawk at without comprehending at all. In the more refined, academic anticults of beauty ceremonially tended and purveyed by so-called multiculturalists and adversaries of Eurocentrism, the proles are harangued headlong about the sins of enjoyment and reminded of the hecatombs of colonized corpses atop which such delicate, but guilt-infected adumbrations of the elegant have always been sitting. Inasmuch as the proles are taught that they must become avid consumers of culture in order to keep professors handsomely paid, all the while wallowing in its disgusting etiology without showing any hint of delight in it, we may be so bold as to name this new, "deconstructionist" approach to aesthetic literacy as something like the *shit-eater's hermeneutic* of the arts and humanities. Deconstructionism in art and literary criticism is but one more surge of the savage naturalism and the accompanying default of all aesthetics that characterizes a culture in disintegration because it is traumatized by its own commercial success, and excess. As Camille Paglia has so pointedly made us understand in her book *Sexual Personae,* the struggle for the beautiful emerges out of a horror of the natural. Western culture had its genesis in the will to power of the "Western eye," through which the ideal of the beautiful halted "the melting flux of nature." "Beauty is the art object's license to life."[5]

But what sort of beauty? With an explosive genius that Paglia's narrative of the titanic combat between nature and culture embodies, *Sexual Personae* discloses how the creation of the beautiful in art and culture has little to do with the usual, textbook account of fine minds and imaginations transcribing their heavenly visions onto some tangible medium as stone, canvas, or paper. On the contrary, it is more a question of *making public the mysteries.* Mythographer Carl Kerenyi has convincing shown that much of the language surrounding the classic Greek concept of the "love of the beautiful" has its origins in the mystery rites at Eleusis with their torch-lit solemnities and their gripping, but unspeakable climax in the celebrant's vision of the *kore,* or maiden. The Socratic discourses on the erotic and the beautiful in Plato's *Symposium,* as well as the *Phaedrus*—passages, in fact, in which the central project and rationale of Western philosophy itself is stated—are saturated with metaphors from the mystery religions. *To kalon* and *to agathon,* "the good" and the "beautiful," are controlling metaphysical constructs of the Western tradition that, curiously and ironically, are formulated out of a primary, religious experience of the "beautiful child" or "maiden," daughter of the earth mother and grain goddess Demeter. Moreover, Plato's reliance on the vocabulary of Eleusian religion is scarcely idiosyncratic, or accidental. Eleusis in its time was a "universal" religious site for Mediterranean paganism, much like Mecca has been for the Islamic world since the eighth century. The Athenians themselves believed that the ceremonies of Eleusis reflected what today we would call a *global religious consciousness* transcending the particularities of clan and tribal cult and that whatever went on in the fire-illumined, underground chambers somehow "held the world together."[6] The sight of the *kore* may have in its own time have been the dazzling, "cosmic" vision of the unity of all humanity that is later assimilated in St. Paul's theology of the church as Christ's body in which there is no male nor female, no slave nor freeman, no Greek nor Jew.

We cannot take time here to analyze the Kerenyi thesis, which remains highly controversial and is not immediately relevant to our interest in popular culture. Yet the point here is a simple, yet intricate one: the apparition of beauty, and the "seeing" of woman, is something much more and something for more ancient and profound than what can be construed by political feminism and chic, but cheap, putdowns of popular estheticism in the name of "rescuing" some rarefied gender identity from the armed camp of the patriarchal plotters. In truth, popular cults of beauty, which can trace their metapsychological, if not their direct social and historical, lineage to the types of mystery faith signified by Eleusis, have always had a sacred function. As the historian Lo Duca has written: "In ancient eroticism there is a constant reference to religious myths, to a secret liturgy which allowed it to be represented as the very Mystery of Mysteries opening on the universe, and to see in the extension of carnal pleasures a means for the progression of the soul."[7]

The synthesis of sacrality and "vulgar" eroticism is captured in the work of British pop artist Allen Jones, whose delineations of female legs, stiletto heels, headless torsos in bikinis, and Masochian goddesses swaddled in furs have served as a visual vocabulary for the voyeurism and explicit sexual preoccupations of 1960s culture as well as a running satire on art gallery aesthetics. It has been observed that pop art, including the creations of Warhol, was in many ways a "new classicism" with its emphasis on the simplicity, commonality, and reproducibility of the figure. And just as classical iconography derived from what we may term the *sanctity of the erotic* and the *piety of the beautiful,* so much of pop art has drawn its fervor from strategic depictions of stereotypical sexual fantasies.

Jones's work evinces an obsession with revealing styles of female clothing, which from a psychological vantage point may be characterized as fetishism, but from the painterly perspective intensifies the "erotic charge" of the forms and materials themselves to the extent that the sexual theme of the work becomes the occasion for hierophany. Such fetishism is used by Jones "to create a sensation of human presence rather than a likeness of a particular person."[8] Pop art, as Jones has conceived it, therefore, functions as its own, Eleusian-like commoners" cult of beauty. As Paglia has proposed, the sign-devices of popular culture themselves are not postscript, but continuous "text" with the ciphers, pictures, and narrations of the classical idiom. "Popular culture is the great heir of the western past."[9] There is, however, both an identity and a difference within this unbroken mesh of signification. The difference lies in what might be described as the "textures" of the respective cultures—what we may call *classical* and *superclassical* or, in more familiar wording, *ancient* and *postmodern*.

The classical is concerned with density, with solidity, with perdurance, with the indivisible "essence" of things, as the parade of artifacts from the standard bas-relief to Aristotle's *Metaphysics* shows. The superclassical, or postmodern, dwells upon the luminosity of surface and the ephemeral glance of the eye. Moreover, the classical aesthetic focused on human nudity because of its interest in the ideality and purity of all that is "human." In contrast, the signature of the superclassical consists in a continuous dialectic of veiling and unveiling, of revealing and concealing, as the thought of Martin Heidegger, the philosopher of the "postmodern," underscores. At the same time, there persists a distinct identity among the two cultural styles. Just as classical values are impelled, as Plato's middle dialogues make clear, by the "intentions" of eros in its quest for the beautiful, so the "postmodern condition" derives in large but not exclusive part from the reach of the sexual imagination.

The sexual imagination, in turn, zeroes in—as it has throughout the modern period—on pictures of woman. Yet it is not the nakedness of woman, signifying subordination and dependency, but "clothedness" that manifests the ideality of the female body in the postmodern context. The postmodern *kore* is a "Madonna" figure, who is neither mother, virgin, nor slut—the usual patriarchal personae. Rather, as her namesake in the pop music ironically conveys, she is the queen of costume, the perpetual mistress, not the "slave" of fashion. She is sexuality projected as outrage, as cabaret sensuality, as carnival. According to Paglia,

> The history of costume belongs to art history but is too often regarded as a journalistic lady's adjunct to scholarship. There is nothing trivial about fashion. Standards of beauty are

conceptualizations projected by each culture. They tell us everything. Women have been the most victimized by fashion's ever-turning wheel, binding their feet or bosom to phantom commands. But fashion is not just one more political oppression to add to the feminist litany. Standards of beauty, created by men but usually consented to by women, ritually limit women's archtypal sexual allure. Fashion is an externalization of woman's daemonic invisibility, her genital mystery. It brings before man's Apollonian eye what the eye can never see.[10]

The intentions of eros, projected into the idiosyncrasies of fashion, are indeed the force behind clothing as the genuine popular, and postmodern, art form. The sacrality that hovers within what are decidedly postmodernist cults of beauty can be discerned in the aesthetics of clothing design and the ubiquitous rhetoric of the "fashion mags" that ballasts it. Such rhetoric is enforced by the subtle messaging of Goffman's "gender advertisements" or "gender indications." Although Goffman and Berger interpret the history of such advertisements as an archive of male domination, historians such as Lois Banner adopt a different stance. According to Banner in her book *American Beauty,* the growth of a mass cultural fashion discourse and of "beauty literature" mirrored the emergence of an articulate self-identity for women that had never existed in the past. The message inherent in such discourse was that "beauty" represented "not morality, but power."[11] Popular cults of beauty in this sense were more in keeping with "feminist" attitudes than the feminists of the day were wont to promote, insofar as the latter then, as well as now, were more concerned with instantiating a society of self-abnegation and virtue. For Banner, the "fashionable woman" is distinguished by heightened self-awareness, in opposition to the "natural" woman who gives herself over to abstract codes of integrity and propriety. Popular cults of beauty among women, Banner suggests, are ultimately more egalitarian in their membership and "multicultural" in their application than the ascetic politics and quasi-Marxian moralism of contemporary feminists who ceremonially criticize the fashion industry. Especially in the Progressive era, "beauty was a liberating force for woman" that marked her "transition from traditional to modern values."[12]

The now, obsolete thesis that popular cults of beauty are hardly more than indices of woman's displacement in the social lattice seems have been falsified by one bald historical fact. As "woman's liberation" in industrial society has advanced, mainly in the last quarter century, the cultural importance of the fashion business has gained, rather than waned. Even if one wants to postulate some all-pervasive, paternalistic cogworks of socio-economic servitude wherein women purchase cosmetics, thigh-high skirts, and body-tight "active wear" to stoke the unquenchable male libido and insatiable lust for cash, the contradiction remains paramount. The "beauty" of fashion has increasingly acquired the image of the dominatrix, of woman as she-wolf, as power-figure. The same is true of fashion's own rhetoric. The December 2, 1991, cover of *W* magazine carries the headline: "Pants Have Power!" The full-color, double-fold portrait of a model for the Donna Karan line shows a raven-haired woman with crystal earrings, dark eyes staring in sultry defiance, the left hand at waist and thumb in the pocket of her Mafia-striped suit pants as if she might be poised to draw some small, hidden weapon. The insinuation is thoroughly phallic. The captions are all intimidating, if not belli-cose: "Big-Time Watches," "Hemline War."

Inside the power imagery is rampant. An ad for a short-sleeved knit dress offered by the department store chain Nordstrom touts woman's singularity, excess, and an almost aristocratic lib-erty. "The genius of Genny. Lining up navy close to the body, then cutting free with a flourish of yellow." Even the syntactics of color is used to suggest female independence and a kind of hauteur that is available to anyone, irrespective of class. Only a rich woman can be decked out in pearls. A shop clerk can feel superior by flaunting yellow. Another edition of *W* shows off "New York's Best Clothes." The poses of all the models are sexy, yet aggressive and confrontational. A fashionable blonde in chiffon is dressed like a cowboy, sporting leather brimmed hat and gloves that convey toughness and ruggedness. A simulation of a tintype for a Macy's model displays a "night white" pleated skirt and jacket that crows: "pure sophistication lights your way." The picture hints far more of the power of wealth than of glamor. The model, whose face is little-girlish, has yet a look of barbarian fierceness in both mein and posture. One hand is behind her back, again as if she is concealing her ability to strike back at any affrontery. The other hand is tucked into a large, metallic-looking glove wreathed with jewelry and clenched into a menacing fist—the gesture of a war-rior before battle.

Missing entirely from the iconics of today's fashion is the seductive girl-child, the scrubbed and wholesome typology, the inconsequential and mascaraed mannequin that political feminism is so accustomed to berating for its pollution of the national mainstream of role models for young women. An advertisement for a Rena Lange skirt from Neiman Marcus mixes the Nordstrom's "power" combination of blue and yellow, seating a brassy but boyishly coifed model in the backseat of a plus limousine where her hand raised in a kind of hesitant salute communicates an incorrigible sense of strength and mystery. Even the goddesses of lingerie are self-contained, partaking in their own new-found sexual puissance. A "gender indication" from Christian Dior exhibits an "intimates collection" in skimpy, black lace. If the picture were for men, it would have a "come hither" look, which of course it does not. The model is both serene and secure, her folding of her arms about herself providing a gesture of self-sufficiency. Her eyes are closed in quiet ecstacy. She may be thought to having an orgasm, but it is from the delight of her own form and body.

The verbal language of the fashion industry also follows such a trajectory. Just as *W* represents the high craftsmanship of the pure, visual statement, *Mirabella* magazine is the gallery of fashion's *bon mots,* its "word bytes." The February 1991 pages of *Mirabella* features "pearls," which it reminds us, have always been "pretty and romantic" but now are ocular vocabulary for the "daemonic invisibility" of gender power intimated in the ideals of postmodernist beauty. Pearls are a "strong design element" in the very symmetry of superclassical woman's projected personality. No matter how they are clustered or conflated with clothing styles, "they have a naturally luminous presence," perhaps to match the feeling of only partial perceptibility, fleeting disclosure, and an immanent, street-legal sort of sacrality that such "superclassical" cults of beauty foment.[13] Contemporary cults of beauty that an-chor the world of fashion have transited rapidly from the old, Hollywood ideal of woman as everybody's ready-to-order pin-up to the post-1960s, stylized totem of private female preference and emancipated selfhood. The distinction resides in what Julie Baumgold has described as the decline of the "glamor girl." Ac-cording to Baumgold, the "glamor girl," who dominated Holly-wood and to a lesser extent Madison Avenue from the First World War to the Vietnam era, was not so much a creation of patriar-chal perversity as the longing of the new American ethnics on the way to assimilation. First, she was blonde and Nordic (Ginger Rogers or Grace Kelly), then voluptuously Mediterranean (Gina Lolabrigida). But she was always a roughly condensed emblem for the "American dream itself." She was the quintessence of *what,* not who, you would marry at the country club once you were allowed in there. She was "glamorous," meaning that she was remote and untouchable. She was beyond all real individuality.[14]

The decline of glamor comes with the rise of woman in the social setting. Images of women are no longer strictly "gender advertisements" in the sociological sense, which is probably why academic theories of fashion have habitually been scarce, irrelevant, overly tendentious, politically correct, or all of the above. Woman becomes, as the Sartrean existentialists might say, both *en soit* and *pour soi*. She has money. She has power. She no longer has glamor. She has her own "style." She is beautiful. The obvious, and remaining, "political" critique of this unabashedly revisionist reading of the fashion literature and its commercial paragons of woman is that, even though the industry has moved beyond the crass "sex-ploitation" of earlier eras, it still yokes the female self-concept to the imperatives of production in the "beauty business." Such a view, and route of attack, can be found in the thesis of neo-feminist and Marxist writer Naomi Wolf, who in *The Beauty Myth* assails woman's continuing obsession with standards of female "looks." Wolf blames the obsession not on the cultural hegemony of men, but on the economic clout and social sway of the cosmetics and clothes manufacturers.[15] In response to her adversaries, Wolf advances her "materalist analysis" by positing that "the real impetus behind the production and dissemination of images of [female] 'perfection' is the need to maintain intact the pool of cheap . . . docile and literate . . . female labour upon which the modern service and information-processing economy depends."[16] The beauty industry inculcates in women "low self-worth" to keep the costs of their labor low. The "ideal of thinness," as one illustration, "can be seen for what it is—not beautiful aesthetically, but beautiful as a political solution to women's threatened empowerment: pre-emptive counterstrike."[17]

Wolf's doctrine of political causality is, to say the least, not very convincing. Yet as a "neo-feminist" who castigates the class biases of the older, Betty Friedan cadres while declaring that "women's issues" have more to do with social position than with gender, Wolf lets slip what the social controversy over popular cults of beauty is really about—wealth and access to the tools of adornment. The problem, of course, lies in the fact that historically the nonelite classes have been the most "self-conscious" about their willing participation in the cult. And the most cogent explanation may have less to do with the familiar, and extremely torturous, theory of predatory capitalism as with Veblen's more nuanced notion of "emulation"—a principle that Marxist dogma in both its "soft" and "hard" renderings has systematically, and conveniently, ignored.

Popular cults of beauty, in fact, hinge not so much on the diminution of female individuality and assertiveness through the power of Paglia's phallic, photo-en-gendering eye as on the differentiation of femininity by a latent appeal to the culture's deeper narcissism. A sequence of images in *Cosmopolitan* magazine under the bare subheading of "Beauty" tells such a story. "Have you ever thought of changing your style?" the article asks. To be a woman is to be a poseur. Life is interminable Mardi Gras. "She" can choose from a trendy but finite menu of "appearances," all of which come with describable behavior codes and consumption tendencies. First, there is the "vamp" who wears magenta lipstick, serves champagne for dinner, and "moisturizes her breasts every morning." Second, we have the "downtown diva" who sports false eyelashes, wears hot pink lipstick to the gym, and "knows the lambada." Third, there is "corporate queen" with her male secretary, purchases panty-hose "by the dozen," and orders salmon with pesto sauce at power lunches. Finally, there is "nature girl," a combination of overgrown girls scout, Rebecca of Sunnybrook Farm, and eternal hippie who boycotts tuna fish, refuses to wear fur, and "won't give a man a chance unless her dog likes him."[18] The implication behind such fashion diction is that the "beautiful" must somehow be whimsical and that, moreover, it must profiled within a wild windscape of Protean, social identity. The particular personae featured by *Cosmopolitian* do not have the ancillary effect of selling costumes and accessories as much as of promoting female self-fascination. These kinds of gender advertisements are sheer street theater. They are not at all for men. They are only slightly more for other women. They are for the voracious, post-1960s narcissistic self with its unlimited capacity for self-construction and unbearable appetite for "experience." They are "divine" in the sense that the ancient Greeks, according to Walter Burkert, meant the phrase, that is, ephemeral but extremely memorable manifestings of the luminous and striking, as "when a mysterious light shines into the chamber."[19] They are visions of the *kore*—ineffable moments of initiation—by which class tensions are relaxed, the anxieties of the everyday are put in suspended animation, and postmodern culture is blissfully, if not necessarily morally, sanctified.

An ad in *Mirabella* puts today's *kore* of fashion's cult of beauty in her proper element. The young model with cropped hair slouches in her pin-striped man's suit, hands stuffed into large, baggy pockets as though she were both a syndicate mol and an oversexed tomboy. Her eyelids are closed. Her face is thick with makeup. She appears almost dead. Stencilled across the phantomlike, black-and-white photo is the teasing subtitle: "Mystery." On the adjoining page is a perspiring and perplexed female face. Here the hands are no longer hidden. They cover the face with a kind of frantic amazement, or possibly grief. The "mystery," reveals the ad, is "for everyday." The mystery of the postmodern *kore* is the highly superstitious sort of "epiphany" that occurs when the well-dressed New York woman appears amid the crowd on Seventh Avenue. It is both the signification of a reverent, quasi-religious "vision" and the unconscionable celebration of the excessive.

It is a simulacrum for the Eleusian higher mystery or *epopteia*, the ecstatic sight of the maiden as she appears out of the void of social anxiety and anticipation. It is raw spectacle made available to every onlooker. It is a structure of master social symbolism, connoting elegance, achievable status, and the "beauty" of personal self-possession. As in today's Eleusis, it binds "commercial civilization" together. It is the procession of the "fashionables." Our present day *kore*, however, is no longer bearer of the mysteries of grain and harvest, as she was in ancient Eleusis. She is the manifestation of the hyperidealized feminine with its many cultural vagaries and in all her tawdry, self-absorbed, histrionic, sensationalist, and voyeuristic splendor. She is neither housewife nor wage laborer, as the Marxist critique proposes. Nor is she some inaccessible, incommensurably affluent duchess of the executive suite—a stunning and overweening Artemis in the masquerade of Ivana Trump, for example—who by her utterly refulgent bearing touches off earthquakes of self-loathing and eruptions of envy in the cerebral cortex of every properly manicured receptionist from Winnemucca to Wall Street.

The view that fashion is but a sullen, overarching conspiracy of the "beauty" industry and that it is simply the Pygmalion-like transmutation of woman by the caprices of masculine desire is supported neither by demographics and sociology nor by the obvious, popular aesthetic values that couple collective self-aspirations and gender fantasies with the frenzy of the marketplace. It also overlooks an apparent "anomaly": fashion magazines are written almost exclusively for women and read by women and increasingly the industry itself is run by women.

To dismiss the universe of fashion, as most scholars do, as an inconsequential carnival of frivolity and as a shocking extravagance of the too rich and scarcely sensible, aided and abetted by

Madison Avenue specialists in social brainwashing, is to vent certain unexamined prejudices while missing a fundamental fact. As the celebrated economic historian Ferdinand Braudel has pointed out, to know the clothing styles of a particular culture is to know the culture. We might add, it is to understand as well the evolution and eventual triumph of woman in the struggle between culture and nature. But, no matter what may be the operative "gender politics" of a given generation, the cultural theory of beautiful women in beautiful clothes is integral to shifting, aesthetic *epistemes,* if we may borrow a term from Michel Foucault. As Quentin Bell has pointed out, art history and fashion history are not at all analogous to natural mother and disfigured foundling. On the contrary, he says, "fashion in fact is the grand motor force of [artistic] taste."[20] It is a system of socially distributed sign-values for broader and far less measurable paradigms of beauty itself. Or, as Roland Barthes tells us, fashion is not the same as clothing. Nor is it equivalent to some kind of ever-shifting, visual calculus. It is the transformation of the object into words, into what we call a *fashion statement.* The point of fashion is to "circulate Fashion broadly as meaning,"[21] as a code of what we might call *sacral totality.*

The human being, according to Lawrence Langer, is the "tailor-made god." Clothes were probably invented not for comfort or warmth, but as "a desire to be godlike."[22] At the same time clothing covers the animal parts, it transfigures the "daemonic invisibility" of erotic longing into a symbology of the beautiful, which culturally speaking also constitutes power. The greatest god is the *deus absconditus,* the god that is hidden. If, as the elder, patriarchal adage goes, clothes are what "make the man," even more importantly they disclose the goddess in woman.

But the goddess is a dual spectacle. She is both the *kore* who redeems, who supplies immortality, and the ancient furies, the stalkers of Orestes, the harvesters of the black night of anxiety that overcomes the body that has been torn by passion rather than saved through eros. To understand the postmodern as a play of somatic signification, we must also venture into the darkness itself. We must envision its tragic potential, if only to deconstruct the very signifiers of the tragic vision. We must take a walk on the nightside where the strangeness and horror of the abyss is dispelled through the apparition of beauty. We must imagine the body crucified and dismembered if only to recognize that it is no longer our fate, that it is but a Dionysian illusion. We must think the thought of the body tragic.

Notes

1. Marina Warner, *Monuments and Maidens: The Allegory of Female Form* (New York: Atheneum, 1985), p. 331.

2. Ibid., p. 331.

3. In Berger's famous line, "men act and women appear. Men look at women. Women watch themselves being looked at." John Berger, *Ways of Seeing* (New York: Penguin Books, 1972), p. 47. Man looks at woman, because he is the "spectator-owner" (p. 56).

4. Thorsten Veblen, *The Theory of the Leisure Class* (New York: Penguin Books, 1967), p. 82.

5. Camille Paglia, *Sexual Personae: Art and Decadence from Nefertiti to Emily Dickinson* (New York: Random House, 1991), p. 57.

6. See Karl Kerenyi, *Eleusis: Archetypal Image of Mother and Daughter,* trans. Ralph Manheim (New York: Schocken Books, 1977). For other accounts, see Alexander Liberman, *Greece, Gods, and Art* (New York: Viking Press, 1968), pp. 49–53. See also G. M. A. Richter, *Korai: Archaic Greek Maidens, A Study of the Development of the Kore Type in Greek Sculpture* (New York: Phaidon Publishers, 1968).

7. Quoted in Marco Livingstone, *Allen Jones: Sheer Magic* (London: Thames and Hudson, 1979), p. 48.

8. Ibid., p. 83.

9. Paglia, *Sexual Personae,* p. 31.

10. Ibid., pp. 32–33.

11. Lois W. Banner, *American Beauty* (Chicago: University of Chicago Press, 1983), p. 13.

12. Ibid., p. 14. A similar point is made by Claudia Brush Kidwell, "Gender Symbols or Fashionable Details," in Claudia Kidwell and Valerie Steele, *Men and Women: Dressing the Part* (Washington, D.C.: Smithsonian Institute, 1989), pp. 124–143.

13. *Mirabella* (February 1991), p. 169.

14. Ibid., pp. 28ff.

15. See Naomi Wolf, *The Beauty Myth: How Images of Beauty Are Used Against Women* (New York: William Morrow, 1991). For a review of Wolf, see Barbara Hey, "Portrait of an Obsession," *Health 23* (June 1991): 68–71. The same kind of argument Wolf uses can be found in the chapter entitled "Consumption and Seduction" of Stuart Ewen, *Captains of Consciousness* (New York: McGraw-Hill, 1976), pp. 177ff. Ewen ties the rise of the beauty industry to the influence of the "ideologues of mass

consumption," who broke down the authority of patriarchy to "liberate" woman as a purchaser of capitalist surplus goods—a typical Marxist argument. Idealizations of the feminine, therefore, are inherently designed for the increase of distribution mechanisms in the interplay among the forces of production and consumption. By seeing herself as an "attractive" icon, woman would therefore be motivated to purchase more consumer produce. Interestingly, Ewen bases his argument almost exclusively on patterns of advertising in the 1920s, which stressed feminine domesticity and the skewing of female taste toward alleged male "corporate" prerogatives. The argument reflects a kind of naivete, familiar to such "Marxist" readings of popular iconography, about the history and social function of advertising. Much of commercial art, including fashion drawings and photography, have followed changing styles of decorative aesthetics, in which images of women have also fluctuated with the times. The same is true of fashion, which can be viewed as "wearable art." For a thorough, and nontendentious survey, of the history of advertising in the context as popular art, see Phillipe Schuwer, *History of Advertising* (London: Leisure Arts, 1968). For a good anthropological study with illustrations about how art as adornment and as a form of signatory of wealth and prestige has roots in primitive culture, see Phyllis Rabineau, *Feather Arts: Beauty, Wealth, and Spirit from Five Continents* (Chicago: Field Museum of Natural History, 1980).

16. Naomi Wolf, "Exploding the Beauty Myth: Naomi Wolf Replies," *Sparerib?* p. 7.

17. Wolf, *The Beauty Myth,* p. 18.

18. *Cosmopolitan* (June 1990): 192ff. The same use of multiple and stylized fashion scenarios as a "breviary" for fantasizing can be found in a popular text for young girls by Lorraine Johnson. See *The Book of Looks* (New York: New American Library, 1983).

19. Walter Burkert, *Greek Religion,* trans. John Raffan (Cambridge, Mass.: Harvard University Press, 1985), p. 272. For an excellent set of essays on the interpatterning of "iconographic" tracings, the Greek sense of the sacred, and semiotics, see Jan Bremmer (ed.), *Interpretations of Greek Mythology* (Totowa, N.J.: Barnes and Noble, 1986).

20. Quentin Bell, *On Human Finery* (New York: Schocken Books, 1976), p. 89. See also Rene König, *The Restless Image: A Sociology of Fashion* (London: George Allen and Unwin, 1973).

21. Roland Barthes, *The Fashion System,* trans. Matthew Ward and Richard Howard (New York: Hill and Wang, 1983), p. 10.

22. Lawrence Langer, *The Importance of Wearing Clothes* (New York: Hastings House, 1959), p. 15.

Section II

The Body Tragic

Chapter 6

The Deconstructive Imagination:
Text as Body, Body as Text

Who will be kind to Oedipus this evening
And give the wanderer charity?
Though he ask little and receive less,
It is sufficient.

Suffering and time,
Have been instructors in our contentment.

—Sophocles, *Oedipus at Colonus*

Although we revere and regale with commemorative discipline the genre of tragedy, we scarcely comprehend it. The tragic, as Nietzsche constantly reminded us, is an aberration and a scandal for both modern morality and esthetics. "The sense of the tragic gains and wanes with sensuality."[1] The tragic vision hovers above a cultural psychology in which knowledge is preeminently crafted from desire, in which the iconography of value and the symbols of divinity all belong to the strange, irrational pulsations of what Nietzsche himself named the *will to power*.

Both Nietzsche and Heidegger, who in the generations before Derrida rough cast the tasks of "deconstruction," understood the tragic not only as a spectacular interlude in Greek thought, but as a kind of "pre-text" to Western speculative philosophy. The tragic conceals a total, primitive world perspective, which comes to be eclipsed by the "moralizing" tendencies that begin with Plato. Tragedy bespeaks a prephilosophical space of engagement between the religious, or archetypal, imagination and the darker mystery of time. The universe of tragic discourse is one in which the codes of language crash against the perplexity of what the Greeks knew darkly as *moira*, or fate, and Freud inelegantly called the *reality principle;* it is one where every alleged denotation is reduced to a mere cipher. However, the tragic is also a straight derivative of what today might be diagnosed as the *pathology of pure freedom.* The tragic arises when human "excellence" (Greek = *arete*) is destroyed by the power of instinctuality and by godlike forces that are no longer subject to the calculus of ritual and supplication. We find the transition from the ancient poetry of the heroic to the definitively tragic at precisely that juncture in history when the myth of intimate dealings between humanity and the gods, corresponding to tradition of social deference between blood relations, is suddenly shattered and a new, dangerous era of moral license and psychic adventure commences. Aeschylus' *Oresteia* is shot through with the theme of parricide. The Oedipus cycle turns on the dilemma—that is, the "double sentence"—of intentional behavior and hidden motivation.

The flowering of tragedy as art, according to Herbert Müller, grows not out of disenchantment with heaven, but out of the imagination of liberty. It is a lump payment for "the fulls costs of consciousness."[2] We might add that the genesis of the tragic imagination, its own primal scene, lies in the dismembering of myth and the movement toward self-disclosure. It is, therefore, not at all accidental that Freud selected the saga of Oedipus as the point of departure for psychoanalysis. Furthermore, the passage from epic to tragedy is bound up inextricably with the discovery that the "divine" is not simply fickle, it is wholly opaque as well. The epic unfolds as the logic of eternity plays itself out in the theater of moral behavior. Tragedy becomes possible precisely when what were hitherto (in the words of Mircea Eliade) timeless, "paradigmatic gestures" all at once dissolve into the ambiguities of temporal experience and coping. "Suffering and time," the twin parameters of the struggle toward self-consciousness, replace the ministry of the immortal divinities as "instructors" in what could be dubbed *education for transcendence.*

The disclosure of the tragic background to Western thought, which Nietzsche profoundly understood, gives rise to the contemporary necessity of "deconstruction." For what is de-constructed is the multitextured symbology of "eternal presence," which the tragic summarily calls into question. As Octavio Paz phrases the matter with metaphoric incision, "it is the sun that has rotted, as gold is congealed light."[3] Drawing upon Nietzsche's well-known typology of the Apollonian versus the Dionysian, we can say that the moment of deconstruction arrives when the permanent representations of the salvific—whether they be heroic narratives, Platonic ideas, or effigies of dying gods—are disclosed as projections, "constructs," transient abstractions. Just as tragic awareness enlarges at exactly the instant (as in the case of Oedipus) when the surface of things suddenly fissures to afford a glimpse of a deeper perplexity, when an unproblematic instantaneity is shown to have a murky and uncharted history, so the movement of "deconstruction" begins when the old sureties of conversation and argument—the system of apodictic notations that modern philosophers from Kant to Collingwood have characterized as metaphysics—are construed as temporal and conditioned in their origin. The temporalizing of timeless presence, on the other hand, which constitutes both the "birth of tragedy" and the dawning of deconstruction in language, is not at all identical with the historicizing, or relativizing, of truth that took root in the early nineteenth century. Hegel's so-called speculative science, the effort to comprehend "dialectically" the full panoply of historical intelligence, was a full leap beyond the habit of reducing knowledge to its social and cultural determinants, a peculiar method of interpretation now described as the "hermeneutics of suspicion" that can be traced back to the French Enlightenment. Hegel's vision of "absolute knowledge," which Derrida deflates into a lowly pun, was a grandiose effort to overcome historicism in this most elementary sense. Hegel's "phenomenology" closes with the well-known passage in which "Spirit," grasped as the infinity of conscious reflection that the older metaphysicians had identified as God, "descends" into, and permeates, the abyssmal reaches of "time." As Hegel proclaims in his famous coda to the *Phenomenology of Spirit,* "the other side of its Becoming, *History,* is a *conscious,* self-*mediating* process—Spirit emptied out into Time; but this externalization, this kenosis, is equally an externalization of itself; the negative is the negative of itself."[4]

The "speculative" truth of Hegel's system, therefore, is that the ancient metaphysical antimonies of "time" and "eternity" are now abolished and "taken up" *(aufgehoben)* as the movement of historical knowledge. That is why Hegel could assert, quite sententiously, that the "philosophy of history" is equivalent to the "history of philosophy." The cinema of "representations" (i.e., the ideas of different epochs) that wheel across the stage of recorded culture and constitute reflective history becomes in itself the text that reveals the mind of the Creator. In Hegel, temporality becomes actuality. Derrida, who in a peculiar manner of speaking belongs to the lineage of radical Hegelianism, strips bare the idealistic overlay of the speculative dialectic and homes in, almost brutally at times, on the "incision" that the new hermeneutics of time has made on the study of history as the relentless play of signification. For Derrida, the evidence of "spirit" has vanished, but texts, and the immense terrain of textuality, remains.

The text, which continues on in time because of the custom of writing, is a "creature" of time. Hence, Taylor reminds us that "the task of thinking at the end of theology is to think and rethink the wound of time." Theology is no longer, as it was even for Hegel, the comprehension and self-comprehension of eternal presence. Theology per se becomes *theological thinking,* which is to say that talk concerning the "holy" or the "sacred" must begin with the modes of temporality. "Theological" language is no longer a privileged tradition of speech, but constitutes a special mode of discourse that reveals the textuality—that is, the unbroken symbological weave—of the world as such. The sense of the world as text and the text as world gives rise to a new kind of "ontology" that surpasses the standpoint of classical metaphysics in which "being" was contrasted with "becoming," the enduring with the ephemeral, the spiritual with the corporeal, the changeless with the changeable.

The strictest application of the insights of the deconstructionists lies in the development of an unprecedented, philosophical intuition of the ultimacy of time that overcomes most of the theoretical dilemmas of Kantian subjectivism, Husserlian phenomenology, Deweyean pragmatism, and process metaphysics. The provenance of deconstruction is, oddly enough, the twentieth century preoccupation with language as the rosetta stone of reality. What Ferdinand de Saussure, the founder of structural linguistics, referred to as the *primacy of the signifier* anticipates the deconstructionist's radical critique of the metaphysics of presence or what Derrida not all that felicitously dubs the *logocentrism* inherent in classical Western architectures of thought. The *primacy of the signifier* suggests the essential detachment of meaning from reference, of explication from denotation, of intelligibility from the rule of correspondence.

Strangely, this early structuralist insight, which became the chief instrument in the assault on "metaphysics," paralleled the program of linguistic analysis in its effort to collapse philosophical issues into forms of "grammar." Starting with G. E. Moore and culminating in the later work of Ludwig Wittgenstein, linguistic analysis had sought to transform philosophical conversation into the unraveling of semantic puzzles. Although the tradition of analysis, in contrast to French thought, was never sufficiently informed by the empirical science of language itself, the heirs of Wittgenstein proposed many of the same "therapeutic" strategies for ridding philosophy of its "reifying" and "speculative" tendencies that deconstruction would later adopt as its own very *modus vivendi.* As critical students of Derrida recognize, the "method" of deconstruction rests upon a new, probing hermeneutic in which the concept of interpretation shifts from homage to ageless icons with cereal offerings of the *Zeitgeist* to an appreciation of texts as texts, of the act of signification as something autonomous and important in its own right. The argument of Derrida's *Speech and Phenomena,* which is one of his earliest and clearest statements of philosophical commitment, urges us in this direction. *Of Grammatology,* while complicated with the sundry salon trifles and ripostes that intimidate the casual reader of his later essays, also sustains the same general drift.

It should be noted, of course, that the more familiar publications of Paul Ricoeur, appearing about a decade in advance, break some of the same ground as Derrida. Ricoeur's theory of metaphor, together with his notion of the "polysemic" quality of nonreferential communication whereby language is infected with a "surplus of meaning" transcending common usage, takes us down a similar road. Indeed, Ricoeur himself may be responsible for introducing the term *deconstruction* during the 1960s in the context of his endeavor to "dismantle the fortress of consciousness." The move toward deconstruction in the current generation must be viewed as a yearning to complete without remainder the century-long process of the dissolution of the classical (i.e., "metaphysical") framework of theoretical knowledge in which truth, or meaning, is posited as a correlation between proposition and fact, representation and world. The contemporary enchantment, particularly in English criticism, with the Derridean style of word sporting, innuendo, cryptology, and excursus unfortunately obscures this underlying philosophical purpose.

Yet, it is also the elaboration within the literature of deconstruction of the view that *reality equals textuality,* that revelation in the postmodern idiom always appears as writing, which calls forth an appreciation of the "wound" of time and temporality. Derrida's "joke" that "absolute knowledge"—*savoir absolu*—should best be abbreviated as *sa, it* in French, underscores the total inversion of metaphysical speculation that the program of deconstruction implies. The *id-it* of Freudian desire, what is always unthought and unavailable to cognition, what is "outside of logic," according to Derrida, becomes an irresolvible remainder in any project of thinking and reflection. The remainder remains, because no idea or representation can be perfectly divided into itself. No analysis of the idea can truly generate the "that for which" it stands. The remainder is time, which consists in the unthought thought of thoughts. The text unfolds in time; the chain of signifiers that constitute the basis for the Derridean skein of meaning and interpretation are embedded within the temporal process. Unlike classical metaphysics, where the instant of signification (as in Plato's allegory of the cave) constitutes an evolution of mere impression or appearance into a radiant vision of its immutable essence, deconstruction confronts the reader with the finality of reading and conversation. The finality of reading and conversation is, therefore, a testament to the sovereignty of time, the reign of Kronus. Time becomes its own "ultimate presence," a substrate, a metaphysical "first principle." It is not just the "death" in Hegel's sense of absolute spirit in time, but its corpse and rhetorical calcification.

Generally speaking, the sensibility of "deconstructionist" writing has stark affinities with the Sartrean nihilism of a preceding generation of both Gallic and American intellectuals. Sartre's notorious characterization of human self-understanding as a "useless passion" foretokens Derrida's "kenotic" theory of language. The identification of "Being" with "nothingness" in Sartre's own anti-metaphysics, which is at the same time an anti-psychology, anticipates the Derridean redescription of presence as absence. Sartre's "humanistic" existentialism, deployed upon the notion that the radical freedom of the indeterminate subject permits an unbounded, amoral praxis, gives hint of the central premise in deconstruction that writing and rewriting to an interminable extent (what Derrida archly terms *the end of the book*) is our most somber task once the substance of language and interpretation has forever been effaced.

Taylor's "a/theology" employs the stones and mortar of poststructuralist linguists to revive in an entirely different vein the strains of the Sartrean ontology of radical freedom. The enterprise of a/theology is, in actuality, a quite sophisticated and trenchant reworking of what Altizer many years ago classified as a "Christian atheism" that grasps the cross as a signature of God's extinction. Derrida's grammatology, which builds upon Saussure's principle that intelligibility in language depends heavily on the broad and complex orchestration of syntactical relations rather than the immediate referencing of particular terms themselves, is turned inside out to become a metaphysics of nothingness. Derrida's denial of "presence" to the *ordo significationis* is transposed into a fundamental repudiation of "total presence" (Altizer's expression) as a meaningful concept for articulating the *ordo entis*. From Taylor's vantage point deconstruction is a semantic lure to recapture not so much the older, postwar mood of nihilism and absurdity as the far more ancient tragic imagination with its passionate valorizing of "suffering and time."

Deconstruction as an integral gesture in the protocols of "theological thinking" demands a profound self-criticism of both ecclesial and academic theology, which since the denouement of neo-orthodoxy nearly three decades ago have sacrificed the "existential" dimension of religiosity for the sake of sundry intellectual fads, causes, and formalisms. In a most peculiar way Taylor's suggestion of a/theology, which arises out of his earlier preoccupation with the thought of Kierkegaard, is a call to faith. As one or two commentators have already observed in passing, the deconstructive imagination harbors some kinship with Tillich's "God beyond God." To some degree Taylor is flailing a scarecrow when he accuses Tillich of "onto-theological" orthodoxy. The faith of deconstruction is, in a most poignant sense, the faith of the disciples as the darkness descended upon Calvary. At the same time, it is certainly no manner of faith in the refulgent Easter morrow, for that requires both knowledge and memory. The faith of the disciples at Golgotha is the self-asseveration of speech *despite* what appears as the closure of the onto-theological signifying process that had been the "sacred history" from creation to Good Friday. Taylor's a/theology betokens this sort of darkling faith. It is the reaffirmation of the tragic insight as the sun sets over the place of the skull. The historical narrative of God's redemptive legacy is suddenly dissolved into the transcendent horror and joy (Nietzsche's "dancing song") of concomitant dissolution and recreation. "The end appears," as Taylor observes, "to be the parousia, which restores or even surpasses the fulfillment and plenitude of the beginning. Although not necessarily circular, the course from origin to conclusion inscribes a 'closed' circuit of departure and return."[5]

The deconstructive imagination rides ironically on the religious myth of eternal recurrence, the disclosure of sameness within difference, the "retrospective" gaze of the ideal observer who envisages truth as the turning back of discourse upon itself, the death of God and gods, the reinscription of the *proton* at the site of the *eschaton*. This reinscription of the *proton,* of the *archai* or "first things," is what Taylor denotes as the *sacred*. For "the sacred is *not* God but is that which remains and approaches when gods fail . . . fail to arrive, to be present, or to be present again in our re-presentations. The failure of God betrays the sacred."[6]

The failure of God is pari passu the instantiation in world history of sheer *difference*. From both a theological and a literary standpoint Good Friday can be read as the most radical moment or "differencing" that occurs within the regime of both historical and cosmic totalization. It is more than "failure," it is the death of the absolute. And this death, as Hegel recognized, stakes out the liminal territoriality within which the "metanarrative" of universal history is both displaced and effaced.

The cross of Christ is the first, genuine "deconstructive" breach of the "cosmotheandric" chain of signification that compasses archaic myth and reaches back toward the plenitude of nostalgic reminiscence. It breaks once and for all, as Biblical theologians have reminded us for several generations, the self-implicating cycle of divine return. The cross is ineradicably *death*. But its embodiment as the totalism of human mortality constitutes at once its transgression of the myth of reoccurrence. In its preoccupation with the mystery of Good Friday, the deconstructive imagination fails to step back from the myth it has reconstructed as the grammar of the self-enfolding text, as the mystique of endless reinterpretation. Good Friday symbolizes the final monumentality of the method of representation.

The "empty tomb" of the Gospels becomes simulacrum for the logocentrality of absence as a kind of pseudonymous, unreflective self-presencing. The "letter," not the spirit, is valorized as redemptive. Salvation is by documentation alone. Theologically speaking the Gospels obtrude into the kingdom of coherent semantics. "The pastness of events is replaced by the presentness of narrating, a present that is already past when we read it and was never present to itself."[7] The *kerygma,* so to speak, can never be "present to itself" and therefore constitutes an absolute rupture, a lack, an abyss of "unverifiability" codified as the stone that was rolled away. It finds its "supplement" in writing, in the "tradition" of discourse and commentary. Yet this tradition "re-members" something that remains beyond the mnemonic, that celebrates the truly originary and undecipherable, not to mention the indemonstrable. The theological past has historically been founded on the "spacing" of the nexus of sacral signifiers. And for that reason it can be described only as the utterly unthought possibility of all thought itself—not so much as Taylor's "altarity" but as the pre-textuality of all texts themselves, as the untruth that comes to unconcealment, as *eschaton* in opposition to what is re-collected as *proton*.

Taylor's a/theology is the enshrinement of Hegel's "speculative" Good Friday. Yet all speculation is "reflection," and reflection takes place through the micrology of the body. The theological tradition is always in danger of running aground on the shoals of a "theologism," that is to say, a reification of the sacral disruptions of remembrance in the form of the "positive principles" of doctrine. The deconstruction of doctrine in the guise of an "a/theological" hermeneutic serves the unintended, but salutary, purpose of returning the understanding of religious tradition to its unmediated and secessionist beginnings. But it also functions as a "recalling" of the paradoxicality of embodiment in which the tradition itself is anchored, of the mysterious and historical "double sentence" in which the desire for the eternal "kingdom of heaven" is traduced by the insuperability of a tortured corpse, even while its compelling nonessentiality is overcome through the "fact" of its glorification at Easter sunrise. The problem with Taylor's a/theology is that it is neither playful nor serious enough to "comprehend," as Hegel would say, this extremity of dialectical reversal. But the dialectical overcoming of the "metaphysical" contradiction between life and death is possible only because we are dealing here not with the unfolding of a "concept," but with the incarnality of the body itself. The deconstructive imagination can surpass the Golgothan wail of finitude only if appropriates the seemingly unbearable tension between body as intractable and corruptible self-presence and the body as infinite immaculation, as parousia.

The remembrance of Good Friday in the tradition is the wandering, or "errancy," of the textual corpse-corpus through time. The tradition itself is the body nomadic. The body nomadic forfeits by its very representational transcendence the erotism of the body of desire. Yet what David Michael Levin terms the *body's recollection of being* remains the indissoluble a priori of religious analysis, even those Christian dogmas that claim a kind of superhistorical priority in the act of reflection. According to Levin, "thinking of being needs an appropriate vessel: a body of perception whose *Befindlichkeit,* a primordial, bodily felt sense-of-being-in-the-world, grants us the potential in an implicit pre-understanding of Being."[8] Stripped of phenomenological jargon, Levin's argument is straightforward, albeit quite "strange" to the sort of logico-metaphysical accounting that for centuries has suffused theological writing. The "pre-understanding of Being" corresponds to the contextual involvement of the soma within a multiplicity of signifying projects and possibilities.

If we return to the efforts of the early Heidegger to redraw the "horizons" of metaphysical inquiry in *Being and Time,* we find that Levin's somatological hermeneutic approximates the "existential" starting point of the former's so-called analysis of Dasein. The move beyond Heidegger, however, derives largely from the realization that the "body" can no longer be understood philosophically as a peculiar "thing" with clear, ontic boundaries, as it has been since the time of Descartes. The new, poststructural view of incarnality puts to rest the so-called mind-body dilemma with its irresolvible metaphysical aporia. Just as Kant "overcame" the seemingly unanswerable question of causal connectivity by positing a table of "transcendental" categories according to which judgments of experience are made, so the type of phenomenological shift Levin suggests allows us to decipher the "body" as a kind of radical context of interpretation within which economies of representation and desire can be mapped.

The self-datum of "embodiment" to which most "poststructural" or "postmodern" readings refer back as a site for deconstructive operations becomes the depot for different forays on either side of the double sentence. To be embodied means to be situated in such a way that discourse can no longer reference itself as the pure source of signification, but that there remains an "unspoken" dimension to every system of denotation and every loop of inference. This dimension is what Merleau-Ponty most likely had in mind when he talked about redescribing the phenomenological "percipii." The act of perception, according to Merleau-Ponty, is not "an intellectual synthesis." The synthesis is "primordial." Furthermore, it is our relationality to others, which can take place only through embodiment, "outside of which the realm of the ideal appears as an alibi."[9] Embodiment means that "alterity" is removed from its abstract form and enters into a concrete reciprocity with the "subject" of experience. The alterity of the embodied other is truly plurisignificative; it cannot be easily "read."

The problem of the deconstructive imagination in matters philosophical, as opposed to the simple theory of the text as text, resides wholly in what might be termed the *subscription* of significatory acts, which are somatic rather than linguistic. The subscription of the signified has almost exclusively to do with the manner in which grammatical codes are dissolved into the intelligible aims of desire. The reflective explication of such desire amounts to a true "fundamental ontology" that lurks behind the crypto-metaphysical agenda of twentieth century philosophy of language. This reflective explication of desire is what really remains at stake when we talk about the "deconstruction" of the chain of signifiers. And such an explication is impossible without a "transcendental" synthesis of the imagination we can deduce from the self-presence of the embodied consciousness.

The transcendental standpoint of self-reflective desire begins with Lacan. Yet desire is never self-descriptive. That is, it cannot view itself per se; it can probe only beyond the horizon of immediate representation. The "body" is neither immediate to itself nor can it be completely mirrored in symbols. "Among the things we do not, in the end, know is what nakedness—or clothing—is."[10] Both the body erotic and the body nomadic in the form of textual extension remain highly ambiguous so far as the act of interpretation is concerned. The body can never by a *Ding an sich* nor can it be defined in terms of its coverings. In the history of culture the erotic is constituted by the insuperable dialectic of concealing and revealing. To be clothed in a certain way is to invite dis-closure. Similarly, the body as "text" is simultaneously manifest and hidden. The recognition of this dys-function of all signification is what we mean by *deconstruction*.

The "anti-Oedipus" precept of Deleuze and Guattari, therefore, can be glimpsed in the same light. The anti-Oedipal signifies a disruption of the primitive constellation of parental nurture and desire. In the familial economy desire is always directed toward the maintenance of temporal relationships via the castrating authority of the father and the seductiveness of the maternal source. The Oedipal economy, contrary to psychoanalysis, is not counter-historical; it remains the basis of the genealogical tradition and, as the myth itself shows, of civil order. The anti-Oedipal hermeneutic, however, allows for a reappropriation of desire in terms of liberating praxis. This liberating praxis, on the other hand, need not be strictly "social," as Deleuze and Guattari are commonly construed. It can also refer to the release of the embodied consciousness from the fetishism of the double sentence together with the reinscription of a new *esthetic* order of signifying action. Anti-Oedipus can also mean the irreversible "deconstruction" of the somatic drive so far as it achieves purely "unconscious" satisfaction and fails to attain the lucidity of language.

The deconstructive imagination works, therefore, not just upon the "literality" of sign-events but on the formalism of all representative acts, inasmuch as it evidences a *body-text* that supplies the range of vision for all reflective and interpretative initiatives. The primacy of the body-text, which remains implicit in all signifying operations, also serves as the transcendental condition in accordance with which "knowledge" in the phenomenological, as opposed to the strictly metaphysical, sense becomes possible. The body-text is itself a "schema" of fluid possibilities of signification and representation that are extrapolated from the somatic economy of drives, wishes, and fantasies. In this manner the body-text—or what for purposes of clarification we shall hereafter refer to as the *someme*—serves as a pre-representational architecture of "purposeful" sensuality that becomes self-aware.

At this level, therefore, the someme is comparable "epistemologically" to Kant's transcendental imagination, except that it can no longer be regarded as a critical philosophical "synthesis" of the operative faculties of the mind, but as a field of dialectical mediation between conscious and unconscious, between language and desire, between world and "will" as Nietzsche understood it. The crucial passage from a modern critical philosophy of the faculties to a postmodern semiology of embodiment does not occur with Derrida, but Deleuze and Guattari. The semiology of Deleuze and Guattari rests on what they have called *haeccities,* a word borrowed from Duns Scotus. A heccity is a "body" in the sense that it constitutes a Protean and sometimes ephemeral constellation of movement, affect, and purpose. The haeccity may also be seen as a postmodernist version of the Aristotlian entelechy, although the latter is constituted by the structural or "morphological" interchange between "act" and "potential," or form and substrate, rather than a hidden intentionality or infraprocesses, as is true of the former.[11] The haeccity may be described as what we have termed the *someme,* precisely whenever the bio-schematized play of energies is capable of "symbolization" in the Lacanian sense and therefore can construct both an order of heteronomous signification and a reflexive domain of subjectivity.

The emergence of the someme jibes with the recognition of a unique, "Platonic" problem that has generally been ignored by Western philosophers but underlies the odd, and tortured, meditations of the Eleatic stranger in the *Sophist.* This Platonic "problem" is exactly the question of embodiment, which the Western tradition with its myriad "footnotes" to the founder has forgotten. According to Deleuze, what we may regard as origin of the great metaphysical amnesia that Heidegger has so exhaustively characterized lies not in the Platonic dialectic per se, but in Plato's anxiety concerning "false" images or *simulacra,* likenesses that deceive rather than likenesses that emulate. The trouble centers on the mode of "production" of signs or images. Certain instances of dissimulation are inevitable in "the region of discourse, making it possible to impose upon the young who are still far removed from the reality of things, by means of words that cheat the ear, exhibiting images of all things in a shadow play of discourse, so as to make them believe that they are hearing the truth and that the speaker is in all matters the wisest of men."[12] Contrary to the customary reading of Plato, the "sophist" is not the trafficker in "copies." Copying or imitation, says Plato, is the very nature of the discursive art, which includes philosophy. There are, however, "two kinds of production," one of which is "divine" and the other merely "human." Divine production gives us "likenesses" or *eika.* Human production, which easily errs, gives us "semblances" (*phantasma* in Greek, *simulacra* in Latin), flitting shadows of things. This "division of the kinds of forms" is what the philosophical inquiry into knowledge is really about.[13] The sophist "mimicks" wisdom insofar as his making or *poesis* is not divine, and thereby given to distortion and dissemblance.

But this dissemblance has little to do with a conflict between the truth of the "material" versus the "spiritual." The "gigantomachy" between the partisans of earth and heaven, which Plato uses in the *Sophist* as a metaphor for the most basal epistemological disputes and which Heidegger takes as synecdochal for the struggle against metaphysics, has much deeper ramifications. It has to do with the structure of the double sentence. That is to say, it is not the battle between "truth" and "fiction," but between intelligibility and velleity, or between productive and unproductive possibilities. The stranger notes cryptically, "I am proposing as a mark to distinguish real things that they are nothing but power."[14] He goes on to say that these sorts of "partisans" are simply "friends of forms," meaning that they desire the more durable representations of speech rather than the episodic and fleeting. To be "real" is to be "powerful," because the criteria for "realization" are commensurate with the capacity for production of stable likenesses. The sophist's "art" is that of "conjuring" illusions that immediately disintegrate before the eye, like cloud forms on high. The philosopher, on the other hand, is skilled at "making" discourse that abides and is subject to rigorous scrutiny and analysis over time.

The relationship between truth and untruth is not, as the metaphysical legacy has stressed, the same as the dissymmetry between the sensible and the ideal. The danger in the sophist's "shadow play of discourse" does not lurk in a deferral to some false order of objects which his language somehow mirrors. After all, a close reading of the Platonic dialogues show us that so-called eidetic truth is not the same as sheer abstraction. The universal always has a concrete veneer in Plato—hence, the easy transit back and forth between philosophy and myth, as we find in the *Timaeus* and the *Republic*. The "poetic" power of Plato's writings is further testament to this correlation. And the "deconstructive" aim of overcoming metaphysics has little real validity when it comes to trekking from end to end of a Platonic dialogue. Indeed, the stranger himself ends up dismissing the "gigantomachy" as a kind of spurious dicotomy that impedes the advance of philosophy: "it seems that only one course is open to the philosopher who values knowledge and the rest above all else. He must refuse to accept from the champions either of the one or of the many forms the doctrine that all reality is changeless, and he must turn a deaf ear to the other party who represents reality as everywhere changing. Like a child begging for 'both', he must declare that reality or the sum of things is both at once—all that is unchangeable and all that is in change."[15]

If reality is "both at once," in the same way that the sophistical statement "what is is not" that occupies the dialogue can be understood not as a trick of language but as the key to the very ontology embedded in the Platonic corpus, then a whole new—postmodern—"interpretative" interface with ancient philosophy becomes conceivable. An actual, as opposed to a virtual, Platonic "theory of experience" comes nearer than we have admitted to the early Heideggerian phenomenology of *Zuhandenheit* ("readiness-to-hand") to which in some way most postmodernist "body studies" must hark back. Freudian psychology provides the "hermeneutics of suspicion" that somatizes the claims of both idealist moral philosophy and extremely rationalized hermeneutical economies, such as structuralism and new criticism.

Deconstruction offers a true, postpositivist and post-Wittgensteinian philosophical linguistics that allow for open, textual response that at last is faithful, and reciprocal, to the genius of the author. Yet the deconstructive imagination is rightly accused of contributing to a "nihilism" in the sphere of culture if it cannot situate its own self-knowledge within the interstices of the body-text by which reality is "read."[16] Deconstruction has "marginalized" itself within the community of letters, only because it had failed to deconstruct itself as a kind of proto-text that projects the erotically embodied, as opposed to the politically embodied, which in itself remains a metaphysical self-construct that requires a critical dismembering. Deconstruction can, and should never, be used for political purposes, for it then becomes a pernicious metapolitics in its own right. The recent alliance in some quarters between Marxism and deconstruction is a marriage made in hell, not in heaven.[17] For the two are ultimately incompatible, insofar as one constitutes a second-order theory of social change and the other a challenge to all grand theory and "metanarrative." Deconstruction, however, does in the final analysis unmask all pretensions of the "body politic" to linguistic totality, while pointing up the pure, lived, somatic con-textuality of all language and knowledge.[18]

As the stranger himself remarks toward the end of the *Sophist,* "being" and "not-being" are not contrarieties, but interpenetrating moments in the signifying web. Ontology is the play of difference, and this "diference has existence and is parcelled out over the whole field of existent things with reference to one another, and of every part of it that is set in contrast to 'that which is' we have dared to say that precisely that *is really* 'that which is not.' "[19] Indeed, "discourse" itself "owes its existence to the weaving together of *eidoi,*" to the mutual embrace and interconnectivity of the representative powers of desire. "Platonic dualism" strangely cannot be found in most of the Platonic dialogues. The body is not the adversary, for the someme in its Platonic integument as the body-text that produces both sensible and transcendental frames of signification, which gives rise to a desire for the "good" not because the latter is morally authorized but because it is beautiful and enduring, is the one, honest broker who oversees the economy of exchange between the body erotic—the body of pure desire— and the body nomadic—the textuality of "thought," the text of history. Indeed, Derrida himself has been moving in this direction. He first raised it an essay that linked "sexual difference" to "ontological difference" and later sought to chart the question of *differance* in terms of the Heideggerian problem of "handedness," where we find the binding of "thinking, and not only philosophy, to a thought or to a situation of the body."[20] Or, put another way, "the thinker is unceasingly occupied with a thought of the hand."[21]

The Eleatic stranger in an important sense wears the disguise of Hermes. His "hermeneutic" is utterly un-Platonic and unmetaphysical in the classic meaning of the word. The stranger gestures toward what genuinely remains "unthought" within Western, and theological, thinking. He gestures to the body. If the deconstructive imagination has not imagined the body, it has not imagined its own genealogy. It has neither felt the warmth of the fire nor smelled the fragrance of the rose. It has become the dead letter.

But the deconstructive imagination perhaps still has a function to perform within the general economy of desire and representation. This economy can be found not within the political state of discourse, but as part of the very "founding" of that discourse, within the "archaic" religious site of representational system that form the symbology of violence to the body. At that site the destruction of the body results through a metonymic alchemy in the formation of the "body politic." Religious violence becomes the proto-act of inscription for the political itself. The illusions of both the body tragic and the body politic are traceable within a dialectical system of logic that the archaeologists of religion have mapped in terms of the practice of *sacrifice*.

Notes

1. Friedrich Nietzsche, *Beyond Good and Evil,* trans. Walter Kaufmann (New York: Vintage Books, 1966), p. 90.

2. Herbert J. Müller, *The Spirit of Tragedy* (New York: Washington Square Press, 1955), p. 48.

3. Octavio Pax, *Conjunctions and Disjunctions,* trans. Helen R. Lane (New York: Seaver Books, 1982), p. 21.

4. G. W. F. Hegel, *Phenomenology of Spirit,* trans. A. V. Miller (New York: Oxford University Press, 1977), p. 492.

5. Mark Taylor, *Erring: A Post-Modern A/theology* (Chicago: University of Chicago Press, 1984), p. 155.

6. Mark Taylor, *Tears* (Albany: State University of New York Press, 1990), p. 231.

7. Derek Attridge, *Peculiar Language: Literature as Difference from the Renaissance to James Joyce* (Ithaca, N.Y.: Cornell University Press, 1988), p. 225.

8. David Michael Levin, *The Body's Recollection of Being* (London: Routledge and Kegan Paul, 1985), p. 62.

9. Maurice Merleau-Ponty, *The Primacy of Perception,* ed. James M. Edic (Evanston, Ill.: Northwestern University Press, 1964), p. 25.

10. Stephen W. Melville, *On Deconstruction and Modernism* (Minneapolis: University of Minnesota Press, 1986), p. 33.

11. The question of infraprocesses was first raised by dramatically by Foucault, although his own fading Marxist hermeneutic of power-domination blinded him to envisaging the actual "scene" of discourse, which is not the "body politic" but the body erotic in the Phaedrian sense. Foucault's rage against poststructuralist formalisms kept him, like Oedipus himself, from achieving the authentic vision of postmodernity. Foucault writes that he has sought a whole new "teleology" fumigated of all lingering "transcendental narcissism." "For it is to it now—and we are determined never to abandon this—that we will now pose the question of the origin, the first constitution, the teleological horizon, temporal continuity." Michel Foucault, *The Archaeology of Knowledge and the Discourse on Language*, trans. A. M. Sheridan (New York: Pantheon Books, 1972).

12. *Sophist* 234c.

13. See *Sophist* 234e–236c.

14. *Sophist* 247e.

15. *Sophist* 249d.

16. For examples of such indictments that are more than rhetorical, see John M. Ellis, *Against Deconstruction* (Princeton, N.J.: Princeton University Press, 1989). For a good review of the controversy, see Christopher Butler, *Interpretation, Deconstruction, and Ideology* (Oxford: Oxford University Press, 1984). For an introduction to the important issues concerning "deconstructive" criticism, see Mark Krupnick (ed.), *Displacement: Derrida and After* (Bloomington: Indiana University Press, 1983); Derek Attridge, *Peculiar Language: Literature as Difference from the Renaissance to James Joyce* (Ithaca, N.Y.: Cornell University Press, 1988).

17. For a sympathetic reading of the relationship between these two forms of "critical theory," which yet insists on their final incommensurability, see Michael Ryan, *Marxism and Deconstruction* (Baltimore: Johns Hopkins University Press, 1982).

18. Derrida himself warns of the political use of deconstruction. Challenging Foucault, Derrida writes: "The words 'force' and 'power' which I have joined you in using, also pose . . . enormous problems. I never resort to these words without a sense of uneasiness." *Limited Inc.* (Evanston, Ill.: Northwestern University Press, 1988), p. 149.

19. *Sophist* 258d–e.

20. Jacques Derrida, "Geschlecht II: Heidegger's Hand," trans. John P. Leavy, Jr., in John Sallis (ed.), *Deconstruction and Philosophy: The Texts of Jacques Derrida* (Chicago: University of Chicago Press, 1987), p. 171. The earlier essay by Derrida is "Geschlecht: Sexual Difference, Ontological Difference," *Research in Phenomenology* 13 (1983): 65–83.

21. "Geschlecht II," p. 177.

Chapter 7

The Dialectics of Sacrifice

Sacrifice, of itself, effects and exaltation of the victims, which renders them directly divine.

Henri Hubert and Marcel Mauss

It is a peculiar pass that scholarly investigators of religion since the close of the Second World War, particularly in America, have as rule ignored the subject of sacrifice. There are several possible and cogent reasons for this inadvertence, however. In an age of triumphant scientism and secularism the ancient, "barbaric" rites of sacrifice have perhaps posed an embarrassment to those in religious studies commissioned to expound the perennial worth and significance of the religious attitude. Historians of religion, to whom the examination of sacrificial practices would be properly assigned, have been wont instead to busy themselves with various "hermeneutical" tasks, focusing on patterns of myth and symbol evinced in composite, literary traditions. Such an emphasis on the cognitive elements of religious life is understandable, of course, inasmuch as contemporary research is automatically wary of drawing inferences from modest amounts of data, and the symbolical contents of ancient religious cults are more accessible to inquiry than the forms of conduct. Moreover, the importance of ritual sacrifice declines, if it does not vanish altogether, in the major "historic" religious traditions of which there are copious written remains.

The literary preoccupation itself suggests perhaps a tactic. So much of the erstwhile probes and speculations concerning the phenomenon of sacrifice, out of which stemmed a number of still influential "classical" theories on the topic, were undertaken by a generation bent on unearthing the "primitive" or "prescientific" underside of religious belief and worship. The work of Sir James Frazer, which inspired a whole school of ritual specialists during the period between the wars, was possibly the benchmark of that generation.[1] Frazer's *The Golden Bough,* which assembled more ethnological data on sacrificial customs around the globe than any previous treatise, was a self-conscious endeavor to expose what the author labeled the *black thread of magic* in the evolution of human thinking. Frazer's positivistic and antireligious leanings remained something of a bogey to subsequent investigators, who might otherwise have incorporated a treatment of sacrifice in their own relatively sympathetic evaluation of a good deal of the speculative anthropological research of its day. Freud's *Totem and Taboo,* which appropriated for the project of psychoanalysis Robertson Smith's earlier hypotheses about the interrelation of totemism and sacrificial offerings, may have enlarged the threat even more.[2] The study of sacrifice was easily borrowed as a subterfuge for dropping scandalous hints about the character of religion, and it was only to be expected that defenders of the religious standpoint would want to give short shrift to the matter, if not censor it completely.

Yet the paramount difficulty with the study of sacrifice goes beyond the modern moral perception that the taking of life, especially animal or human life, seems at stark variance with the "humanizing" function so often ascribed to religious devotion. The problem of sacrifice is more an anthropolitical puzzle than an apologetic task. The dark implications of the universal existence of sacrifice, insofar as sacrifice belongs to a significant phase in the growth of religious expression, are perhaps of a magnitude not sufficiently plumbed by even the well-known debunkers, such as Frazer and Freud. The fact of sacrifice bespeaks something riddlesome, fascinating, and disturbing not just about the role of religion in human development, but about the constitution of the human species as well. The presence of sacrifice may well intimate an awesome truth, acknowledged dimly by archaic humanity, but glossed over or even suppressed by modern, "enlightened" sensibilities. It may suggest, as Jan de Vries has commented in conjunction with his brief appraisal of sacrifice, that all human religiosity depends ultimately on a *killing.* "In life there is an antinomy; it persists by destroying other life."[3] Sacrificial killing is accomplished, in contrast to the slaughter of animals for food, or warfare, or in many instances the crime of homicide, for no tangible or practical objectives.

Sacrificial killing is "senseless" except in the sacerdotal frame of reference, where it comes a supreme gesture of piety. The institution of sacrifice persists as a kind of surd, unless the contemporary theorist is prepared to confront the unsettling inferences that can be credibly drawn from the widespread occurrence of the practice. A more honest reckoning with the observance of sacrifice may direct the research straightway toward a hidden dimension of religion that has not been adequately surveyed. It may also throw into relief a perspective that was not within reach heretofore; namely, an outlook on the beginning and end of religion itself.

The eclipse in the postmodern era of what classically were known as *theological studies* had resulted in an increased prestige, within that rather diffuse field known as *religious studies,* for the social sciences, chiefly anthropology. In the past the bulk of the primary data on sacrifice has been gleaned by cultural anthropologists, and it is not surprising that a growing regard for that special discipline might at last stimulate new scrutiny of a longstanding issue. Victor Turner's oft-cited investigations of ritual have moved toward his analysis of sacrifice itself as a "quintessential process."[4] The most signal contribution to scholarly deliberations on sacrifice has been Rene Girard's *Violence and the Sacred,* which has also exercised a significant influence over poststructuralist, or postmodernist thought. Girard attempts to come to terms with the psychology of religious sacrifice, using anthropological models. The key to sacrifice, according to Girard, is the ineradicable nisus toward violence. Girard, therefore, unlike Turner, addresses himself to deVries's pressing question. It is religion itself, for Girard, that regiments within permissible biological and social boundaries the violent proclivities of humanity. Girard writes: "A unique generative force exists that we can only qualify as religious in some sense deeper than the theological one. It remains concealed and draws its strength from this concealment, even as its self-created shelter begins to crumble. The acknowledgment of such a force allows us to assess our modern ignorance—ignorance in regard to violence as well as religion. Religion shelters us from violence [that] . . . seeks shelter in religion."[5]

Sacrifice is thus a transference and redistribution into a signifying totality of what would otherwise be unbridled and socially destructive outworkings of violent passions. In some respects Girard's discussion is a more sophisticated and less tendentious version of Freud's analysis of religious phenomena as "substitute" satisfactions or oblique resolutions of instinctual conflicts. Girard's approach, like Freud's, compasses much of what the conventional academic wisdom has frequently swept aside. Yet Girard's account still suffers from a tendency to recapitulate, or restate more precisely and with expended documentation, the theoretical propositions of earlier researchers, as does Turner's, although the two discussions have unmistakably different slants.

If we were to factor out the differences, however, and pinpoint the crucial distinction between the two approaches, we might underline one of the enduring themes of contention in the whole body of publications on sacrifice. Girard accents the conservative and equilibrating features of sacrificial rites, whereas Turner highlights the transformative ones. Sacrifice, in Girard's estimate, has by and large what Turner denotes as a "prophylactic" purpose; it protects the existing order of things from upheaval and dislocation, it safeguards what is holy from profanation and pollution. Sacrifice constitutes a "dam against violence," a violence that constantly swells against the bulwarks of society. Like any dam, of course, the effectiveness of sacrifice hinges on the construction of a spillway to carry off the overflow and relieve the back pressure; furthermore, this controlled release of violent instinctualities, a part of the sacrificial protocol, makes that rite itself a stabilizing agent. Society itself is placed in jeopardy whenever the sacrificial regulation of violent tendencies falters. Turner takes note, to be sure, of the prophylactic components in sacrifice, but he seems to give more weight to its dynamic qualities, to the circumstances under which it becomes a medium of psychic and symbolic transmutation.

Sacrifice is not merely a single, isolated type of corporate ceremony that attains its significance exclusively within the circle of worship nor is it just, as many nineteenth century scholars believed, a universal mode of etiquette—a rather superficial and thoroughly Victorian conjecture that fails to consider the curious fact that humanity pays homage to its gods not by friendly greeting but by immolation or butchery. The very character of the god, or gods, who would demand such an unseemly reception is in this instance not brought into serious question. Contrary to the conception of sacrifice as etiquette, we must explore the fashion in which the rite involves a much broader, complex, and richer set of psychosocial changes underlying the religious experience of the event. The "whole process of sacrifice," Turner contends, represents a moment in a "longer ritual process," which in turn "may be a phase in a protracted social drama or crisis that overlaps with the secular sphere of human activity."[6]

Turner's elaboration of the more extensive ramifications of the sacrificial deed, though handicapped by a few deficiencies already suggested, is still more versatile than Girard's, principally because it accounts for the transformative as well as the disciplinary office of sacrifice. Although Girard's hypothesis penetrates more directly into what we might term the *kratotic* (from the Greek *kratos* = violence, force) origin of sacrifice, it takes the violent strain in sacrificial ritual only as a kind of blind puissance that must be kept in rein, like Freud's id. Turner's analysis, which on the main ignores the kratotic origin of sacrifice, nevertheless grasps what is even more important in the performance of the rite. Turner describes the dialectic through which violence becomes an instrument of abrupt, qualitative change in the essence of what is sacrificed, through which a kind of transformation is facilitated.

Furthermore, this "transformation as the mode of sacrifice is not . . . a gradual remolding of the human essence." Rather, the "sacrifice transforms, like revolution in some modern doctrines, more violently and rapidly by an act of slaughter that both ends and begins."[7] As a vehicle of transformation the sacrifice resolves an urgent "crisis" of disunity or incoherence in the human relationship with the divine. The crisis is surmounted through a symbolic drama of death and transfiguration, whereby the "victim" in his or her sudden metamorphosis into spiritual power now reconciles his or her own mortal kindred with the claims of the sacred, just as in the Christian myth the "risen" savior acts as eternal intercessor between creatures and the Creator.

We can compare Turner's views on sacrifice as a medium of transformation with Girard's idea that the rite is primarily prophylactic. Although for Turner the sacrifice serves to overcome the social and religious crisis, for Girard it amounts to the root of the crisis itself, because violent discord is the immediate consequence of the breakdown of the sacrificial system rather than its cause. The key to what is really at stake in these two contemporary theories is the problem of religious duality. In a sense, the religious outlook itself rests on the experience of duality; it is molded and sustained by a basic awareness of discontinuity between facticity and aspiration, between giveness and value, between sensible and supersensible, between finite and infinite, between the "sacred" and the "profane." Such a scission can be represented psychologically, mythologically, metaphysically, or ultimately thematized, as in the case of Platonism and certain dualistic Hindu philosophies like Samkhya-Yoga, as an ontology. Altogether, religious discourse itself constitutes its own "syntax of oppositionals," if we may paraphrase Merleau-Ponty; and this syntax is fundamental to the very "articulation" of the sacred that the history and phenomenology of religions has spun out as its own metalanguage of "transcendental" codes and symbols.

The problem of religious duality arises, however, when the fragile, day-to-day ecology linking the two qualitatively distinct "worlds" of humanity and divinity is disrupted by various happenstances or fatalities. Such fatalities may be described as the "differencing" of the significatory action of the syntax as a whole. The "primal" doubleness of the significatory moment tenses into a seeming metaphysical dualism. Darkness wars against light, the evil against the good principle, Satan against God, the pollution of sin against immaculate righteousness. If dualism is not delineated as an active struggle, it is ofttimes portrayed as a state of estrangement , in which the "flow" (as Turner puts it) of comingling of human and divine substances is prevented. The dualistic world picture can be the outgrowth of innumerable, different sorts of shifts in the religious balance of forces; or quite frequently it becomes the symbolic reflection of entrenched antagonisms between groups in society, as Mary Douglas has argued.[8] In any event, the dualistic disjunction widens into a crisis and demands a swift resolution. The implicit harmony of opposites found in the original duality must be wrested from an intractable condition of enmity. Ether God or the Devil must emerge triumphant or the power of the latter must somehow be held in rein.

The sacrifice resolves provisionally, if not once and for all, the mode of tension, either by expelling the disruptive agency as part of the prophylactic strategy or by reconciling the two contrarieties through "transubstantiation." The prophylactic strategy is largely regressive, inasmuch as it seeks to return to the order of things that was dominant at the outset. The second movement, which we shall call *dialectical,* returns also to the beginning, but only after having come full circle. In the circular process there is a dynamic exchange of properties, a veritable *communicato idiomatum,* between the two different substances. The enmity is lessened not by the one element vanquishing the other, but by a reciprocal transmission of qualities so that an act of renovation, a synthesis, takes place. Just as in the Hegelian dialectic there is a resolution of two, antithetical moments that are mutually canceled and "taken up" *(aufgehoben)* into a higher unity, so in the sacrifice the opposition of the dual elements is transcended through a process of reciprocal negation. The force of negation is, of course, the sacrificial slaughter.

The scheme of dialectical reciprocity in the sacrifice was adumbrated in the writings of the nineteenth century and early twentieth century theorists, even though the role of violence was glossed over and inadequately understood. The notion of sacrifice as a "gift" to the gods, first advanced in 1871 by E. B. Tylor,[9] was a crude conspectus of this scheme. And it remained by and large the leading strand of thinking about sacrifice throughout the period in which the "classic" theories were evolved.[10] The so-called gift theory regarded sacrifice as the enactment of a basic contractual formula—*do ut des* or "I give to you, so that you may give to me in return." The early, more literalist version of the gift theory saw sacrifice as something of an attempt to curry favor with, or even offer an outright bribe to, the gods.

Yet the rationale for this interpretation was not as transparent as adherents of the gift theory might have presumed. If the sacrifice was inherently a bargain struck between mortals and divinities or between the European imperial administrators and the native chiefs, with the gods themselves holding the best negotiating position, why did the immortals invariably receive less (i.e. some mutable commodity or specimen of corruptible flesh) and give up more (i.e., their own lordly strength) than their human clients? A major hint of this incongruity can be discerned in the archaic Greek story of Prometheus. Prometheus is the father of the human race who dupes Zeus in the sacrifice by fobbing off on him the less attractive fat and bones, while keeping the tasty meat for himself. In the gift theory the "contractual" arrangement between gods and mortals turns out really to be a shrewd business deal carried off by the human sacrificer. It is the kind of transaction where, as Marcel Mauss says, "the gods who give and repay are there to give something great in exchange for something small."[11] One may wonder whether the gift theory itself was little more than an unwitting analogy with the social models of classical economics (as Darwinism had, to a certain extent, been in biology) that underscored rivalry and competition between individuals, the virtues of cunning and expediency, as well as the underlying equipoise of such relations.

As a theoretical paradigm that mirrors the general social milieu of its age, the first theory may very well, in retrospect, prove to be an illustration of Douglas's dictum that "people's behavior to their god (or in this case we should say people's perception of other people's behavior too) corresponds to their behavior to each other."[12] The trouble with the gift theory was that, like classical economics and social Darwinism, it not only rationalized to an excessive degree the inveterate fact of violence and dissension, it also could not allow for the possibility of sudden, cataclysmic transfiguration. Or, to put the matter differently, it erroneously described the dialectics of sacrifice as a polite give and take, as a form of commercial haggling in the religious domain.

If the gift theory can be faulted as an empirical reading of the ethnological evidence, it also suffers grievously from a lack of psychological insight. Persisting as what Eliade has called a "cultural fashion" in the interpretation of comparative data in religion, the gift theory has crowded out any comprehensive examination of the connections between the ritual expression and the inner symbolic dimensions of the sacrificial process.[13] What may appear as convenantal dealings from observation of external rites may on inward inspection show itself as a clash and melding of psycholinguistic vectors, as a struggle toward self-overcoming. The "rational" motives of the sacrifice may perhaps be visible even to the sacrificers themselves; yet like the ad hoc reasons or excuses individuals supply every day to justify their actions, these motives may not be definitive, or even instructive, as theoretical principles. Again, the explanation that sacrifice is mainly a transaction with a god begs the theoretical question, because it does not account for the peculiar personality of a deity who would exact the destructive gesture of sacrifice in the first place. Moreover, the gift theory runs aground, because it does not locate the formal structure of reciprocity and dialectical movement characterizing the sacrificial ceremony within the more complex psychosignifactory architecture.

Within the context of the gift theory, nonetheless, an effort was made by Hubert and Mauss to make some connections with the overarching complex of symbols. Their famous monograph, in a departure from the data collecting methods of Frazer, did not concern itself with further cataloging of the numerous instances of sacrifice, but concentrated on what they called *typical facts* that reveal some of the intrinsic forms and structures of sacrificial performance. Hubert and Mauss did not, of course, make any strict, psychological judgment about their subject matter. Their methodology, in fact, approached what later came to be dubbed *phenomenological.* Yet some specific conclusions can be drawn about the intentionality, and the "interiority," of the sacrificial act. Sacrifice, according to Hubert and Mauss, is preeminently a "religious act." It is an act of "consecration," wherein "an object passes from he common into the religious domain."[14] While Hubert and Mauss retained Tylor's framework by discussing the sacrifice as a donation the gods "demand," they still clarified some essential issues that were not really raised in the gift theory. They pointed out, for example, that in all sacrifice there is, in addition to the element of exchange, an achievement of "redemption." The redemptive outworking of the sacrifice is brought about by its deeper, dialectical constitution. The sacrifice yields an apotheosis of the consecrated victim, a metaphorization of its mundane marrow into a spiritual "essence." Through the procedure of immolation—which may involve dismemberment, eating, burning, interment, or other means of destruction—the spiritual substance of the consecrated victim is "liberated" from its corporeal factity and the sacral "power" is released for the benefit of the sacrificer.

According to Hubert and Mauss, the transmogrification of the victim is a kind of magical substitute for the spiritual and somatic changes that the sacrificer wishes to attain. The sacrificial victim is a specially empowered proxy for the sponsor of the sacrifice. The sacrificer and the personality of the god to whom the victim is presented are "merged." The sacrifice serves as an opportunity for the sacrificer through the mediation of the victim to be transformed. For human beings to have genuine commerce with the realm of divinity, to transmit "gifts" successfully to them and to receive them back in return, they must take on some guise of deity themselves. "All that touches upon the gods must be divine; the sacrificer is obliged to become a god himself in order to be capable of acting upon them."[15] The foregoing statement naturally bears a striking similarity to Nietzsche's contention that the "'murderers" of God must become "gods" themselves to be "worthy" of the deed.

What presents itself in Hubert and Mauss's theory is a switch in emphasis from appropriate decorum in the court of the deities to the "spiritual" predicament of the human agent. Hubert and Mauss preserve the rhetoric of the gift theory, while in the same vein they succeed in altering its underlying grammar. The former stress on the condign "giving" becomes a concern with the sacrificer's "redemption." The reciprocity of the "external" relations between human and divinity is changed into a reciprocity of internal connections between the sacrificer's finite condition and infinite possibility. The sacrifice allows the transcendence of the immediate dualism apparent in these connections. The sacrifice confers a proleptic immortality, the mimetic securing of eternity within time, the achievement of authentic "life" in the midst of death.

If the goal of sacrifice is to accomplish an apotheosis, then it is easy to understand why sacrifice has been consistently linked in terms of both myth and ritual to the promotion of fertility in agricultural societies. The seasonal renewal of life that follows upon the disappearance of vegetation in winter becomes the closest analogue to, and thus an archetypal representation of, a laboring toward immanent divinity. The drama of invigoration staged in the world of plants and animals suffices as symmetrical symbology for the inward transmutation of spiritual energies, for the dissolution and reintegration of the schemae of consciousness.

For that reason it is not really true, as Frazer held, that sacrifice consists for the most part in a form of sympathetic magic used to guarantee the growth of foodstuffs by imitating the life-in-death cycle of nature. Of magical impregnation were the foremost incentive for the sacrifice, then the same end could be reached without the act of killing. Ritual copulation, or the ceremonial sowing of seeds, or its surrogates—such as the sprinkling of corn meal in Pueblo Indian religion—would seem a more "rational" recourse. The practical objective of fecundation does not require sacrificial killing any more than animal husbandry necessitates animal slaughter. From the "technological" standpoint the two activities are mutually exclusive. In the commonsense, empirical level, even among "savages," life and death may supervene on one another, but they do not necessarily convene in a causal chain. If the two events were causally codetermined, the primitive mind would not be prone to construe death frequently as something accidental or "unnatural," as anthropologists have reported. The association of fertility with the immolation of a victim cannot be an observational inference, only a secondary indication of a more profound identification. The identification is "representational," and the symbols themselves mirror the dialectical operations of the sacrificial syntax itself. The act of sacrifice is a ritual expression of these semiotic transformations. The violence associated with the act is not patterned after the "brutishness" of nature, but instantiates the transgression implicit in the "inversive" character of the dialectical significations themselves. Murder and death are integral moments in the sacrificial process, not because they have an instrumental value in enhancing "life," but because the process itself is an immanent replication of the sacrificer's struggle for self-transcendence. And self-transcendence is possible only by a dialectical movement from affirmation to negation to a "higher" affirmation. Only in the universe of myth, rarely in the domain of phenomena, is the dialectic of self-transcendence authentically operative.

The ritual enacts the myth. In Girard's term it becomes a dramaturgy of the violent. It certainly does not "imitate" nature.

The "structural" correlation between the "violent" and the "natural" in myth studies can be understood not as a form of representation or reproduction but as a kind of "poiesis" through which the self-disruption—or self-diremption in Hegelian language—of primitive desire in its positing of the transcendent object can be brought within the universe of signs. One could, of course, object here that for *homo religiosus* nature and myth are experienced in terms of each other. This objection is precisely what one might anticipate from partisans of that method of investigation which has made a significant impression on cross-cultural religious studies. Nature and myth as seen in a kind of circular logic as self-implicating idealities, as styles of autogenesis, as "constructions." We are speaking here of the so-called phenomenology of religion, including its kindred and more reductive method known as the *sociology of knowledge,* which seeks to uncover the meaning of religious acts through description and morphological comparisons while avoiding all theoretical presuppositions, including psychological ones.

"Phenomenologists" are concerned with the structures of the religious "experience" itself, which in principle at least is supposed to enable them to lay bare the formal comparisons between the multifarious symbols of different cults and cultures, between beliefs and actions, between mythic prototypes and ritual exhibitions. With respect to the problem of sacrifice, phenomenology of religion is interested only in the structural correlation between the ceremonial pattern and the religious assumptions of those performing the rite. It displays a deliberate reluctance to interpret or redescribe the set of religious assumptions in keeping with the patterns of religious action itself.

Thus the phenomenology of religion can retain a traditional "theological" manner of talking about the sacrifice, inasmuch as it employs the parlance of "gods" as protagonists in the rite without making any overt claims concerning the "reality"—or unreality—of these transcendent beings. The "gods" are taken simply as representations that can be subsumed under a broader, structural rubric. The gods, as they were for Plato, mere *eidoi,* traditional denotations for what can be easily classified in terms of the *essence* of the religious experience, which phenomenologists of religion have alternately labeled the *sacred,* the *holy,* or what Gerhard van der Leeuw has termed *power.* Hence, the conception of an encounter between the human and divine that is typical of the religious person's own account of the sacrifice does not have to be translated into some alien, theoretical idiom. It can be appreciated in the contest of religious belief itself, providing we recognize that the sacrifice is not so much to the "gods" in the literal sense of the word as it is a concrete mediation of the divine in some manner.

Indeed, the major phenomenologists of religion have tended to characterize the sacrifice in this more general fashion. Phenomenology focuses on the aim that sacrifice appears to satisfy from inside the horizon of the cult. And structural analysis of the various cultic perspectives reveals that sacrifice has a cosmic significance; it is an indispensible activity for the maintenance of the balance between sacred force and human volition; it constitutes the interface between the two fundamental "worlds" that spring from the religious experience of the universe as a duality.

In the estimate of the phenomenologists, sacrifice is the supreme ritual for safeguarding the cosmos against the menace of chaos; it is an assurance of "life" in the face of a perpetual menace of death or nonexistence. As van der Leeuw puts it, the sacrifice is "the working of the power of life itself,"[16] it is a kind of "cosmic necessity" that "ensures the uninterrupted circulation of life," according to Eliade.[17] The sacrifice is effective, insofar as it serves to harmonize human existence with the dynamic power of the sacred. It is, as W. B. Kristensen declares, humanity's "sacramental participation in abiding, divine life."[18] The sacrifice facilitates an infusion of divine vitality into the organs and limbs of the cosmic body. Without such an infusion the universe would inevitably wither, disintegrate, and collapse into nothingness. Life is an ongoing energy transfer that keeps the world system in motion. "Life" and the "sacred" are interchangeable concepts. "Life" is the animating power not of physical entities alone, but off souls and divinities as well.

Phenomenology of religion, of course, pointedly eschews "explaining" anything about sacrifice. Nor does it trace the historical genesis of the rite. It merely endeavors to redistribute the experiential and symbolic properties of sacrifice. And hence it does not furnish us with a plausible "understanding" of sacrifice, because all "theory" in some measure contains explanation. This shirking of explanation reinforces three conspicuous defects in the approach. First, the phenomenologist of religion is constrained to view the act of sacrifice, if only for the sake of renouncing all "presuppositions," from the perspective of the cultic experience itself and is thereby barred from drawing any extensive anthropological conclusions. This stance results in a fundamentally conservative reading of the sacrifice. Like the priest who superintends the sacrificial enterprise the phenomenologist can describe it only as a liturgical sustaining of the cosmic rhythms. And the conservative interpretation becomes unavoidable, because the phenomenologist will heed the "transformative" liturgy, which may very well be the integral clue to the meaning of the sacrifice that earlier theorists either skirted around or completely overlooked. Second, the typological method of description seized on by the phenomenologists forecloses any examination of the direction of historical change and variation in both the mode and intent of the sacrifice. Third, phenomenology of religion cannot give sufficient consideration to the "generative" force of violence that is at the "core" and radiates throughout the semantics of sacrifice. If sacrifice is *au fond* a mechanism for promoting the "circulation of life," then doubtlessly the nurturance of vitality must have as its corollary the necessity of death. But under what circumstances is the death imperative transposed into the sacrificial demand for murder? This question, above all, has not been matched with an adequate answer in the general theories and researchers of the past, particularly within the history of religions. Whereas such researchers have called in an abundance of data on the subject, they have been somewhat remiss in addressing themselves to the "grammatology" of sacrifice itself.

The history of religions, therefore, must give way to a *cultural semiotics* of religion that treats the sacred neither as pure formality nor as projection or epiphenomenon, but as a dynamic and substitutional sign process whose "cipher" lies in the deconstructive reading of the history of the body and desire. The anthropological "puzzle" of sacrifice is integral to the "question" concerning religion itself, because it not only serves as an "epiphany of darkness" in the midst of a metaphysics of the luminous, but because it "re-presents" the dialectical movement, which in truth is but a metonymy, of the existential duality: death and divinity, body and transcendence, desire and quiescence, fragility and perdurance. This metonymical "secret" is discovered at the conclusion of Euripides' tragic drama *The Bacchae*, which Girard has fruitfully "misread" in terms of mimesis and a duplication of the transcendental signified. In *The Bacchae*, Dionysus, who both psychologically and philologically signifies the presencing of hitherto unbounded and inarticulable desire, is placed by the tragic writer in dialectical "antithesis" to Pentheus, the Apollonian archon, the bearer of all civic and "political" virtues. In Euripidean tragedy, as opposed to the Aeschyliean and Sophoclean, the Dionysian-demonic no longer lays siege without victory to the architectonic of the "cultural"; it condenses it into its metonymic signature, in this case the slapstick personage of Pentheus, then devours it.[19] But the final act in which the Dionyisac *sparagmos* engulfs the illusion both of Pentheus and tragic art, so that horror can be viewed and ultimately turned rational, the symbolic transformation supposedly inherent in the event of sacrifice proves fraudulent. Ecstasy becomes holocaust. Wisdom becomes grisly spectacle. The "absolute knowledge" of the sacrificer is revealed as trance-possession. Pentheus is slain by his own mother, who mistakes him for an animal. The "self-knowledge" of the sacrificer, which supposedly comprehends a greater, sacred totality, is deconstructed in terms of a profane and repugnant segment of the human psyche: murder and madness. The Hegelian "truth" of the whole is reappropriated metonymically as the shame of the part. The victim is not deified, but rather God dies—absolutely!

The more cryptic message of *The Bacchae* is thus subversive of the transcendentalist project that all along we have called the *study of religion*. The message turns not only on the Girardian relationship between "sacrifice" and "sacrality," but on the recognition that the founding moment of all religiosity is an act of unspeakable, and perhaps unsearchable, violence. The "violent origins" of the experience of the sacred can already be grasped in Kristeva's vision of the "thetic" character of all language and signification. According to Kristeva, the natural signifying processes that make up the constant formation and reformation of desire are subject to sudden irruptions and interferences. This "redistribution" of signifying intentions separates subject form object and constitutes the sign in its existential duality. "There is no sign that is not thetic."[20] The moment of the thetic is also the apparition of alterity, the evanescence of the "other" out of the play of drives and fantasies. It is the realization of "drive heterogeneity." Without the thetic "break," language cannot occur. In short, the romantic longing for another is what makes for the possibility of discursivity in the first place. It is the basis of an endless "semiotization" that mutates into the structure of representation.

It is not, therefore, the case, as Heidegger insists, that "Being speaks," but "bodies speak" and occasion the act of speaking. Furthermore, the radicalization of the disruptive terrain of the body generates the speaking of not just the other, but the "wholly other." The disfigurement of the body through sacrifice creates at a primitive level the illusion of the holy because it is a leap from semiosis to stasis, from inclination to representation. Sacrifice is the "theologization of the thetic."[21] It puts an end to "semiotic violence" and focuses instead on a victim through a metonymic recasting of the somatic syntax. The creation of the "sacrificial" order is similar to the valorization of the outsider, the denomination of a "chosen people" who are also history's eternal sacrificial victims, the scapegoats, the Jews. The possibility of eternity necessitates the temporal victimization of foreigners, strangers, wayfarers—those who "thetically" appear within the endless flow of history. The "stranger as guest" is also the metonymical realization of an ontology of the symbolical and therefore, if we may speak metaphysically, of "Being" itself. *Christ* is the word for "parousia," the fullness of being, because "Christ" is the stranger, the Son of Man who has nowhere to lay his head. The foreigner is always reviled under the "name of the father," because he has "lost his mother."[22] He lives in a *civitas peregrone*. He is persecuted, because he is the ultimate possibility of signification. His having been named comes through violence, through the thetic. In Greek religion the stranger was Dionysus.

The "birth of religion" at the primal scene of a Dionysian orgy has further implications than some new and uncanny "hermeneutics of suspicion" conjured up by a poststructuralist form of catachrestic spell casting. Religiosity is a kind of reversible alchemy between violence and the purity of representation, between *kratos* and *eidos,* between Dionysus and Deus, as the "tragic" Greeks understood it, according to Nietzsche. If that is the case, then it is indeed imaginable how theological thinking must be interchangeable with somatological self-reflection. The "divine" can be comprehended only in terms of both power and the transcendence of the body. The problem of sacrifice is ultimately the problem of religion, because it points up the dialectical and nonlinear patterning of the gesture of the sacred, while at the same time it challenges at the core the unbearable metaphysics of presence that has dominated, and retarded, the development of a real theory of the "religious." The interconnectivity between the erotic and the tragic, between desire and cathartic suffering, between love and sacrifice, between Krishna and Christ, between passion and "The Passion," indicates the profound ways in which the religious sense emerges from the *disjunctiveness of the signs of the body.*

While "classic theories" of sacrifice were based on social metaphors of negotiation and exchange, poststructural models have their source within what might be termed *analogies of commutation.* In the poststructural setting the religious concept of "sacrifice" serves as a chain of signification leading from single wish-fantasy to the types of complex symbolic ordering found in collective ritual. Derrida's preoccupation with the *pharmakon,* or

surrogate victim, as the metaphor of deconstructive readings reinforces this interpretation. If in the deconstructive reading the "text
is victim," as Mark Taylor puts it, in the sacrificial paradigmatics
of religious theory, the slaughter and extirpation of the *pharmakon*
amounts to a cycle of semiotic substitutions through which the
"real" violence of the collective and the self-surpassing strategies
of somatic existence are represented as "holy" and "redemptive."[23]
Religious values then are metonymic codings for the disquiet of
the body. Religious theory must begin, as it ultimately does for
Plato, in the analytic of desire. The "flower" of religious thinking
is rooted in the "flames" of passion. If sacrifice is "neurotic" in the
psychoanalytical context, it is such because it seeks to render the
impossible: it aims to transform the finite into the infinite through
what in the writing of Lacan is called the *deconstruction of the
drive,* the ultimate project of language. It endeavors to make the
sacrificer immortal and the victim a "metonymic," rather than a
mimetic, double. In the production of the victim the ritual of
sacrifice produces religion, the shadow of violence. It is not historically coincidental that the advent of the discipline known as *religious studies* in the 1960s coincided with both the Nietzschean
"murder of God" and the liberation of body throughout Western
culture. It is also far form coincidental that the formalization of
the discipline in recent decades has proceeded apace with the
identification of deconstructionism as a kind of *pharmakon.* But
that is a subject for another discourse.

The "study of religion" itself is ultimately the study of the
Luciferian energies of violence. Barth's rejection of a modernist
faith in the salvific characteristics of "religion," therefore, was
more prescient than many realize. But this modernist faith has
not yet been deconstructed because its founding myth has not yet
been encoded. It is the myth of the transformative.

Notes

---

1. The Cambridge ritualists wer pioneer researchers in the early
history of Greek religion, which also commanded significant attention in
Frazer"s work. Among the most important works of this school are Jane
Harison, *Prolegomena to the Study of Greek Religion* (London: Merlin Press,
1961) and *Themis* (New York: World Publishing Company, 1962). See also
F. M. Cornford, *The Origin of Attic Comedy* (Garden City, N.Y.: Doubleday
Books, 1961); Gilbert Murray, *Five Stages of Greek Religion* (Oxford:
Clarendon Press, 1925).

2. W. Robertson Smith is noted for his theory that the origin of sacrifice is to be found in totemism. The sacrifice, according to Smith, was initially the practice of communally eating the totem animal, which represented the god. "Eating" the god was an expression of the sense of intimacy between human and divinity. Later, when humans became estranged from gods (especially in the development of the Semitic myths of divine transcendence), the ritual form of slaughter was retained, but now the sacrifice became an offering of conciliation with a distant deity, rather than a ceremony of immediate communion. See W. Robertson Smith, *The Religion of the Semites* (New York: Meridan Books, 1956), especially Lectures 6–12. See also his article "Sacrifice," *The Encyclopedia Brittanica,* 9th edition, 1887. It is not too difficult to draw the connection with the theories of Freud.

3. Jan de Vries, *The Study of Religion,* trans. Kees W. Bolle (New York: Harcourt, Brace, and World, 1967).

4. See Victor Turner, "Sacrifices as Quintessential Process: Prophylaxis or Abandonment?" *History of Religions* 16 (February 1975): 189–215. See also Victor Turner, *The Ritual Process* (Chicago: Aldine Publishing Co., 1969).

5. Rene Girard, *Violence and the Sacred,* trans. Patrick Gregory (Baltimore: Johns Hopkins University Press, 1977), p. 24. For Girard, the prototypical form of the social crisis is a "sacrificial crisis," which arises when the institution of sacrifice no longer provides an outlet for inherent violence. The ritual of sacrifice is basic to society, because human beings are inherently violent and require a legitimate, "structured" expression of violent proclivities. There comes a point in many socieites, however, when the sacrificial discipline of violence crumbles, the violence can no longer be sublimated ritually and thus surges unchecked.

Other works by Girard include *Decit, Desire and the Novel: Self and Other in Literary Structure,* trans. Yvonne Freccero (Baltimore: Johns Hopkins University Press, 1965); *The Scapegoat,* trans. Yvonne Freccero (Baltimore: Johns Hopkins University Press, 1986); *Things Hidden Since the Foundations of the World,* trans. Stephen Bann and Michael Metteer (Stanford, California: Stanford University Press, 1987). For a good series of secondary treatments, see Paul Dumochel, *Violence and Truth: On the Work of René Girard* (Stanford, California: Stanford University Press, 1988). Feminist considerations can be found in William Beers, Women and Sacrifice: Male Narcissism and the Psychology of Religion (Detroit: Wayne State University Press, 1992), pp. 105–111.

6. Turner, "Sacrifice as Quintessential Process," p. 189.

7. Ibid., p. 202.

8. See Mary Douglas, *Natural Symbols* (New York: Pantheon Books, 1970), pp. 102–124.

9. See E. B. Tylor, *Primitive Culture* (London: John Murray, 1871), vol. 2.

10. See Richard Hecht, "Sacrifice and Interpretation: A Study of Time and Humanity in Ancient Israel and Vedic India," unpublished Ph.D. dissertation, University of California at Los Angeles, 1977.

11. Marcel Mauss, *The Gift: Forms and Functions in Archaic Socieites,* trans. Ian Cunnison (New York: W. W. Norton and Co., 1967), p. 13.

12. Douglas, *Natural Symbols,* p. 15.

13. See Hect, "Sacrifice and Interpetation," pp. 91ff.

14. Henri Hubert and Marcel Mauss, *Sacrifice: Its Nature and Function,* trans. I. D. Hails (Chicago: University of Chicago Press, 1964), p. 9.

15. Ibid., p. 20.

16. Gerhard van der Leeuw, *Religion in Essence and Manifestation,* trans. J. E. Turner (New York: Harper and Row, 1963), vol. 2, p. 354.

17. Mircea Eliade, *Myths, Dreams and Mysteries,* trans. Philip Mairet (New York: Harper and Row, 1960), p. 189.

18. W. Brede Kristensen, *The Meaning of Religion,* trans. John Carman (The Hague: Martinus Nijhoff, 1960), p. 480.

19. The distance between "God" (Zeus) and Dionysus was not all that great in the cultural sense of ancient Greece, contrary to the dualistic contrast between the Apollonian and Dionysian that has grown up under the influence of Western puritanism. Bernhard Zimmerman has pointed out the essential "bipolarity" of the Dionysian cult, the rhythmic oscillation between "overpowering beauty" and "inhuman cruelty." See *Greek Tragedy: An Introduction,* trans. Thomas Marier (Baltimore: Johns Hopkins University Press, 1991), pp. 127–128. This bipolarity may have been both the source of play's fascination and the covert message of *The Bacchae,* where the seeming "contest" between Pentheus and the "savage god" dissolves dramatically and climactically into the scene where self-knowledge is attained through the unleashing and outpouring of instinctual violence.

20. Julia Kristeva, *Revolution in Poetic Language,* trans. Margaret Waller (New York: Columbia University Press, 1984), p. 44.

21. Ibid., p. 78.

22. Julia Kristeva, *Strangers to Ourselves,* trans. Leon S. Roudice (New York: Columbia University Press, 1991), p. 5.

23. For a comparison of Girard and Derrida, see Andrew McKenna, *Violence and Difference: Girard, Derrida, and Deconstruction* (Urbana: University of Illinois Press, 1992). "The victim is the issue of violence and the origin of the sacred" (p. 69). Derrida's "mystification" of writing is similar

to Girard's, where "the law" that is writing, inscription, Torah is the heir to "sacrifice and its contradictions," in this came the metonymical reversal that amounts to the banishment of the signifier. See ibid., p. 50. Along these lines see also John D. Caputo, "Heidegger's Scandal: Thinking and the Essence of the Victim," in Joseph Margolis and Tom Rockmore (eds.), *The Heidegger Case: Philosophy and Politics* (Philadelphia: Temple University Press, 1991); Walter Burkert, *Greek Religion*, trans. John Raffan (Cambridge, Mass.: Harvard University Press, 1985).

Chapter 8

The Transformation Myth and the End
of the "Myth of History"

The sacred is a fetid, sticky object without boundaries.

Georges Bataille

The so-called Hymn of Man *(Purusa Sukta)* from the *Rg Veda*, is the locus classicus for examining the relationship between mythology and the ritual of sacrifice.

Thousand headed is Man.
With thousand eyes and feet.
He envelops the whole earth
And goes beyond it by ten fingers.

Man indeed is all that was and is,
And whatever may come in the future,
He is the master of immortality,
Of all that rises through nourishment...

From that cosmic sacrifice,
Drops of oil were collected,
Beasts of the wing were born,
And animals wild and tame.

From that original sacrifice,
The hymns and the chants were born,
The meters were born from it,
And from it prose was born...

By sacrifice the gods sacrificed the sacrifice.
Those were the original and earliest acts.
Those powers (of the sacrifice) reach heaven,
Where the Sadhyas and the gods are.[1]

The texture of the myth contains major clues as to the meaning of sacrificial performances. In the Indian hymn, as well as in
a medley of other passages from the Vedas, the intimate connection between the act of sacrifice and the event of creation is firmly
established. Historians of religion are cognizant of the premier
position of sacrifice in the priestly cult introduced by the Aryan
conquerors of the Indian subcontinent, and this exaltation of the
ritual endowed it with a cosmogonic significance in the eyes of its
ancient stewards. Yet rituals of sacrifice have been incorporated
into the ceremonial ambience of other religions without receiving
overt representation in the arrangement of mythic icons. The
converse is true also: where no evidence of cultic sacrifice is discernible, there still linger as part of the mythology certain echoes
of sacrifice having been undertaken, as in the Greek saga of Cronus
devouring his children recounted in Hesiod's *Theogony*.

It is, therefore, difficult to explain the character of the Vedic
myth purely in terms of its ritual context. Rather, the prominence
of sacrifice itself may be adduced in some measure from the content of the myth; or we may be persuaded to view both the myth
and ritual en bloc as mutual expressions of an underlying religious complex. In any event, the Vedic imagery can be treated as
the outcropping of a more primitive mythologem subsisting within
a virtually forgotten stratum of religious culture. And this
mythologem possibly divulges something quite telling with respect
to the archaic intuition both about the make-up of the universe
and about human destiny.

Historian Bruce Lincoln has made a compelling case for the
genuine antiquity of this particular mythologem.[2] According to
Lincoln, the Vedic account, which portrays the creation of the
world as the sacrifice of the first human being Purusa (literally,
"person" or "human being") is in actuality only a slight variant
on a proto-Indo-European story. The original Indo-European myth
is now lost, yet it can still be reconstructed after a fashion from
various residues present in such diverse materials as the creation
tales of Persia and Scandinavia and the legend of the founding of
Rome. The Indian rendition, Lincoln argues, is nonetheless the
closest we have to the archaic prototype. Whereas most of the
other variants have expurgated or made substitutions for the sacrificial motif, the Vedic hymn retains it. The theme of sacrifice

thus lurks behind certain Indo-European narratives of the beginnings of the world, the parturition of the human species, and the confirmation of the order of society.

According to Lincoln, sacrifice is "the most prominent of all Indo-European rituals," the performance of which in its universal context "was felt to re-create the world, dispersing material substance from its microcosmic form to the macrocosm, and thus sustaining creation."[3] The prestige of the myth has been tied by anthropologists to the view that sacrifice is an instrument of fertility magic. According to the theory, popularized by the Cambridge school of anthropology, the dismemberment of the consecrated victim—the nucleus of the proto-Indo-European myth— could be interpreted as a symbolic act of distributing the energy concentrated within the god's body. The ritual slaying of the *meriah*, a ceremony of fecundation enacted in precolonial India that Frazer documents, would be such an illustration.[4] The slain *meriah*, whose fragments are buried in the fields, or mixed with the grain, thus becomes a kind of life-enhancing manure. The dissemination of his divine substance promotes the growth and harvest of crops. A second example would be the myth of Hainuwele among the tribes of West Ceram. Hainuwele, the virgin, is buried alive by her people, but in her sacrificial death she becomes the continuing source of vitality for the food plants of the area.[5] The Indo-European account of the cosmos as having been composed out of the immolated corpse of a primordial victim could be regarded in this connection as an etiological myth to legitimate the fertility ritual. The myth could be dated perhaps in the early Neolithic period, when fertility sacrifices seem to have been popular in the primitive agricultural villages of the temperate zone.

Attempts to link the proto-Indo-European mythologem to the communal rites of prehistoric farmers, however, are an obvious misadventure. First, the dismemberment motif seems to be older than the Neolithic age, and it seems to have its genesis in the Paleolithic era when all human economies revolved around hunting. The same motif also reaches beyond the Neolithic into the Greek mystery religions. The symbolism of dismemberment is at the heart of the Dionysian revel as well as the Orphic initiation, both of which had only a derivative relationship to agricultural ceremonies. Second, such symbolism is built into the psychology of shamanism, which has nothing to do with fertility magic.[6] Finally, the original Indo-European myth, as Lincoln shows, was the invention not of sedentary tillers of the earth, but of nomadic herders.[7] Therefore, any exposition of the myth that dwells exclusively on its agrarian, or chthonic, facets must be challenged.

A second account derives from socio-psychological considerations and are tacit in Girard's discussions. Sacrifice is necessary
if the different, refractory segments of the social order are held
together. Some of the material Lincoln cites support such an interpretation. He cites Tacitus's story of the ancient Germans in which
"all people of the same blood" convene in a wooded spot and
perform "barbaric rites," recalling an "ancient dread" while cel-
ebrating the "sacrifice" or "dismemberment" of a human being
"for the public good." The dismemberment signifies the dispersion
of the social group, and the ritual of sacrifice thus becomes a way
of replicating through the corporealization of signs the
deconstitution of the body politic and its symbolic reintegration.[8]
From Girard's standpoint, sacrifice inscribes the sacred by making
the horror of the violent spectacle a surrogate for the randomized
and incoherent destructive impulses of the group. Here it mimics,
while at the same time it totalizes, the actions of the social body.
The difficulty with such a theory is that it presupposes an exact
correlation between ritual structures and indigenous concepts of
social solidarity, whereas it does not explain how the violent spectacle, as opposed to an "affirmative" celebration such as ritual
copulation, performs a socially integrative role. The Girardian
identification of "spectacular" representations of violence with the
sacred turns on a fundamental misunderstanding of the way in
which popular ideas of the holy are bound up with the body. The
mutilation of the body is not itself a gesture of sacrality. The
mutilation destroys the representational system of popular religion and reinscribes the "signs of the body" with respect to the
forms of authority. That, of course, has been Foucault's argument
all along.[9]

The third avenue of approach, of course, is the phenomenological one. A phenomenological description of the myth yields
not so much a serious anthropology of origins, but a new metaphysics of presence, as we have shown. Such a metaphysics can be
discerned in Eliade's valorization of the ancient Indo-Europeans,
who supposedly made the discovery that "nothing can be created
without immolation, without sacrifice."[10] The Vedic writings in-
scribe poetically the notion that "the texture of the universe is
sacrifice."[11] Sacrifice is "that which preserves the universe in its
existence, that which gives life and the hope of life."[12] By and
large this exposition parallels the general phenomenological mode
of portraying sacrificial operations. Through sacrifice the viability
of the cosmos is restored, the parts are reinvigorated. The creation

is drawn back into the substance of the creator. The diffused energy of nature is gathered together and compressed in the object of sacrifice, then broadcast anew as the power of creativity and the force of life. The sacrifice forestalls the drift of life toward immobility and death.

What is most intriguing about the Indo-European myth is the preeminent figure of "human being" (*Gayomart* in the Zoroastrian version). The primal human being, as the victim of the sacrifice, is the very embodiment of its redemptive power. Indeed, as the Brahmana says, the "sacrifice *is* Man."[13] The sacrifice is not cosmic in its essence so much as "anthropocosmic." It is the *via regia* whereby humanity is raised to the status of godhood.

> Daily the sacrifice is spread.
> Daily the sacrifice is completed.
> Daily it unites the sacrificer to heaven.
> Daily by sacrifice to heaven he ascends.[14]

The Indo-European myth is less a statement about the origins and evolution of the universe than an affirmation of the incipient destiny of humanity. The myth is *about* humanity, who "is all that was and is." The sacrifice consists in the promise of a marvelous transformation of human existence. The intention of the Brahmanic sacrifice is not, as Eliade would have it, "the continual regeneration of the world,"[15] but the apotheosis of humanity who is a veritable *microcosm*. Humanity is not fashioned out of the stuff of the universe. Humanity itself is the prima materia.

It is noteworthy that in the *Rg Veda* fragment, which represents a later theological refurbishing of the older lore, humanity is the victim and the "gods" the sacrificer, whereas in the proto-Indo-European version humanity is both sacrificer and the one who is sacrificed. Humanity creates itself by self-sacrifice or at least by sacrificing an integral dimension of itself. In the primordial act, humanity is split in twain. Humanity transcends this cleavage by the sacrifice of the one half, which in turn leads to the immortalization of the remaining half.

Lincoln contends that, among the surviving narratives that betray components of the proto-Indo-European myth, the story of the "beguiling of Gylfi" in the Old Norse cycle best preserves the original characterization of the primal being. Here the primal being is the giant Ymir (= *Yama*, Sanskrit). The Old Norse version is recounted as follows:

Bor's sons killed the giant Ymir, and when he fell, so much
blood poured from his wounds that they drowned the whole
tribe of frost ogres with it. . . . They took Ymir and carried
him into the middle of Ginnungagap, and made the world
from him, from his bones the mountains; rocks and pebbles
they made from his teeth and jaws and those bones that
were broken. . . . From the blood which welled freely from his
wounds they fashioned the ocean, when they put together
the earth and girdled it, laying the ocean round about it. . . .
They also took his skull and made the sky from it and set it
over the earth with its four sides, and under each corner they
put a dwarf. . . . Then they took the sparks and burning embers
that were flying about after they had blown out of Muspell,
and placed them in the midst of Ginnungagap to give light
to heaven above and earth beneath. They gave their stations
to all the stars, some fixed in the sky; others [planetary] that
had wandered at will in the paths in which they were to
travel.[16]

There is a strange structural affinity between the creation
account in the Vedas, where cosmos and society are forged from
the disjointed corpse of humanity, and the Old Norse reminiscence
of the dismembering of Ymir. But another important inference can
be drawn from survey of the different Indo-European variants. In
the Persian text we find the figure of "Yima" (= Ymir), the first
"king," who in the golden age "ruled over the seven Karsvares of
the earth, over the Daevas and men . . ."[17] Lincoln observes that
from the Indo-European standpoint the king is the "complete man,"
the incarnation of divine power, the simulacrum for the universe.[18]
Creation of the world is linked directly to the sacrifice of the king.
"The king must die," as the title of Mary Renault's famous novel
has it, so that the spiritual potentialities of the human race can
be actualized.

The king poses as the sacrificial victim par excellence, as the
salvific *pharmakon*. But who, then, is the sacrificer? In Lincoln's
estimate a priest, "Manu," or "human being," appears in the
Vedic literature. The priest slays the king to let loose the transformative energies that he possesses. To put the matter in
nonmythological language, we can say that "humanity" as priest
sacrifices a vital aspect of itself (i.e., the "king") to attain a higher
state of existence, to be reunited with the three-quarters that are
"immortal in heaven." The death of the king releases the transcendent spiritual benefits for the sacrificer. Through ritual killing

humanity itself is transmuted into divinity. The discovery of the proto-Indo-European outlook toward creation, narratively signified as the slaying of the primal king, naturally betokens the Frazerian research on ritual regicide. It determines an early mythical matrix for such a ritual, if one in fact existed; but it also impugns Frazer's premier thesis in *The Golden Bough* that the kings were ceremonially murdered so that "their divine spirit may be transmitted to their successors in full vigor, uncontaminated by the weakness and decay of sickness or old age, because any such degeneration on the part of the king would . . . entail a corresponding degeneration on mankind, on cattle, and on the crops."[19]

Clearly, the sacrificial killing of the king involved more than fertility magic. It was the expression of a quest for power and self-transcendence. In the Old Norse sage Ymir's creative power is acquired through the sacrifice by the sons of Bor, who now rule over the world. In the *Avesta*, Yima's "glory" is "seized" by "the sturdiest of the men of strength," including the prophet Zarathustra. As a living figure the king is the finite embodiment of power. In many primitive religions the king is seen as an object of *taboo*, because he has around him an aura of sacrality. The king is the instantiation of the divine energy. Yet this energy remains merely potential, until it is actualized by obliterating the king's mortal frame. In death alone resides life eternal. And only in the king's death can his life-supporting capacity be shared by all. On the cosmological plane it is through absolute destruction that authentic creation can transpire.

Another curious feature of the myth is the implication that the first king and first priest are "twins."[20] Divine twins are prominent characters in many primitive creation accounts, occurring among the peoples of the American Southwest as well as in Africa.[21] Legendary twin personages inhabit the time of beginnings in the traditions of Hebraic and European civilization. One can reference the tales of Cain and Abel, or Jacob and Esau, or Romulus and Remus. There is also the myth of Horus and Set among the Egyptians. In all these accounts the story of primordial twins cradles a plot of fierce sibling rivalry, and the first and third legends relate how one of the pair murdered the other. The study of Romulus and Remus by Lincoln's reckoning is descended straightaway from the Indo-European myth, and it concludes as well with the institution of world order, in this case the founding of the city of Rome. The myth of primordial twins whose competition with each other leads to fratricide redlines the religious sense of an unbridgeable dualism at the bottom of things. In the Vedic context, the dualism is overcome ritually through the Brahmanic sacrifice, opening an immediate route to immortality. In Iranian Zoroastrianism, as in the Hebraic legend of Cain and Abel, the primal killing loses its cosmo-redemptive function and is demythologized to the point where it is depicted as an original *crime* that casts humanity into the torrent of history.

In Zoroastrianism the dualism is preserved throughout time as the war between the Creator God Ohrmazd and the evil spirit Ahriman. When Zarathustra rejected the traditions of animal sacrifice, he also repudiated it as a solution to the problem of dualism. Overcoming dualism and the acquisition of immortality must await the end of history. In the Old Norse mythology a similar attitude is evident. Bor's sons, like Zeus in the Greek myth, have won a temporary victory over the giants, their perennial antagonists. But the power of Bor's sons is continually threatened and destiny is leading them on to the final Ragnarok, the apocalyptic "twilight of the gods," when they too will be vanquished and slain. In the Iranian and Norse sagas we have what amounts to a historical projection of what Girard calls the *sacrificial crisis.*

At another level, however, the twin motif can also be taken to signify a more fundamental dualism: the antimony between life and death. Ingredient in the rhetoric of sacrifice is a rudimentary inkling that life can be secured only through death, and that through surrender to the sway of death, death ultimately loses its power. "Whoever seeks to gain his own life will lose it, but whoever loses his life will preserve it." (Luke 17:33). The power of life can be unfettered only with the abolition of the living form. The crucified Jesus is at least revealed as "Christus Victor," as the heavenly Son of God.

Although creation depends on destruction, it must not entail wanton slaughter. The slaughter must be that of the sacral victim, the metonymic representation or mythico-linguistic "supplement," of divine power. The primal dualism is the precondition for the reconciliation of the forces of life and death into a "dialectical" synthesis. One of the twins must take the life of the other, but in reality each twin is nought but an alternate manifestation of the same, underlying substance. Together they constitute a diptych of the "primordial human," who is both human and divine, mortal and immortal, evil and good. By means of the sacrificial oblation, the living matter is sublimed, converted into its transcendental double. The subrogation of form is the disclosure of "essence," the tearing down of the disguises. In the myth of universal sacrifice we have a basal figuration of a kind of symbol-text that seems to run through or at least leave traces within the larger constellation of mythology. The Indo-European complex is one key orchestral flight through this theme. Although this symbolic thread may not be entirely global, it is consistent and overarching enough to identify it as a kind of "monomyth." Such a monomyth is commensurate with what Erich Neumann has dubbed the *transformation myth*. The transformation myth can be schematized as follows:

• The present world comes into existence through the sundering of a primal being, who may be bisected or dismembered.

• The resulting elements of the act of sundering become the multitude of creatures or entities in the universe, standing in contrast to the original oneness of things.

• The distinction between the One and the Many is at the same time a hiatus between the spiritual and the phenomenal, the sacred and the profane, life and death.

• This duality inherent in the given make-up of the world emerges as an unstable dualism that must be overcome through *regenerative destruction*. In the cultic situation the abolition of duality is achieved through sacrifice. The sacrifice "makes sacred," because it obliterates the material or phenomenal integument of life and reinscribes divinity. Among those religions that reject or downplay the cultic sacrifice, the redemption of the phenomenal world is the climax of certain historical theatrics. The world itself is dissolved in a cosmic battle and out of the rubble emerges a new heaven and earth.

• The sacrifice is, of course, a restitution of the original unity of life, but even more significantly it brings about the unity by *transforming* the scattered shards of the universe into their primordial identity. The sacrifice does not merely rectify the balance of forces, but is responsible for qualitative alterations. The cremated patriarch rejoins his ancestors, the extinction of the body occasions the rebirth of the soul, the fallen hero or martyred saint becomes a pervading and redeeming religious presence for his worshipers.

The transformation myth can be delineated in a nexus of cultural and historical phenotypes from the paleolithic period down through the neolithic era and into the religious matrices of the "higher" civilizations. The myth serves as the enveloping symbolic grammar of sacrificial practices and thus correlates in various aspects with them. The transformation myth is perhaps the master clue to the sacrifice, and it can be uncovered in rarefied guises in those religious symbol-universes where conspicuous sacrificial rites have been abandoned or dismantled. What stands out about myth is that, like the ritual of sacrifice, it mediates and expresses "spiritual" metamorphosis, which yet presupposes an archaeology of violence. Just as the universe takes form through a violent catastrophe, so religious life itself must be governed by the same kind of cosmogenic *tremendum*. "Salvation" is not a gradual, unilinear, and equable process, but a cataclysmic jolt, a sudden metastasis, a dialectical leap in which the previous moments are negated and reamalgamated.

A template for the transformation myth is, as we have seen, the proto-Indo-European story, which very likely is a repatterning of even older symbolic weaves and designs. The proto-Indo-European myth may indeed, as Helmut Hoffmann has convincingly argued, be a second-order elaboration of the worldview of paleolithic shamanism, of which vestiges are apparent in the traditions of the Aryan nomads and in the Bon religion of Tibet.[22] The Bon religion is known to have involved human sacrifice. The motif of violent death and rebirth, which has all too frequently been explained as a simulacrum for the swings of the vegetation cycle first experienced by the neolithic cultivators, actually predates the invention of agriculture. It belongs in all likelihood to the Old Stone Age when wild game was the principal foodstuff and shamans were the custodians of the sacred. The symbolism of violent death and revivification, according to another scholar, is "actually an archaic archetype for the initiation of the most ancient hunters of wild animals, one which is at the foundation of the ceremony for youthful rites of passage. In the shamanic initiation this archetype is combined with an older rite of dismemberment and evisceration.[23]

Eliade has described in exhaustive detail the ritualized tearing to pieces of the shamanic initiate, which consists in a drama of death and mystical rejuvenation. The candidate for the shamanic vocation is killed by the masters of the ceremony. He is symbolically cut up, pierced with arrows, his head smashed open, his brain excised, and his vital organs removed.[24] In some instances the initiate falls into a trance and is compelled to contemplate himself as a skeleton, as a stack of dead bones.[25] The ceremony concludes with the magical revitalization of the lifeless bones and flesh, at which point the initiate has completed his ordeal and now enters into the fraternity of shamans.

Hoffmann interprets the shamanic rite of dismemberment and resurrection as a magical imitation of the killing of game animals. The shaman identifies with the spirit of the animals. He becomes an incarnation of the life-conferring "deer mother," who is the generatrix of all game. He transforms himself into the maternal spirit who is slain and her carcass dismembered and eaten, yet who nevertheless returns to life and dwells as the souls of all beasts.[26] It has been commonly observed among Native American hunters that they do not consider the slaughter of an animal to be its consummate destruction. Instead they regard the killing as a sort of exchange wherein the human receives the meat and the animal's spirit is set free. Likewise, the ancient shaman through the mimetic ritualization of the slaughter of the deer offers up its own body, yet in the same gesture takes possession of its inner life and obtains its gift of immortality.

Both the sacrifice and the transformation myth, henceforth, are derived ultimately from the ritualization of primitive hunting symbols. The act of sacrificial killing, which has remained by and large an enigma for religious psychology, can be reckoned as a symbolic representation of hunting ecology.[27] The fact that systematic sacrifice is rare among peoples whose sole livelihood is hunting, but tends to become prominent among agriculturalists who have been denied a natural outlet for this most ancient "violent" activity, would support such a hypothesis.

In the grand, historical sweep, according to Walter Burkett, "hunting, sacrifice, and war are symbolically interchangeable."[28] The development of human sacrifice and cannibalism can also be understood along these lines. If it is the case, as Eli Sagan contends, that "warfare and cannibalism are inexorably connected,"[29] then the sacrifice of human beings may be regarded as a secondary ritualization of aggression or in this instance as a concomitant of warfare. The most spectacular and ghastly historical incidence of human sacrifice performed in conjunction with cannibalism occurred among the Aztecs. The Aztecs crafted an elaborate martial civilization, whose priests annually liquidated thousands of victims to their sanguinary solar deity Huitzilopochtli. Prior to building an agricultural city-state in the Valley of Mexico, the Aztecs had been nomadic hunters and warriors. Like the Indo-Europeans, who were also nomads, the Aztecs had a myth that looked upon the creation of the world as a sacrifice. In the beginning there took place a colossal sacrifice of the gods, whose death and blood became the power of life symbolized in the sun.[30] The priestly sacrifice of victims captured in constant warfare was not so much a stylized reenactment of the myth as a device for preserving the sun's power.

Here we discern a striking variation of the Paleolithic transformation myth within Mesoamerican civilization, while the shamanic initiation rite lurks in the background. The emblem of the Aztecs was an eagle devouring a serpent. The serpent is the archetypal symbol of agricultural fecundity as well as major divinity among plant cultivators, like those peoples of the central Mexican plateau subdued by the invading Aztec warriors. The eagle, on the other hand, is the archaic token of the shaman's hunting prowess. In the symbol-universe the shamanic initiation can be viewed as an identification by the initiate with the animal, whom the hunter slays. In the initiation the roles of the hunter and the hunted are reversed. The hunter becomes the quarry. He is killed, rent in pieces, and even swallowed by the mythical animal, whom the initiation guides impersonate. The animal may be a representative of the game the initiate will be accustomed to hunting, for example, the deer-mother; it may be a fearsome creature, such as a crocodile[31] or even a mythical monster. This switching of roles, the upending of the familiar order of life, the revelation of a startling and terrifying "underside" to everyday reality, is typical of what Turner has termed the *liminal* stage in the ritual or initiation process. The phase of "liminality" constitutes the point of transition between two entirely different worlds. Everything becomes topsy-turvy. Light becomes darkness, good becomes evil, the real becomes unreal. What was above now sinks to the bottom, and what was at bottom now rises to the top. The conventional hierarchy of things is inverted. The contradictory character of liminal reality is resolved finally in the movement to a higher order of understanding in the third, or completed, phase of the initiation. The initiate is within reinscribed within the cosmos.

The passage through liminality is inherent in the structure of sacrifice.[32] The dialectics of sacrifice encompass the negative moment of death as the threshold of new life. The sacrifice constitutes an exteriorization of the initiatory rite insofar as an alien victim is substituted for the initiate per se. The death of the victim is ritually equivalent to the symbolic death of the initiate. In the initiation proper, which precedes the sacrifice both psychologically and historically, the transit through the sphere of liminality is the necessary prelude to the transformation of the candidate. The initiate's former manner of being in the world must be stripped away and annihilated, so that he or she can be uplifted to a new station. This "resurrection" of the initiate is the outcome of the ceremony. The initiate becomes, as Eliade puts it, the "consecrated man."[33]

The drama of initiation, therefore, serves as the experiential ground plan for the transformation myth. The "raising" of the initiate to a more lofty estate is analogous to the elevation of the sacrificial victim to the status of divinity. The resurrected shaman is the precursor of the immolated king. This "primordial" theme of transformation is woven through the myriad myths of death and rebirth that spring up everywhere in human culture. Yet this symbolic pattern has been seriously misconstrued in the study of religion, perhaps because of the exceptional influence of Eliade. For Eliade, the "consecrated man" attains a "new mode of being" through the initiation only in the sense that "he" wins back what was taken away in humanity's "fall" from the sacred into the province of the profane. Initiation is a kind of homecoming, a return from exile, an *apocatastasis.* The "initiatory death reiterates the paradigmatic return to chaos, in order to make possible a repetition of the cosmogony."[34] The sequence of death and resurrection is nought but a replication of "paradigmatic" divine action. "By imitating the gods, man remains in the sacred, hence in reality."[35]

Platonic metaphysics suffuses Eliade's thinking. We may remember that Plato himself described philosophy as "initiation," as a recovery of humanity's forgotten immortality, and *anamnesis* or "recollection" of his erstwhile spiritual perfection.[36] The whole of myth and ritual, as far as Eliade is concerned, are instances not of any transformation myth, but exemplifications of the "myth of the eternal return;" they are "archetypal gestures," a "reactualization" of primordial happenings that occurred "once upon a time."[37]

The historical context of the transformation myth, is scarcely as consequential for theoretical study of religion as the *theological.* Panikkar observes: "After the creation by dismemberment, the creature must in one way or another reenter its Creator, return to the point of departure, return to the point of departure; in short, it must be divinized. Divinization, however, is not an external activity, like throwing a rope of salvation for the world to catch and so be rescued. It has to be a real reconstruction of the divine body, a total liberation from bondage, from creatureliness. For this, only an embrace between Creator and creature, their total reunion, will solve the problem . . . redemption is not merely an external act, a moral rescue, but an ontological action, a real regeneration, a new life, indeed a divine life."[38] Even creation itself is a "sacrifice of God." The theological hermeneutic behind the transformation myth discloses that "the world is nothing else but . . . [a] demi-reality on the way to becoming God, called to take part in this act of divine 'growth' "[39] The distinction between the divine and human "is not one of numerical order. . . . Inasmuch as Man *is*, God *is* not; insofar as God is, Man is not; the one means the absence of the other. The relation between the temporal and the eternal cannot be expressed in terms of being. Ultimately 'God' and 'Man', as well as the 'Cosmos' are mere abstractions of an all-embracing cosmotheandric reality."[40]

The "cosmotheandric" constitution of both the world and the universe of human experience in its grandest ensemble offers a new rendering of religious salvation, which is not to be conceived as "ontic" rather than juridical, moral, or even psychosomatic. The transformation myth constitutes the linguistico-symbolical pole of what Panikkar dubs the *quest for the supreme experience*. Such a quest refers back, as Panikkar tells us, to the rather nebulous but quintessential search in contemporary religious thought for the apriority of a "'fundamental theology" from which the doctrinal and anagogical statements of the world's religions can be derived. The cognate of the "supreme experience" is the cosmotheandric unity of metaphysical traditions, which is implicit in the transformation myth.

In his recent work Lincoln, in fact, has delineated some of these connections from a critico-literary and epigraphic perspective, rather than from the kind of "perennialist" theology for which Panikkar is most famous. The syntagmatic expression of what we have called the *transformation myth*, which underrides the practice of sacrifice, is found in the ancient cult of Mithra, the god who is both "sun and savior." In fact, Mithraism was such a powerful rival to Christianity in the ancient world, most likely because of certain close morphological and psychological similarities, that, were it not for Constantinian policy toward the church, the former might have become the "official religion" of the Roman state. Mithraism is a "proto-European" complex of symbols and attitudes that spans ages and cultures from ancient India to the late Roman imperium. Mithraic "sacrificial ideology" rests on the view "divine sacrifice" "gives life to men"[41] as well as command over the forces of destiny. The prototypical divine sacrifice is the slaying of the bull by the god Mithra, the so-called tauroctony that in later times, when mithraism became a "mystery religion," was enacted through the ritual of the *tauroboleum,* or the immersion-baptism of the celebrant with the animal's blood. Yet this sacrificial ideology is also intimately associated, according to Lincoln, with the rising of the sun, the triumph over astral fatality, the liberation of the soul from darkness, and its conduct to a greater realm. Sacrifice is necessary to the soul's ascent and in its grimmer Indo-European aspects was commingled with ideas of star worship, astrology, and mastery over the forces of destiny.

Although their religious practices were kept fierce secrets, the ancient Druids, who were celebrated as star gazers and observers of the heavenly cycles, were reported to have routinely engaged in human sacrifice, largely because of this way of thinking. The ancient writer Diodorus suggested that it was possible to divine the future by watching closely the twitching of a dead and dismembered human victim.[42] Such a view is not simply "perverse" or magical. It is established on the notion that there is a homology, or code of correspondences, between celestial patterns and energies and the life of the human body, the so-called man as microcosm principle that permeated Hermetic and Renaissiance thinking and influenced the rise of modern experimental science. The same "homologization" applied in the ancient pagan, particularly Celtic, mind to health and was the opposite of sacrifice. An understanding of the signs and motions of the cosmos could be applied to the restoration of somatic processes. Both sacrifice and astral healing mirrored "a mythic ideology" in which body and universe were regarded as a self-reflecting dyad of all experience. The ideology was "the basic of a unified discourse which the Greeks and Romans called 'physiology.' "[43] As Lincoln puts it elsewhere, "the solution is as stunning as it is simple: the victim can become the cosmos because earlier the cosmos had become the victim."[44]

The ancient standpoint of "physiological" thinking thus constitutes a place of departure for comprehending the myths and themes that have prevailed throughout the "Christian" era and into the time of re-paganizng, which we call the *modern.* The symbolism of the sacrifice of the primal "god-man," which is the human in *potentia,* to ensure creation betokens the critical understanding of life as *tempiternal.* In contemporary theological parlance the sacrifice, or "death," of God is the realization of the dialectical crossover between transcendence and immanence, between the unchanging and the ever changeable, between time and eternity. It is also the moment of the metaphysical constitution of the "human" in its immortal and even "sacred" cast, the founding of Comte's religion of *humanité* on which most "social scientific" praxis rests.[45] The salvific goal of religious activity and the beatitude of the philosopher are most adequately summed up not as a kind of *unio mystica,* but as a moment that religious orthodoxy has designated *incarnation,* the *homousia,* the fusion of substances.

Cosmotheandrism means that there is an intimate bondedness between the myth of sacrificial exchange and the philosophico-theological understanding of the speculative connection between timeless knowledge and conditioned, historical consciousness. From a theo-linguistic standpoint the sacrificial victim becomes a "second self," according to Georges Batailles, the twentieth century's surly theoretician of bodily excess. Sacrificed things "must be destroyed as things."[46] In the sacrifice the thingly perdurance of things is deconstituted through both the seemingly "irrational" violence of the authorized transgression, the perfectly licit consumption of what is otherwise inviolable, the liminal surpassing of objecthood in its routineness and everydayness. Furthermore, the transformation of mortal life into immortality through ritualized killing reflects both the finite boundaries of desire and the overreaching of those boundaries. If desire cannot unite Platonically with its eidetic and "heavenly" representation, then at least it can lay siege to the structure of representation itself as the circumscription of all "mortal experience. In the sacrificial motive it is the "combination of abhorrence and desire that gives the sacred world a paradoxical character."[47] All love ends in "immolation."

But immortalization requires a "victim." The victim in this case is the textual tradition, the "corpus" of linked metaphors and references that refer back in the sacred ideology to the founding event, to the creation of the canon, to "giving" by God or the gods of the great works. But the works themselves were conceived in violence, as we know not only of Homer but of the New Testament. Therefore, the "deconstruction" of texts in the contemporary setting is a reployment of the ancient effort to solve Girard's "sacrificial crisis." Indeed, the broader history of the formation of the "canon" can be seen as an ongoing "Oresteia," a flight from the furies, a continuation of the violent beginnings of the corpus. The resolution of the sacrificial crisis at the philosophical level— the kind of philosophical solution enshrined in the Enlightenment ideal of the encyclopedia—is the subtext of the Hegelian phenomenology. The isotropism with the shamanistic mythopoetry of self-immolation and transformation can be found at the close of Hegel's great, youthful work, where the very postmodern project of the subsumption of eternity in time is rhetorically set forth. "But the life of Spirit is not the life that shrinks from death and keeps itself untouched by devastation, but rather the life that endures it and maintains itself in it. It wins its truth only when, in *utter dismemberment,* it finds itself."[48]

Such a version of the "supreme experience" is a "constant thread" running back through the pre-Socratics to the *Rig Veda* and denoting "the human quest for sacred secularity."[49] It takes origin as the myth of primal sacrifice and returns as the ontology of "God's death"—Hegel's "new shape" of the absolute where "Spirit" is "emptied out into Time" and the "negative is the negative of itself."[50] The transformation myth that involves the self-sacrifice of the divine itself and the apotheosis of the adept points beyond even the classical and the modern to the *postmodern* vision of presencing in and through and as time—Altizer's "total presence." If "deconstruction," as Taylor tells us, is the full reading of the Altizerian myth of Golgotha, of cosmic dismembering, then we are beginning to understand both the power, and the absolute peril, of its implicit a/theology. It is the a/theology of postmodernity is erected upon the sacrifice of spirit, then it is close to the Masonic myth of the primal murder that founded the temple, the blood that sleeps beneath the stones, the fury of the sea and the terror of the fire, like one of Rene Magritte's "surrealistic" paintings, that forces its way into and shows itself within the fissures of the marble facade, the destruction of the human body for the pure textual corpus of "writing." But this writing cannot conceal its sanguinary etiology. The etiology of writing is always desire and sacrifice. And that is why, amid the storm of the postmodern, our cry must resound: "back to the body, back to Freud!"

Notes

1. The Hymn of Man," *Rg Veda* 10.90, translated and cited in Antonio T. de Nicholas, *Four-Dimension Man* (Stony Brook, N.Y.: Nicolas Hays, 1976), pp. 225–226.

2. Bruce Lincoln, "The Indo-European Myth of Creation," *History of Religions* 15 (November 1975): 121–145.

3. Bruce Lincoln, *Myth, Cosmos, and Society: Indo-European Themes of Creation and Destruction* (Cambridge, Mass.: Harvard University Press, 1986), pp. 41–42.

4. See Sir James G. Frazer, *The Golden Bough: A Study in Magic and Religion* (New York: Macmillan, 1951), pp. 506f.

5. See Adolf Jensen, "Die mythische Weltbetrachtung der alten Pflanzer-Volker," *Eranos Jahrbuch* (1949): 440–447.

6. See Lincoln, "The Indo-European Myth of Creation," p. 41.

7. See ibid., pp. 142ff.

8. Bruce Lincoln, *Myth, Cosmos, and Society,* (Cambridge, Mass.: Harvard University Press, 1986), p. 47.

9. Michel Foucault. *Discipline and Punish,* trans. Alan Sheridan (New York: Pantheon Books, 1977).

10. *Myths, Dreams, Mysteries,* trans. Philip Mairet (New York: Harper and Row, 1967), p. 183.

11. Raimundo Panikkar, *The Vedic Experience* (Berkeley: University of California Press, 1977), p. 348.

12. Ibid., p. 352.

13. *Satapatha Brahmana,* 1, 3, 2, quoted in *The Vedic Experience,* p. 388.

14. *Aitareya Brahmana,* IV, 27 (XIX, 5, 4), quoted in *The Vedic Experience,* p. 396.

15. Mircea Eliade, *The Myth of the Eternal Return* (Princeton, N.J.: Princeton University Press, 1971), p. 79.

16. *The Prose Edda of Snorri Sturluson,* trans. Jean I. Young (Berkeley: University of California Press, 1964), pp. 35–36.

17. *The Zend Avesta,* trans. James Darmestater (Oxford: Clarendon Press, 1887), vol. 2, pp. 292ff.

18. Lincoln, "The Indo-European Myth of Creation," p. 131.

19. Frazer, *The Golden Bough,* p. 313.

20. See Lincoln, "The Indo-European Myth of Creation," pp. 134ff.

21. See Charles Long, *Alpha: The Myths of Creation* (New York: George Braziller, 1963), pp. 109ff.

22. Helmut Offman, *Symbolik der Tibetischen Religionen und des Schamanismus* (Stuttgart: Anton Hiersman, 1967), pp. 96f.

23. Matthias Hermanns, *Schamanen-Pseudoschamenen, Erlöser und Heilbringer* (Wiesbaden: Franz Steiner, 1970), vol. 1, pp. xxi.

24. Mircea Eliade, *Shamanism: Archaic Techniques of Ecstasy,* trans. Willard R. Trask (New York: Pantheon Books, 1964), p. 53.

25. Ibid., p. 62.

26. Hoffman, *Symbolik der Tibetischen Religionen*, p. 112.

27. See Walter Burkett, *Homo Necans: Interpretationen Altgriescher Opferriten und Mythen* (Berlin: Walter de Gruyter, 1972), pp. 45ff.

28. Ibid., p. 59.

29. Eli Sagan, *Cannibalism: Human Aggression and Cultural Form* (New York: Harper and Row, 1974), p. 3.

30. Samuel N. Kramer, *Mythologies of the Ancient World* (Chicago: Quadrangle Books, 1961), pp. 463ff.

31. See Mircea Eliade, *Rites and Symbols and Initiation* (New York: Harper and Row, 1958), p. 35.

32. See Evan M. Zuesse, "Taboo and the Divine Order," *Journal of the American Academy of Religion* 62 (1974): 482–504. See also W. E. H. Stanner, *On Aboriginal Religion*, Oceania Monograph No. 11 (Sydney: University of Sydney Press, 1966).

33. See Eliade, *Rites and Symbols and Initiation*, p. 91; also Eliade, *Myths, Dreams, Mysteries*, pp. 208f.

34. Mircea Eliade, *The Sacred and the Profane*, trans. Willard R. Trask (New York: Harcourt Brace Jovanovich, 1959), p. 196.

35. Ibid., p. 99.

36. See Plato, *Phaedo* 69c; *Meno* 76e. See also the discussion of this theme in Plato by J. A. Stewart, *The Myths of Plato* (Carbondale: Southern Illinois University Press, 1960), pp. 339ff.

37. See Eliade, *The Myth of the Eternal Return*, pp. 28f.

38. Raimundo Panikkar, *Myth, Faith and Hermeneutics* (New York: Paulist Press, 1979), p. 77.

39. Ibid., p. 81.

40. Ibid., p. 83.

41. Bruce Lincoln, *Death, War, and Sacrifice: Studies in Ideology and Practice* (Chicago: University of Chicago Press, 1991), p. 77. The argument has its origins in a thesis by John R. Hinnels, "Reflections on the Bull-Slaying Scene," *Mithraic Studies* (Manchester: Manchester University Press, 1975), pp. 290–312.

42. *Death, War, and Sacrifice*, ibid., p. 180.

43. Ibid., p. 181.

44. *Myth, Cosmos, and Society*, p. 59.

45. Bataille can be credited with this particular movement in French letters and in anthropology when he founded the "College of Sociology" after the First World War. For a discussion of Bataille and the "College," see *The College of Sociology (1937–39)* / [texts by Georges Bataille . . . [et al.]; edited by Denis Hollier; translated by Betsy Wing. (Minneapolis: University of Minnesota Press, 1988).

46. See Georges Bataille, *The Accursed Share: An Essay on General Economy,* trans. Robert Hurley (New York: Zone Books, 1988), vol. 1, p. 56.

47. Ibid., vol. 2, p. 95.

48. G. W. F. Hegel, *Phenomenology of Spirit,* trans. A. V. Miller (New York: Oxford University Press, 1977), p. 19. Emphasis mine.

49. Raimundo Panikkar, *Blessed Simplicity: The Monk as Universal Archetype* (New York: Seabury Press, 1982), p. 131.

50. Hegel, *Phenomenology of Spirit,* p. 492.

Chapter 9

Freud and the Psychoanalytic Enigma

> We are faced here by the great enigma of the biological
> fact of the duality of the sexes: for our knowledge it is some-
> thing ultimate, it resists every attempt to trace it back to
> something else.
>
> Sigmund Freud, *An Outline of Psychoanalysis*

The integral tie between religious symbolism and sexual aims was
the consummate discovery of psychoanalysis. The biological polar-
ity of the sexes constituted the bedrock into which was set Sigmund
Freud's lifelong research, not only into the origins of neuroses and
irrational behavior, but concerning the "metapsychological" forces
behind history and the career of civilization as well. Freud was the
great "reductionist" who has been ardently criticized, revised, and
calumniated for securing such a novel and, in its own time, discon-
certing "Archimedian" point for explaining human motives and
actions. Although a good deal of his specific hypotheses and clinical inferences have been overridden or qualified, his "pansexual"
starting point has not been successfully dislodged. Every theoretical
breakthrough, whether in the sciences or the humanities, exhibits
a certain "reductionist" edge. Yet in all reductionistic general theory
there obtrudes a marrow of major insight. Even Jung's disciples,
who in plotting an alternative track in "depth psychology" repudiated what they reckoned as Freud's physiological determinism, still
upheld the primacy of the "male" and "female" components of the
human psyche.

In the study of religion, the psychoanalytic vantage point
has irreversibly prodded theologians into taking serious account of

the sexual implications of religious myths and ethical ideals,[1] not to mention the visible tensions between "matriarchal" and "patri-archal" modes of cultural organization that earlier social anthro-pologists hit upon through analysis of symbolic forms.[2] It might be argued, too, that the vigor, plausibility, and long-range impact of much of the present-day feminist critique of the "phallocentric" Judeao-Christian tradition can be attributed, at least in part, to the achievements of psychoanalytic inquiry in uncovering the sexual conflicts that underlie the formation of human identity. Although Freud's own theoretical resolution of "the great enigma" may make a circuit for a not-so-subtle misogynist agenda, the stark, inalienable fact of sexual dimorphism in the species pre-sents itself as the Gordian knot of human and religious thought that demands to be unraveled.

Freud's sexual hermeneutic was first expounded in a very brief paper he wrote in 1927 evaluating the meaning of "religious experience" reported by an American physician. The physician had dispatched a letter to Freud describing how he had been engulfed with emotion on glimpsing the corpse of "a sweet-faced dear old woman" en route to the dissecting room. The encounter kindled in the doctor extreme anger at God for "allowing" the old woman to be exposed in death to such humiliation. The physician reproved his own Christian beliefs, yet in the course of his self-reflection he heard an "inner voice" assuring him that his long-standing faith was valid and that he could trust in God's word. Afterward, the doctor added, God underscored this assurance by "revealing" himself with "many infallible proofs." In answer to the letter, Freud claimed to have politely acknowledged the sincer-ity of the physician's piety. Yet in the professional paper, in which he recounted the exchange, Freud set forth an unmistakably blunt appraisal of the doctor's case. The countenance of the dead woman, together with the naked cadaver, had simply evoked, according to Freud, in the doctor's unconscious the though "of his own mother," Freud went on:

> It roused in him a longing for his mother which sprang from his Oedipus complex, and this was immediately completed by a feeling of indignation against his father. His ideas of "father" and "God" had not yet become widely separated; so that his desire to destroy his father could become conscious as doubt in the existence of God and could seek to justify itself in the eyes of reason as indignation about the ill-treatment of the mother-object. It is of course typical for a

child to regard what his father does to his mother in sexual intercourse as ill-treatment. The new impulse, which was displaced into the sphere of religion, was only a repetition of the Oedipus situation and consequently met with a similar fate. It succumbed to a powerful opposing current. During the actual conflict the level of displacement was not maintained: there is no mention of the arguments in justification of God, nor are we told what the infallible signs were by which God proved his existence to the doubter. The conflict seems to have been unfolded in the form of a hallucinatory psychosis: inner voices were heard which uttered warnings against resistance to God. But the outcome of the struggle was displayed once again in the sphere of religion and it was of a kind predetermined by the fate of the Oedipus complex: complete submission to the will of God the Father. The young man became a believer and accepted everything he had taught since his childhood about God and Jesus Christ. He had had a religious experience and had undergone a conversion.[3]

In the foregoing diagnosis, Freud touches on all the salient features of his well-publicized assimilation of religious ideology to childhood sexual fantasy. Religious myths and symbols tend to derive from ambivalent feelings toward both mother and father, culminating in the Oedipal dilemma. Mother and father are the crystallizing images, the primary cathexes, of a person's sexual desires because they are the earliest representations of instinctual wishes during an individual's entire biography. Initially, the male child is locked into an incestuous relationship of physical stimulation and longing—what Freud dubbed the *pleasure ego*—with his mother, who is the absolute object of love. The mother is the fathomless and omnipotent font in the child's imagination for gratification and protection.

But, as the child grows older, it encounters a hiatus, from which spring all subsequent instinctual conflicts, between its illimitable desire and the availability of the love object. The hiatus become pronounced, especially in the young boy, with the onset of what Freud referred to as the *phallic* phase of development. In the phallic stage the child discovers the enjoyment present in the excitation of its own genitalia. Such enjoyment present in both the child's delight in masturbation and in the fantasy of sexual seduction by the mother. The child's sexual precocity, however, is counteracted by a threat, usually made by the mother herself but with appeal to the executive powers of the father, that if it continues in its overt genital expression it will be severely castigated.

For boys, the trauma and anxiety over punishment is most severe, since the threat is couched in terms of castration, the peremptory removal of the protruding and highly favored sexual member. The danger of castration is thereby magnified and schematized with respect to the absence in the mother of such an organ. Both male and female children, in Freud's estimate, apprehend the mother as having already been castrated by the father. Little girls react to this brutal perception by taking on a niggling sense of inferiority, which induces them to revile for a time their own feminine anatomy and covet the father's phallic prerogatives through the outlook to which Freud gave the notorious caption of *penis envy*. The girl's penis envy is finally worked out, though not entirely, in the woman's affirmation of her biological makeup by giving birth to children. Small boys, on the other hand, evince a different pattern of response. Their fear of castration, coupled with their horror of the "fact" that women have already been victimized by the same act, coalesces into a strong, erotic attachment to the mother and an attendant hatred of the father, the ambivalence that distinguishes the classical Oedipus complex. The disclosure of the father's "aggressive" role in sexual intercourse merely compounds the ambivalence. The male child cannot realize his incestual longing for the mother, and in the normal, "healthy" transcendence of the Oedipal crisis he overcomes this conflict by identifying with the posture of the father. As Freud stressed in *The Future of an Illusion,* religion is the "universal obsessional neurosis" of humanity. The "formation of religion" resides in the human's "defense against childish helplessness,"[4] against the specter of annihilation and personal impotence in a vast and indifferent universe. For the psyche confronted with its own cosmic inconsequence, the consolation and surety of religious faith in a beneficient power governing the world performs a function comparable to the child's identification with masculine strength rescuing it from the peril of castration. Death and castration are fused symbolically in the adult's psychic ledger. Therefore, it is only natural, in Freud's view, that divine invulnerability and authority are envisioned as attributes of "God the Father," while in the same vein this power and legitimacy take on a malignant aura. When counterposed to the childish yearning for serenity, comfort, and deathlessness in the guise of maternal succor, the father's image appears wrathful, threatening, castrating. The American physician's quarrel with God would exemplify the two religious poles of the more fundamental Oedipal dilemma. The physician renounced his maternal fascination, projected as sympathy for the dead woman, and "accepted" the justice and righteousness of the Father God whose "wisdom" surpasses all human inclinations and preferences.

The religious solution to the Oedipal quandary, however, is intrinsically precarious and unstable. Whereas the development of the child under optimal circumstances leads to an eventual reconciliation with social prohibitions on maternal incest and to a mature personality that waives instinctual impulses for the sake of "higher," cultural objectives, the religious point of view traps the individual in his infantile fantasies and wishes. The "neurotic," according to Freud, is a person who has reached a deadlock between wants and reality. Neurotic symptoms are either "a substitute satisfaction of some sexual impulse or measures to prevent such a satisfaction." Instead of coming to terms with the obstacles to his libido, the neurotic man endeavors to preserve the satisfactions of the childish pleasure-ego by distorting the contradictory messages he receives from his environment. He molds a universe that tallies with his own desires. He weaves about himself a protective canopy of illusory fulfillments. A man who has failed to gain command of his Oedipal lusts will cling to the fantasy of union with his mother, which may betray itself as compulsive and bizarre erotic obsessions or become parlayed in self-defeating relationships with those of the opposite sex. Similarly, the religious believer will continue to rely throughout his or her life on ideas and symbols that reinforce the neurotic compromise with Oedipal pressures. In setting aside the mother as the natural love object, the child may in turn compensate for the withdrawal of feminine nurturance by conjuring up the notion of the all-powerful father who looks after and safeguards his human "children."

Although Freud does not say so expressly, it is possible to deduce from his analysis that the Father God in religion is a replacement, albeit not a totally acceptable one, for the discredited mother who was once the infinite giver of blessings in the infant's imagination. God as almighty, paternal protector serves much the same role in human consciousness as the cherishing mother did originally, although the picture of the Father God contains repressive and vengeful elements. God the Father loves and is gracious toward creatures, but strictly on the condition that they suppress their instinctual demands. This suppression is engineered through the sin-ridden conscience, which makes it extremely difficult to please the father. The religious personality, therefore, remains in a state of dependence on the guidance and tutelage of a patriarchal figure. So long as this dependence is sustained, the individual never expels the antagonism between paternal, super-ego prohibitions and libidinal drives. The upshot is a chronic neurotic struggle between accepting the world as it is and falsify-ing the world in conformance with our primitive proclivities. Freud thought the need for religion was deeply ingrained in the human mind because of dissonance between one's insuperable urges for security and pleasurable stimulation and once's inescapable fini-tude as a mortal being. The advantage of religion is not that it fosters a sense of truth, which only the "educational" methods of psychoanalysis can do, but that it furnishes a socially legitimate framework for neurotic thinking and emotion. Religious people's "acceptance of the universal neurosis spares them the task of constructing a personal one.[5]

In Freud's view the neurotic aims of religion are entwined with human efforts to vent one's instinctual cravings within cul-tural and existential boundaries. The ethical content of religion is a measure of the requirement that one sublimate one's blind desires in the pursuit of the collective goals of civilization. But the contest between human instinctual life and civilization on the historical level has its individual, psychic source in the experience of painful separation from the mother's bouteous body and the subsequent discipline of the instincts through paternal domination. It is inevi-table, therefore, that religion also take origin in the father's expro-priation of the child from the maternal relation. The incest wish is the prototype for every myth of the human "temptation" to attain eternal bliss and immortality. The nostalgia for paradise is the corporate yearning for reunion with the feminine. The human historical submission to the will of God is the grand, Oedipal compromise, the weaning from the mother and the subjection to the father and to civilization.

But the sovereignty of the father can never suffice for the Eden of maternal intimacy. The role of the mother is transferred to certain aspects of the image of paternity. As the same time, the surrender of maternal intimacy is never final; the lure of the mother mounts in strength in proportion to the harshness of the rule of the father. The repressed id bursts its shackles and presses forth to consummate the Oedipal wish, to reclaim the mother and cast out the father with violence. The father is dethroned, even demonized. God the Father comes to wear the mask of the Devil, who is the epitome of the licentious, frustrated, and importunate libido. The Devil as father substitute takes on the sexual characteristics of the mother and becomes the standard or revolt against paternal castration, as Freud in his analysis of the demonological neurosis of a seventeenth century painter contended.[6] Yet the revolt is never successful, and the father reasserts his authority. The supreme Oedipal wish fulfillment is the murder of the father who obstructs the beatific relation to the mother. But the child cannot deal with the father as he stands in his terrible epiphany. The child must imagine the father instead of Satan, as the evil seducer. But in the end he must resist the Devil and pledge himself anew to God, who is his "rock" of salvation.

Freud held that religion will endure so long as civilization enforces a regime of instinctual renunciation for the sake of social harmony. Religion, with its virtue of "brotherly love," eases the "disappointments of genital love by turning away from its sexual aims and transforming the instinct into an impulse with an inhibited aim."[7] The impairment of the genital aim eventuates in the forging of families, social groups, and spiritual communities dedicated to the well-being of their constituents. Religion promotes social solidarity, inasmuch as it exacts "such great sacrifices not only on man's sexuality but on his aggresivity."[8] Freud's use of the word *sacrifice*, as well as the symbolism associated with it, can be construed along Freudian lines as a phenomenon connected with both instinctual repression and the "secondary" hindrance of destructive tendencies issuing from that repression. Both religion and civilization curtail not just the spontaneity of the libido, but check and require compensation for the violent reactivity of the instincts. Both religion and civilization throw up barriers against maternal incest and parry the homicidal rebellion against paternal jurisdiction. Religion and civilization seek not merely to avert genital lawlessness, but to crush the inbred ambition to slay the father.

In *The Ego and the Id* Freud analyzes the formation of the superego—the internal writ of paternal legislation—as "the outcome of two highly important factors, one a biological and the other of a historical nature."[9] The biological influence, of course, is the Oedipal factor. "The superego retains the character of the father, while the more powerful the Oedipus complex was and the more rapidly it succumbed to repression (under the influence of authority, religious teaching, schooling, and reading), the stricter will be the domination of the superego over the ego later on—in the form of conscience or perhaps of an unconscious sense of guilt."[10] Still, the biological and ontogenetic context for the materialization of the superego cannot be the sole determinant of this *inner patriarchy,* according to Freud. Biographical data is useful for explaining the dynamics of individual consciousness, but the perdurance of superordinate symbols and conceptions in the collective regulation of human instinct remained problematic.

Henceforth, Freud in his later years plunged into the field he designated as *metapsychology.* The project of metapsychology consists in a calculation of the correlates among psychic perturbations and the history of culture. In short, it is a grand economy of instinctuality and the proto-narratives of a civilization. Freud's metapsychology became the contextuality for his speculations on the historical purpose and provenance of religion in relation to the superego. The religious "pathology," he observed, appeared to reach back to a more primordial genesis than the familiar "reaction-formations" inferred from clinical observation. Freud regarded religion as a kind of unstable, but almost necessary, entente between desire and experience. This rapprochement must have been compelled by a certain genealogical influence that had left "memory-traces" upon the record of culture and thereby tinged all linguistic responses. "We now observe that the store of religious ideas includes not only wish-fulfillments but important historical recollections."[11] These "recollections" included the Oedipal conflict, together with those agencies inhibiting the child's aggression toward the father, which Freud believed must have been evident at the dawning of the human species.

Furthermore, Oedipal aggression must have its phylogenetic complement in some primeval urge to violence. Freud spotted an analogy between the grammatics of sacrifice and the psychoanalytic interpretation of the Oedipal problem. Both sacrifice and Oedipal tension are founded on the necessity of "giving up" something that is alluring and precious to fulfill a "higher" obligation. Both sacrifice and the post-Oedipal inclination constitute a redirection of the primitive wave of violence toward a symbolics and sacrality and authority. Hence. Freud shifted from his clinical excursions to anthropological studies, in particular Robertson Smith's investigations of sacrifice. "The writings of Robertson Smith—a man of genius—have given me valuable point of contact," Freud wrote in *Moses and Monotheism,* "with the psychological material of analysis and indications for its employment."[12]

Freud recounted Smith's hypothesis that the act of sacrifice, as the nucleus of the archaic religious cult, could be traced back to the rituals of totemism. Like other nineteenth century pioneers in the "scientific study of religion," such as Emile Durkheim, Smith was interested in the general archaeology of religious practice. As was the case with his confederates, Smith took totemic institutions as the starting point for his examination of the "primitive" background to the world's religious traditions. Smith identified the totem animal with the victim of the cult sacrifice. He argued that a "totem feast," in which the sacred animal of the clan was butchered and eaten, was the basis for sacrificial procedures. The animal was a "god," insofar as it appropriated the collective identity of the clan. It was holy and inviolable—that is, "taboo"; it could not be killed or consumed without terrible penalties. Yet, on prescribed ceremonial occasions, it was actually enjoined of clan members to infringe the taboo and share in a corporate meal of the totem animal's flesh.

Smith contended that the slaughter of the totem animal was the ambience in which kinspeople ritually recognized their own unity by partaking of the "body" of the victim, which was their common spiritual ancestor and the incarnation of their own collective substance. The outcome of the feast was "to cement and seal their mystical unity with one another and with their god."[13] The prohibition of the animal's flesh to persons in the clan except during the official ceremony corresponded to the community taboo against release of private impulses. Such a ban on individual expression was the hallmark of preliterate societies. The price of flouting the taboo was severe guilt and punishment. But guilt flourished as well in the "licit" ceremony of sacrifice. Smith accounted for the widespread pagan convention of "mourning" a dead god as a reminiscence of the remorse once felt for having killed the sacred animal, even though the sacrifice itself was mandatory. In Smith's opinion, "a chief object of the mourners is to disclaim responsibility for the god's death—a point which has already come before us in connection with theantropic sacrifices."[14]

Another anomaly for both Freud and Smith was the custom of relaxing other moral restraints during the sacrificial celebration and allowing a certain degree of orgiastic liberty. Freud interpolated from Smith's data that the sanctioning of "immortality" as part of the primitive festival could not be understood in any way than as a devious outlet for repressed instincts. The maintenance of the social prohibitions, manifested in the taboo against eating the totem, hinged on the guilt mechanism, which served effectively to interdict dangerous desires. Yet, if no safety valve for the release of these desires were contrived, the burden of guilt would become so intense that chaos would result. Thus the totem ritual kept intact the overlay of guilt, while at the same time providing a means of discharge for proscribed impulses. The "excesses" of the festival were not due, as Freud put it, to the fact that individuals "are feeling happy as a result of some injunction they have received. It is rather that excess is of the essence of a festival."[15]

Freud sought, therefore, to exploit Smith's anthropological surmises as a bridge to his metapsychology. Freud's theories in *Totem and Taboo* have frequently been dismissed on the grounds that they relied too uncritically on Smith's conclusions, for which other ethnologists found little evidence. Moreover, the more extensive inferences Freud drew from Smith's writings had no anthropological support at all. Freud was not unaware of the objections of anthropologists to Smith's notions, as he made clear in a footnote. But such objections, he reasoned, "have not diminished to any important extent the impression produced by Robertson Smith's hypothesis."[16] A cautious reading of Freud's own discussions, amplified two decades later in *Moses and Monotheism*, raises the possibility that he was not so much concerned with corroborating some theses about primitive society as he was engaged in a though experiment, which would penetrate into the subconscious chambers of human history. Freud was not preoccupied with inductive precision in the interpretation of anthropological information.[17] Rather, he seems to have been bent on delineating a perspective on the data that had not been previously essayed. Freud augmented Smith's considerations with some even more dubious postulates about prehistory from the theories of Charles Darwin. But his grander prospect was that of bringing about a "deeper understanding" of the meaning of the existing "facts" about religious observances and beliefs that had escaped ethnologists.

Freud looked upon his own statements in *Totem and Taboo* as a glimpse of a hypotheses which may seem fantastic but which offers the advantage of establishing an unsuspected correlation between groups of phenomena that have hitherto been disconnected."[18] The validity of the correlation did not have to stand on the empirical confirmation of the sorts of primitive social activity that Freud characterized so much as on the amenability of similar anthropological data to the verdict of psychoanalysis. Freud recognized his metapsychology was more heuristic than definitive. Ethnology might alter the data with which the psychoanalyst operates and thereby disallow the specific historical theses, but the method of applying psychological constructs to historical and cultural evidence would remain unchallenged. Psychological constructs are serviceable tools, not because they represent irrefragible "facts" open to inspection, but because they aid in engendering insight. They are in themselves, as Freud described even the "instincts" that clinical work had already accepted tentatively, "mythical entities."[19] The fruitlessness of the construct for mapping a new range of speculative options was the real issue at stake, and it suggests that in many ways the entire Freudian initiative can be assessed as a "metanarrative" of the body, understood not as a "psycho-physical" content or substrate, but as the generative grammar of desire.

The details of Freud's "paleontological" forays into religion, focusing both on totemism and the Oedipus complex, are quite familiar to students of psychoanalysis. Following Darwin, Freud posited the existence of a "primal horde" ruled by a ruthless father figure, who monopolized the females in the band and fomented passionate sexual jealousy on the part of the young men. Denied sexual satisfaction, the "brothers" of the horde rose up against the primal father, then murdered and ate him. In their eating of the father the brother identified with his dominion and incorporated magically his power, just as cannibals have been reported on numerous occasions to consume the portion of a slain adversary in which is supposed to reside in his *mana*. At the same time, the brother's knowledge of the violence committed issued in a deep sense of guilt. The guilt was magnified by their ambivalence over having attained instinctual gratification in possessing the females, which the father's authority had previously forbidden. One might say that the sons carried out in reality what every male child during the Oedipal phase executes only in fantasy.

As a gesture of atonement the sons reimposed on themselves the same restrictions that had once been decreed by the dead patriarch. The presence of the father was even reinstated symbolically as the sacred animal of totem religion. The sanctity of the totem supplanted the sons' earlier deference to the father's will. But, again, Oedipal lust and jealousy were not completely brought to rein. The instinct for patricide reasserted itself ritually in the sacrifice of the totem. The oscillation between taboo and license in the totemic cult betrayed the contradictory character of Father worship, which lurks in the shadows of all religion. The dynamics of totemism have passed over the primitive state. "We shall not be surprised," Freud wrote, "to find that the element of filial rebelliousness also emerges, in the later products of religion, often in the strangest disguises and transformations."[20]

The "transformations" to which Freud alludes here consist in the consolidation of the totemic pattern into the "civilized" religions, In his papers Freud had already demonstrated how repressed wishes or guilty memories that the patient refuses to acknowledge are neurotically displaced on to cognate objects or reenacted harmlessly by recurrent, obsessional behavior, so-called parapraxes, in keeping with the wider syndrome he termed the *compulsion to repeat*. By the same token, unresolved Oedipal conflicts clustering originally around the ideas of father and mother are played out compulsively in the adult's relationship with his or her own peers. Just as the analyst can locate the source of these adult dysfunctions in "forgotten" childhood traumas, so the psychologist of religion can adduce certain types of historical incidents of which myths and rites are disguised reminiscences. Freud contended that the "concept" of God was born of the Oedipal struggle that eventuated in both the primordial "murder" of the father and in the totemic regime. In addition, the ultimate form of parapraxis is the ritual of sacrifice. "The father is represented twice over in the situation of primitive sacrifice: once as God and once as the totemic animal victim."[21] In the course of history the totem animal was projected as the heavenly Father. But "the memory of the first great act of sacrifice . . . proved indestructible, in spite of every effort to forget it; and at the very point at which men sought to be at the farthest distance from the motives that led to it, its undistorted reproduction emerged in the form of the sacrifice of the god."[22] The sacrifice of the god was the recapitulation historically of, as well as the mythical token of the Oedipal wish for, the murder of the god.

If the specific historical deed that Freud narrated has been disconfirmed by anthropology, then at least the psycho-social underpinnings of primitive religion that Freud describes as reflecting Oedipal urges have recently been documented. In contrast to Freud, Eli Sagan employs more comprehensive and updated ethnographic evidence in stipulating that "sacrifice is a sublimated form of cannibal behavior."[23] He also construes cannibalism itself as a primordial form of religion with roots in the Oedipal reflex of oral aggression aimed at recovering the lost intimacy with the mother. Father murder, however, is not as significant as Freud made it out to be, according to Sagan, because primitives do not "know" the superego in the way modern people do.[24] We might possibly salvage Freud from the criticisms of anthropologists if we understand the "father" to signify not so much a personal figure or even a coherent structure of moral conscience as a symbol of whatever opposes the instincts. The patricidal aim of religion could be read instead in a metaphorical rather than in a literal sense. In any event, Freud thought he had come up with an etiology for the interconnection between sacrifice and regicide—the killing of the king as "father"—that Frazer left as a puzzle in *The Golden Bough*. Such an etiology was also behind the Christian doctrine of the crucifixion. "If this sacrifice of a life brought about atonement with God the Father, the crime to be expiated can only have been the murder of the father."[25] The church sacrament of the Eucharist, in which the "body of Christ" is eaten and his blood is drunk, can only be a translation of the totem feast. Christianity is the faith of the sons who bind themselves in love and guilt to the specter of the deposed patriarch.

Behind Christianity, however, stands Judaism. If Christianity is the faith of the victorious sons who achieve fellowship with each other as "brother in Christ," Judaism is the religion of the jealous males who remain under the heel of the powerful father. Most of Freud's comments on orthodox Judaism, which was his own religious heritage, accentuate this point of view. In orthodox Judaism the emblem of paternal authority is not just Yahweh, a transcendent Deity, but his "law" handed down through the intermediary Moses. Insofar as the orthodox Jew is "yoked" to the "law," he finds himself in the post-Oedipal contest with the exacting, patriarchal superego. Painfully, yet conscientiously, he forswears his wish for instinctual gratification, as exhibited in the ethical ban on fornication and adultery as well as in the prophetic condemnation of the heathen cult of sacred prostitution. The orthodox concern for ritual purity and moral rectitude are manifestations of the patriarchal regimen. In the same vein, the orthodox Jew repudiates all associations with the ancient mother goddesses and excises from the divine personality every vestige of the consoling, feminine element. The orthodox Jew sustains the typical, Oedipal ambivalence to the "law," which clashes with his human inclinations. Although the "law" is intended to fortify the devotee's "self-esteem" and heighten his consciousness of having been "chosen" for a superior calling by God, in actuality it taxes all too heavily one's instinctual expression and reduces one to a profound feeling of impotence and inferiority. Freud's portrait of Judaism, from the standpoint of an historian of religion, is without doubt rather parochial and tendentious. Yet it does illustrate a particular sensibility that infects not just psychoanalysis, but also the psychology of certain "revolutionaries" in the history of Western religious thought. Freud's own disposition toward Judaism can be compared closely with that of Paul.

The difference is that, whereas Paul purported to have effected a solution to the Oedipal contradiction by implying that salvation is to be had through the "death" of God the Father,

Freud regarded Christianity as nothing more than a further neurotic repetition of the ancient patricidal screenplay. The slaying of
the heavenly Father on the Cross merely resulted in a new instruc-
tion of law and authority, in this case the ascendancy of the
"universal church."

The tragedy of our instinctual "vicissitudes," as Freud expressed it, was most honestly depicted in the story of Judaism. It
is against the backdrop of this tragic awareness that we can perhaps estimate why Freud in his last years produced what even his
apologists recognize as a rather fanciful and embarrassing book,
his *Moses and Monotheism*, published in 1939. Although his earlier
reflections on religion in *Totem and Taboo* had generated some
questionable suppositions, *Moses and Monotheism* was erected on
what were prima facie some wild and untenable proposals. Freud
attempted to write with a transparently "revisionist" slant to the
history of Jewish tradition by insisting that there were really two
Moseses, the one Egyptian and the other Hebrew. Freud borrowed
this theses from the German biblical scholar Ernst Sellin, but made
some further qualifications. Both Moses figures were conflated as
the single personage of the Bible. The Egyptian Moses had been a
legislator and civilizer of the Hebrews who, like the biblical God
he represented, "adopted" his people. The second Moses was a
follower of the heathen Midianite religion, which was pagan and
revolved around the cult of Yahweh at Mt. Sinai. The Egyptian
Moses brought to the Hebrews a stern code of law enforced by the
prestige of the new monotheistic faith he had culled from the
legacy of the heretical pharaoh Akhenaten. The ethical monotheism of the Egyptian Moses, however, jarred strongly with the native polytheism and loose moral standards of the "savage" Israelites.
Moses' giving of the law was tantamount to the impressing of the
paternal superego on the child. "When Moses brought the people
the idea of a single god, it was not a novelty but signified the
revival of an experience in the primeval ages of the human family which had long vanished from men's conscious memory."[26]
Just as the primitive sons had rebelled against the father, so the
barbarous Hebrews mounted an insurgency and murdered the
Egyptian Moses. The Midianite Moses then took over and survived
in the tradition as the historical leader of his people, while the
slain Egyptian Moses lurked in unconscious memory as the bearer
of the covenant and the custodian of the law. The Egyptian Moses,
whom the tradition suppressed, functioned in the same manner as
the deified patriarch of totemism. The buried recollection of the
murder of the Egyptian Moses continued to influence the Jewish

self-understanding. Such a recollection gave rise to the ethos of guilt and the demand for atonement. The elevation of the ritual of sacrifice on the priestly cult provided the vehicle for supplicating the angry Father God.

But the "forgotten" crime could not be readily expiated. It crept back into consciousness as the collective version of "the return of the repressed." By virtue of the "gift" of Torah conferred on them by the Egyptian Moses, the Jews raised themselves above the Gentiles as the favored children of God. Yet their "pagan" disposition prevented them from bringing to fruition their greatest religious legacy. Similarly, they have interpreted their own historical misfortunes as "just" retribution for having shunned their ethical obligations. Freud did not live to confront the Holocaust and be affected by the searching reexamination of the old biblical theodicy among Jewish theologians. Judaism has never surmounted the Oedipal dilemma, Freud suggested, though it has been less pretentious than Christianity, which concocted only the semblance of a solution. Both Christianity and Judaism are anchored in the psychology of the father complex and deicide. Freud, however, throws the tragic burden of Western civilization not on Christians, but on Jews. In a strange and disturbing passage at the close of *Moses and Monotheism*, ironically composed after he had fled Hitler's Germany to England, Freud lamented:

> [The Jews] were obliged to hear the new [Christian] religious community (which, besides Jews, included Egyptians, Greeks, Syrians, Romans, and eventually Germans) reproach them with having murdered God. In full, this reproach would run as follows: "They will not accept it as true that they murdered God, whereas we admit it and have been cleansed of that guilt." It is easy therefore to see how much truth lies behind this reproach. A special enquiry would be called for to discover why it has been impossible for the Jews to join in this forward step which was implied, in spite of all its distortions, by the admission of having murdered God. In a certain sense they have in that way taken a tragic load of guilt of themselves; they have been made to pay heavy penance.[27]

If Freud had lived six more years he would, in all likelihood, have retracted such a statement. The "heavy penance" could no longer be regarded as tolerable. Was Freud so "guilty" about his own Jewishness or so alarmed by the resistance of the Gentile world at that time to psychoanalysis, as some critics have accused him, that he would debunk the Jewish tradition in a fashion that would readily resonate with the obloquy of anti-Semites? Or, when Freud spoke of "Judaism," which he knew better than any other religion, did he really have in mind the religion of the "Father" with all its repressive violence and its demand for atonement and scapegoats that summoned forth the primordial urge to murder even God? Was it this religion, which embraced Christianity as well, that cowered behind the crisis of civilization? Had the Jews paid "penance" not because they had failed to be absolved of a "crime," in which Christians also were conspirators, but because they were the first to shoulder, psychologically and theologically, the Oedipal conflict that no religion or culture had yet worked out?

The intricate, concealed intentions of Freud's thought is a subject that cannot be encompassed here. Nevertheless, we can detect certain motives that may have deflected the development of Freud's views on religion in a key direction. The passage cited previously, once read in conjunction with Freud's other remarks on the problem of Judaism, cannot be lumped with the self-serving arguments of the anti-Semites. Yet Freud did view anti-Semitism, which he categorized as a peculiarly Gentile pathology, as arising out of the same universal psychic turmoil that suffused the Jewish heritage. The Jews were the pariah of Western civilization, not because they were responsible for its "discontents," but because Judaism's own internal contradictions expressed those discontents. The Jewish experience may have been the tacit framework of his theorizing, but it is a well-established position that Hebraic values and symbols have been preeminent in Western culture. And Freud's indictment of his own heritage was simply a gambit for analysis of the larger issue of Western religious attitudes.

David Bakan has assigned the Freudian outlook to that of Jewish mysticism.[28] Bakan does not show with any measurable success that Freud was consciously inspired by mystical thinking, but he does demonstrate how Freud had commerce with the ideas of that strand of Judaism and how there is an overall symmetry between his intellectual projects and the weltanschauung of the mystics. Bakan asserts that Freud, like Jewish Sabbatianism, which flowed from Medieval Kabbalah and constituted a protest against rabbinic orthodoxy and legalism, sought salvation through the Romantic strategy of "self-realization." Bakan submits that there is a sense in which "the whole burden of psychoanalysis may be regarded as a fulfillment of the Sabbatian ethos."[29] Sabbatian mysticism advanced the notion that there is a primordial Torah, inscribed in nature and intuited as esoteric wisdom, that precedes Mosaic religion. The language of primordial Torah is an occult symbolism that bespeaks a hidden harmony of life and cannot be reduced entirely to the idiom of Halakah, or system of talmudic legal precepts. The goal of the Sabbatian devotee is to be able to see through the structures of orthodoxy, without violating them in practice, and "harmonize" the development of self-consciousness with the paradoxes of sexuality. Likewise, psychoanalysis assumed that there exists a biological subtext for every narratology that is anterior to the emergence of the superego, of religion, and cultural supplements. The "grammar" of our instincts is ciphered into our fantasies, dreams, myths, and artistic productions, which cannot be interpreted in accordance with the conventional rules of discursivity but must be read as glyphs or nonsequential descriptions, through the clinical method of free association. The task of psychoanalysis is to make the patient aware of his or her instinctual biography in much the same way as Sabbatianism tried to achieve a unanimity between the body and the "law." Moreover, psychoanalysis was built on the presupposition of "pansexuality," because Jewish mysticism itself in both symbolism and ritual stressed the physical union of male and female as the perfect analogue of the relation between God and humanity.

The erotic imagery of Kabbalah was the clue, which Freud transposed into naturalistic and "scientific" parlance, to the rift in human consciousness and historical upheavals. The primordial communion between man and woman has been distorted by the history of patriarchy and thereby falsified in terms of the collision between "nature" and "morality," between the "primary processes" and the rule of God and superego. The primordial communion mirrors God's own sexual nature, which was a principal tenet of Jewish mysticism. And the "mystery" of God's sexual nature, as conceived by the Kabbalists, became the "great enigma" of human sexuality that Freud took as his methodological prius.

In the Kabbalah, all cosmic dualism is overcome by the affirmation of God's bisexuality. Perhaps the idea of God's bisexuality was reflected in Freud's firm conviction, usually ignored by his feminist detractors, that human beings are also born bisexual in their psychological propensities. The acquisition of distinct sexual identities is the outcome of the Oedipal phase. The cultural prohibition on maternal incest is what gives issue to, particularly under conditions of patriarchy, the positive estimation of the male, superego structure and the concomitant devaluation of femininity, which comes to be ranged with such concepts as "instinct" and "flesh" on account of the child's primal relationship to the mother's body. Psychologically speaking, patriarchy amounts to a repression of women as a consequence of the Oedipal assimilation of representations of "woman" to the purely somatic.[30]

But such repression is never complete. The orthodox exclusion of the feminine side of the deity was counteracted in Jewish mysticism by a concerted stress on the maternal facet of the Godhead. In the mystical tradition, the concealed "other" face of God is the Shekinah (literally, the "one who dwells"). The Shekinah is the intimate, nurturing, feminine, and motherly manifestation of divine reality who sojourned with Israel throughout its history and may, in fact, be a mythic transfiguration of the ancient mother goddess whom the Jews, to the consternation of the prophets, worshipped in Canaan.[31] When Israel goes into exile as chastisement for having disobeyed the Father's commandment, the Shekinah stays with her people. The exile of the people is the exile of the Shekinah. Likewise, the age in which the name of the Father predominates is the epoch of the Shekinah's estrangement. The coming Messianic era will be marked by the return of the Shekinah from her exile and the reunion between male and female in both heaven and earth.

But the Jewish mystics gave a concrete expression to the expectation of the Messianic era with a proleptic ritual of "sacred marriage" performed always on the eve of the Sabbath. On the mythic plane the hierogamy is between God and his Shekinah. It was enacted liturgically in the family setting and consummated at night through intercourse between husband and wife.[32] Bakan notes that "the conception of sexuality as the source of all energy" pervade Sabbatianism.[33] Sexuality both alienates humanity from God and reunites it with the holy. The revelation of the Shekinah is the uncovering of the "nakedness" of the feminine that signifies the primal and ultimate human wish. The messianic redemption of the Jews by the return of the Shekinah corresponds in the Freudian vision to the liberation of humanity from its Oedipal neurosis, to the reapproachment of instinct and conscience, to the concord between mother and father. So long as humanity remains under the sway of the Oedipal neurosis, it will persist in a state of alienation. By the same token, acknowledgment of the "truth" of father murder would perhaps emancipate humanity from the turbulence and cultural contradictions of patriarchy, while clearing the way for the messianic climax.

Freud's gloomy appraisal of the "future" of the instincts, at the same time, is well known and was challenged by Jung. Jung's radical revalorization of the instincts was the watershed in his development of his own brand of psychoanalysis, which he called *analytical psychology*. Such a revisioning of the libido, as we shall see, made possible not just a more hopeful prognosis for the ills of civilization, but a more sanguine assessment, too, of the role of religion and a different understanding of sacrifice as a means to "spiritual transformation." In his review of the precepts of psychoanalysis, Jung contravened Freud's tenet that the libido is something definite and quantifiable. "I maintain that the libido," Jung wrote, "with which we operate is not only not concrete or known, but is a complete X, a pure hypotheses, a model or counter, and is no more concretely conceivable than the energy known to the world of physics.[34] Libido, Jung argued, is merely "a name for the energy which manifests itself in the life-process and is perceived subjectively as conation and desire."[35] It is "an energy-value which is able to communicate itself to any field of activity whatsoever, be it power, hunger, hatred, sexuality, or religion, without ever being itself specific instinct."[36] The libido is the full ensemble of instincts in their psycho-physiological totality. The physiological urgings can be "depotentiated" in favor of the psychological instincts. The psychological instincts are oriented teleologically, not toward the release of sexual tension or at slaking feelings of hunger or thirst, but toward the articulation of symbols. Religious and mythic symbols, which spring from the deep-reaching, presomatic repository of tendencies, Jung dubbed the *collective unconscious*.

The mythologization of consciousness is crucial for both the canalization and the transmutation of the instincts. Once blocked in its physiological flux, the libido may well obtain expression in a desexualized, religious mode. This alteration is not "sublimation" as Freud precisely had meant it. Freud's concept of sublimation rested on the premise that the refractory instincts could be harnessed in the service of moral and cultural objectives. The harnessing of the instincts, for Freud, constituted a salutary negotiation of the conflict between the please and reality principles. Jung saw the transformation of the instincts, however, as the yield of the ego's inherent struggle for independence and self-determination. The child's break with its infantile, narcissistic attachments comes about through an internal coantus. It is not culture, but the evolutionary push of the psyche, toward its own mature efflorescence that establishes the ego with its self-sufficient goals and boundaries. Even morality is not something "imposed" from without, for "men have the laws which they make for themselves."[37] The generation of symbols is attributable to the internal

laws of the transpersonal psyche. And the leading set of transformative symbols are those that have to do with sacrifice.

For Freud, the phylogeny of sacrifice can be glimpsed in its
ontogenic correlate, the Oedipal stage. The sacrificial imperative
arises from the demand for renunciation of infantile wish fulfillment exacted by the authority of the paternal superego. The sacrifice is the arena of the persistent tension between the instincts
and conscience. The sacrifice is the ganglion of patriarchal repression. In effect, the sacrifice is the foundation of the "universal
obsessional neurosis" that impedes humanity from growing up. It
arrests the libidinal impulses without translating them.

Indeed, Martin Bergmann's recent research supports both
historically and ethnographically the speculations of Freud. According to Bergmann, the Judeo-Christian form of "ethical monotheism" in the West derives from an epochal struggle between "the
religion of Moses" and an older stratum of devotion in the Ancient
Near East, centered on worship of the god Moloch and the sacrifice of children. Bergmann argues that the worship of Yahwheh
itself may have been a cultic transform of Molochism, as exemplified in the numerous passages from the Old Testament where
"sacrifice of the first born" is an issue and a challenge before the
"new" deity. The sacrifice of children can be understood from the
standpoint of collective psychology as a ritualizing of the violent
instinctuality of the Oedipal stage and the refusal to make the
necessary libidinal renunciation that results in the formation of
the higher, "Mosaic" moral consciousness. Hence, notes Bergmann,
the "covenant" between Israel and Yahweh, which is also the "core
myth of Judaism," needs to be reread "as an example of a highly
disguised oedipal victory."[38]

So far as Jung was concerned, however, the sacrifice is not
coordinate with the phallic misadventures of early childhood, but
with the postpubertal manifestations of genital sexuality. "The
symbol of sacrifice" comes to bear "when the problem arises of
detachment from the parents."[39] "The fantasy of sacrifice means
the giving up of infantile wishes."[40] But the relinquishment of
such wishes depends on more than the paternal threat of castration, It is supported by the religious ideal of sacrifice, leading the
"libido away from the infantile objects (parents) towards the symbolic representatives of the past, i.e., the gods, thus facilitating the
transition from the infantile world to the adult world."[41] The sacrifice overpasses the "incest barrier," not simply by acceding to the
prohibition, but by transforming the instinctual energy originally
cathected toward the pleasure bond with the mother.

In his *Symbols of Transformation*, a work often given lesser weight by "orthodox Jungians," Jung expounded at length the elements and constellations of myth that can be interpreted as the transfiguration of the libido. In the myth, the emblem of the libido on its voyage of transformation is the "hero." According to Jung, the libido "symbolizes itself in the sun or personifies itself in figures with solar attributes."[42] The libido emerges from the womb of the unconscious and radiates the world with the light of consciousness. It is the *sol invictus* that descends into the earth and returns triumphant with the dawn. The darkness and formlessness of the earth signifies the maternal matrix of life in which the primordial libido is sheltered. Union with the earth is incest. But when the hero "goes down" into mother earth, he does not encounter the maternal in its beatific simplicity, but as *mater horribilis*, as a beast, as a serpent, as a dragon, as hell, as death. The submergence in the underworld is the regression to incestual beginnings, the fulfillment of the prepubertal wish. But, instead of finding unrelieved bliss, the hero is thrown into a tiatanic struggle. As the nascent ego, as the libido on its way to self-formation, the hero confronts the mother as the power of dissolution and death. The luminosity of the ego is sunk in darkness; creativity is threatened with annihilation. Although he may be momentarily overcome by the mother's destructive power, the hero manages to slay and vanquish the monster. The hero's embrace with the mother becomes a fight to the death. The ego will either disintegrate in a tragic finale of instinctual regression or subdue the claims of the instincts and climb back to the light of day and to the state of spiritual transformation of the libido.

The hero's agonistic involvement with death and the material "monster" of the instincts parallels the ritual of dismemberment, which is the transitional moment of sacrifice. Jung observes: "We can say that the hero unites himself with the mother in death and at the same time negates the act of union, paying for his guilt with deadly torment. This act of supreme courage and supreme renunciation is also an earnest of supreme salvation, because such a deed alone seems adequate to expiate Adam's sin of unbridled instinctuality. The sacrifice is the very reverse of regression—it is a successful canalization of libido into the symbolic equivalent of the mother, and hence a spiritualization of it."[43]

The "rebirth" of the hero is the liberation of spiritual humanity from the autocracy of the instincts, from the "savage mother of desire." It is the wresting of "consciousness." The achievement of consciousness, however, rests on the emancipation of the ego from the maternal fixation in both a biographical respect and a historical respect. "The world comes into being when man discovers it. But he only discovers it when he sacrifices his containment in the primal mother, the original state of consciousness."[44] Hence, sacrifice is not, as Freud would have it, the vehicle of repression, but the threshold of the actualization of humankind's "higher" possibilities. "Sacrifice brings with it a plenitude of power that is equal to the power of the gods. Even as the world is created by sacrifice, by renouncing the personal tie to childhood, so, according to the teaching of the Upanishads, will be created the new state of man, which can be described as immortal."[45] The self-sacrifice of Christ on the Cross should not be read only as the Oedipal murder of the divine patriarch, but as the "liminal" entryway. The *hieros gamos*, which completes the heroic adventure and the deed of sacrifice, is the goal of maturation. It is the eschaton, or "end," of humanity's quest for realization. In the Christian myth the "first" coming of the Messiah concludes with his sacrificial crucifixion. The "second coming" is in "glory" and is depicted as the sacred marriage of the heavenly bride and the suffering lamb, according to the Book of Revelation. In the hierogamy the male and female duality is overcome, not in the regressivity of Oedipal satisfaction, but as an egalitarian covenant of men and women.

The tragedy of civilization, Freud believed, lies in the bondage of the "feminine" to the obstreperous instincts. But in the Jungian picture the metamorphosis of the libido is commensurate with the transformation of the mask of womanhood from instinctual violence—the imago of the terrible mother—into the creative or "spiritual" feminine. Freud, however, was haunted by the phantom of the castrating father and Oedipal rage. From the Jungian vantage point, the terrible father is only a shadow of the terrible mother and is therefore feckless. The submission to the terrible father under the coercion of patriarchal imperatives and symbols is au fond an abdication of the will to be transformed, to complete the pubertal rite of passage, to come of age. Like a gang of swaggering adolescent boys, the band of sons is never able to accept the reality and dignity of women. When, as Erich Neumann remarks in his application of Jung's insights to the sweep of human culture, "the hero-bearing goddess is blotted out by the Terrible Father," the upshot is "a sterile conservatism and a reactionary identification with the father, which lacks the living, dialectical struggle between generations."[46]

Transposed out of the idiom of Jungian idealism, the adventure of the hero is no longer a "masculine" simulacrum for the formation of personal identity, but corresponds to the rupture of signification and the eventuality of language into the turbulent play of the erotic. But this "adventure" is far more problematic than a transformational theory of the instincts would allow and tends to circumvent the fatality of Oedipal rage, which has its discourse as well. Such a discourse can be detected in the Greek chorus. It is the discourse of the "savage mother" itself. The synecdochal displacement of the erotic that discloses itself as the bathos of the tragic points to the limits of the transformation myth and the "dialectics of sacrifice," which mythically ensure an immortality through violence. In effect, the "tragic hero" of the ancient genre is the metonymic secret of the myth. Tragedy unfurls precisely as the discursive units of "egoautonomy"—Oedipus the king, in effect—are deconstructed as the revelations of a perverse past. If the name *Oedipus* signifies the "lame footed," a colloquialism for the penis, it also implies metaphorically the incestual vectors of phallic desire. In this sense the "Oedipus complex" is far more fundamental than Freud imagined. The "tragedy" of Oedipal consciousness can be found in both the innocence and ultimate disfigurement of eros itself. Western culture is inherently Oedipal, and therefore misogynist, to the degree that it is "phallocentric." But its phallocentrism is also the basis of its discursivity, its reflexivity, and hence its memory.

The "hero myth," therefore, coincides with the metaphysics of the transcendental signified. All disruptions of the dominant grammatics must be resolved through hermeneutical intervention and struggle into a new and supreme "order" of meaning that is inviolable. "Truth is a woman," as Nietzsche said; but the winning of her hand in the last analysis—grammatologically understood, that is—depends on a savaging of previous syntaxes, a reaming of previous fabrics of implication, a rape that is also incestual in the measure it is a union with the very text out of which the longing for it emerged. The signifying of what is "real" and "truthful" is at once a transgression, and if the transgressor is to become conscious of the truth, there must be a "self-binding." The desire of language in and for itself, together with the drive toward its own unfolding, is at the heart of the Oedipal conflict. Desire is of the body, but this "choric" dance of instinctual energies, as Kristeva calls them, becomes both the pretext and context for all that is spoken and thought. As soon as the dance ends in speech, the objects of desire become confused and misdirected. Oedipus "knows" he has slept with mother and murdered his father. All the "names" become confused. The order of philosophical reflection is upended.

Tragic art culminates, while at the same time psychology is the resultant. Psychology or the theory of interiority results because the systems of conventional signification have broken down. Just as Job in the biblical saga is only a "sinner" from the standpoint of an outworn moralist hermeneutic, so Oedipus is not in any sense simply a "criminal" or an ignoramus. The tragedy of Oedipus underscores "the failure of rationality" as ordinary language. Oedipus "interprets all the signs correctly," but he fails "at the level of desire."[47] This failure of desire is the occasion for a new realization of what lies behind the surfaces, what is an intimation of darkness.

The overcoming of Oedipal rage demands the sacrifice, because discursivity itself requires a consolidation of violence, the violence of interpretation, the violence of the transgressive movement toward "truth." If we transpose the notion of a Freudian "instinctual economy" into the register of signification and erasure, then the inscriptions of language are ultimately the inscriptions of "the body." It is when the body erotic is dialectically transfigured through the desire for the undying into the body tragic that "truth" can be reconciled with "method," when the endless Platonic "symposium" that constitutes the project of Western thinking at last comes to an end, when the love of God and the death of God are comprehended as dual dimensions of a signifying totality, in effect, as the *eschatology of the instincts.*

The Freudian, as opposed to the Jungian, project is cognate with the iconoclasm of textual deconstruction. But it also has a larger purpose. We might even say that Freud is the first "deconstructionist" in the postmodern sense because he understands not only the intimate, ontological connection between the act of signification and the moment of desire, but also the relationship between the order of "presence" and the "appearance" of meaning through the experience of absence and the amnesia of origins. The Freudian project, later refined by Jacques Lacan, relies upon an underlying grasp of this relationship to the extent that it assesses the "tragic" quality of both truth and discourse, resulting from the dismembering of the previous context of readings. As Albert Cook comments, the "logos" of tragedy "restructures the Freudian internal myth-dynamics of emotion [and the instincts] into the logical patterns of dialogue and dialectic."[48]

Tragic "catharsis," as Aristotle defined it, is the outcome of a while new symbolic ordering of experience through the myth building and affect engendering design of the play itself. Catharsis is the release of feelings and illusions for the "silent spectator," just as the drama of insight and self-recognition caps the venture into tragic awareness for the "hero" of the enactment. Because tragedy is thoroughly "performative rather than designative,"[49] the movement toward catharsis expresses the total "deconstruction" of all routine signifiers in both the text of the play, and the meta-text of the culture, culminating in a silence of sublime recognition of the power of the gods, the ineluctability of destiny, and the web of desire.[50] Freud's observation that the therapeutic task must be an affirmation of the goddess *ananke*, the underlying force of "necessity," is in reality little more than a modernist adaptation of the "purgative" functions of tragic drama to the scene of analysis, a transfer of the principles of "enactment" from theater to couch.

In psychoanalysis the "performative" aspects of contemporary culture and the language of the body are at last restored to the stage and with much the same "religious" purpose. The recovery of tragedy is the recovery of the signifying power of desire surging behind the textual monolith, in keeping with Freud's archaeology. This is because tragedy itself was enacted, and written down, in ancient times as a kind of *meso-textuality* bridging the immediacy of phallic ritual and the new, "civilizing" literacy of the poets, philosophers, and orators. That may be the reason the tragedians themselves, as Charles Segal has suggested, were fascinated with the origins of language and the genealogy of writing.[51] The "thing" of the play was recognized as problematic in its own right, as caught between two layers of signification, as concealing a Dionyisian past and an Apollonian present. It was a "stranger" in the Athenian house of culture and could be performed only to the degree that it was constantly searched for its forms of concealment.

Freud's "tragedy of the instincts" is at once a prelude to the triumph of reason in its dialectical trajectory and an explanation of what is often identified as the "schizoid" character of his attitude toward somatic nature. The post-Oedipal "sacrifice," the wailing of regret for what is now known and the rending of innocent sight, that every "man" makes on the altar of the "god" logos is necessary if the tragic cycle of unmediated desire can ever be broken. The "law" of the father causes deep rage and conflict, but it is also the occasion for the transformation of desire into symbol, for the "deconstruction of the drive" in the "tragic" instant of self-knowledge and the achievement of discourse. Girard's metonymy of the scapegoat, which is also the production of the sacred as a representation of "authorized" violence, thus is turned on its head. The "metonymic secret" of the act of sacrifice is quite the opposite of Girard's view that violence is now socially contained in the power of representation. On the contrary, the secret is lodged in the de-potentiation of the signified itself, in the collapse of the "immortal" referent into the tragic condition of humanity rather than the glorification of the hero. Here we also find the more essential meaning of Hegel's "Gologotha of Absolute Spirit," which foretokens a philosophical world beyond the *disiecta membra* of desire, beyond the "theological" imagination, beyond the totalism of representation—the world of truth in its "speculative" unveiling.

If deconstruction is the death of God as writing at the end of theology, philosophy as Hegel understood it must be a thinking more deeply than thought has ever ventured. It must be a thinking the "truth," a *thinking the body*. But it must be a thinking through of the body to its very eschatology, to its disclosure as divine representation, the "new Adam," the personality that coincides with the *parousia*. It must be a thinking of the body as transfigured. The transfiguration of the body is *prefigured* in the mobilization and pure movement and unity of the soma through eros to its clarifying representation in the "next" dimension, through the artistry of temporal disclosure that in itself symbolizes the immanence of the eternal, through the sudden entrainment of all signifying processes and intentions within the final night of writing and at the dusty nadir of Ezekiel's valley of "dead bones," through the power of the ecstatic coordination of flesh and desire so that death is no longer the transcendent sign of the erotic— *through the dance.*

Notes

1. See *inter alia* Peter Homans, *Theology After Freud* (Indianapolis: Bobbs-Merrill, 1970) and Richard Rubenstein, *The Religious Imagination* (Indianapolis: Bobbs-Merrill, 1968).

2. The most important of these works are J. J. Bachofen, *Myth, Religion, and Mother Right: Selected Writings*, trans. Ralph Manheim (Princeton, N.J.: Princeton University Press, 1967); Robert Briffault, *The Mothers* (New York: Grosset and Dunlap, 1963).

3. Freud's theory of sexual development is summarized in *An Outline of Psychoanalysis*, trans. James Strachey (New York: W. W. Norton, 1949).

4. Sigmund Freud, "The Future of an Illusion," in *The Complete Works*, vol. 21, p. 24.

5. Ibid., p. 44.

6. See Freud, "A Seventeenth-Century Demonological Neurosis," in *The Complete Works*, vol. 19, pp. 72–108.

7. Sigmund Freud, "Civilization and Its Discontents," in *The Complete Works*, vol. 21, p. 102.

8. Ibid., p. 115.

9. Sigmund Freud, "The Ego and the Id," in *The Complete Works*, vol. 19, p. 35.

10. Ibid., p. 35.

11. Freud, "The Future of an Illusion," p. 42.

12. Sigmund Freud, "Moses and Monotheism," in *The Complete Works*, vol. 22, p. 132.

13. Robertson Smith, *The Religion of the Semites* (New York: Meridian Books, 1956), p. 313.

14. Ibid., p. 412.

15. Sigmund Freud, *Totem and Taboo* (New York: W. W. Norton, 1950), p. 140.

16. Ibid., n.1, pp. 139–140.

17. Freud comments in a footnote: "The lack of precision in what I have written in the text above, its abbreviation of the time factor and its compression of the whole subject-matter, may be attributed to the reserve necessitated by the nature of the topic. It would be foolish to aim at exactitude in such questions as it would be unfair to insist upon certainty." Ibid., n. 1, pp. 142–143.

18. Ibid., p. 141.

19. Sigmund Freud, "New Introductory Lectures on Psychoanalysis," in *The Complete Works*, vol. 22. p. 95.

20. Freud, *Totem and Taboo*, p. 145.

21. Ibid., p. 147.

22. Freud, *Totem and Taboo*, pp. 151–152.

23. Eli Sagan, *Cannibalism and Human Aggression* (New York: Haper and Row, 1975), p. 52.

24. Ibid., pp. 64–66.

25. Freud, *Totem and Taboo*, p. 154.

26. Freud, "Moses and Monotheism," p. 129.

27. Ibid., p. 136.

28. See David Bakan, *Sigmund Freud and the Jewish Mystical Tradition* (New York: Schocken Books, 1965).

29. Ibid., p. 158.

30. For a discussion of Freud and the "feminist" issues, particularly as they relate to patriarchy and the repression of women, see Dorothy Dinnerstein, *The Mermaid and the Minotaur: Sexual Arrangements and Human Malaise* (New York: Harper and Row, 1976). Freud, as is common knowledge, did not deal with the kinds of questions raised both then and now by feminists concerning sex rolse and the social position of women. Many of Freud's obiter dicta about women mirrored the conventional prejudices of his day. Yet the revolutionary implications of Freud's basic theories actually work against these sorts of prejudices. As Marie Jahoda has noted in defense of Freud's psychoanalytic insights about sexuality: "When Freud, with all his contradictions, deliberately turned his great mind to an examination as a radical and revolutionary thinker, no longer tied to the status quo, no longer essentially conservative as he was in accepting the stereotype about women . . ." *Freud and the Dilemmas of Psychology* (London: the Hogarth Press, 1977), p. 89.

31. See Raphael Patai, *The Hebrew Goddess* (New York: KTAV Publishing House, 1967), pp. 289ff.

32. Gershom Scholem, *On the Kabbalah and Its Symbolism*, trans. Ralph Manheim (New York: Schocken Books, 1969), pp. 138ff.

33. Bakan, *Sigmund Freud*, p. 278.

34. C. G. Jung, "Freud and Psychoanalysis," trans. R. F. C. Hull, *The Collected Works of C. G. Jung*, ed. Herbert Read et al. (New York: Pantheon Books, 1961), vol. 4, p. 124.

35. Ibid., p. 125.

36. C. G. Jung, "Symbols of Transformation," *Collected Works*, vol. 5, p. 137.

37. Jung, "Freud and Psychoanalysis," p. 154.

38. Martin S. Bergmann, *In the Shadow of Moloch: The Sacrifice of Children and Its Impact on Western Religions* (New York: Columbia University Press, 1992), p. 88. Evidence that human sacrifice itself was relatively widespread throughout the Ancient Near East is presented in Alberto R. W. Green, *The Role of Sacrifice in the Ancient Near East*, American Schools of Oriental Research Dissertation Series 1 (Missoula, Mont.: Scholars Press, 1975).

39. Jung, "Freud and Psychoanalysis," p. 154.

40. Ibid, p. 155.

41. Ibid., p. 156.

42. Jung, "Symbols of Transformation," p. 207.

43. Ibid., p. 263.

44. Ibid., p. 417.

45. Ibid., p. 420.

46. Erich Neumann, *The Origins and History of Consciousness*, trans. R. F. C. Hull (New York: Pantheon Books, 1954), pp. 189–190.

47. Simon Goldhill, *Reading Greek Tragedy* (London: Cambridge University Press, 1986), p. 221.

48. Albert S. Cook, *Enactment: Greek Tragedy* (Chicago: Swallow Press, 1971), p. 36. The Freudian argument is also developed in a much more sophisticated way by C. Fred Alford, *The Psychoanalytic Theory of Greek Tragedy* (New Haven, Conn.: Yale University Press, 1992).

49. Cook, ibid., p. 49.

50. One might argue, as Jon D. Mikalson had done, that, because Greek tragedy is preoccupied with strategies of desire and the complexity of myriad forms of representation, rather than the "unities" classicism with its aristocratic biases always spoke of, it is one, important key to the semiotics of popular culture. Although Mikalson's exposition is not very sophisticated methologically, it is very suggestive. See *Honor Thy Gods: Popular Religion in Greek Tragedy* (Chapel Hill: University of North Carolina, 1991).

51. See Charles Segal, *Interpreting Greek Tragedy: Myth, Poetry, Text* (Ithaca, N.Y.: Cornell University Press, 1986), p. 96.

Section III

The Body Transfigurative

Chapter 10

Rhythm Is a Dancer

I have discovered the dance.

Isadora Duncan

Nietzsche's last written words were a disjunctive proposition: "Dionysus" or "the Crucified?" The genesis of Nietzschean philosophy, and hence of all postmodernism, resides in many respects in this question. Eric Blondel has dubbed Nietzsche the philosopher of "tragic knowledge," a knowledge deracinated and destructured by virtue of its reduction of reality to appearance, of science to art, of discourse to mimesis, a "double discourse" that "subverts itself through metaphor."[1] In *The Birth of Tragedy*, Nietzsche set forth his strange form of "cultural hermeneutic" as a preparation for his signature attack on the Western metaphysical tradition, which he identified with a Christianized Platonism. The "art" of the tragic derives from the Dionysian dithyramb, according to Nietzsche, even though such a view has been rejected by the majority of "modern" classical scholars. It is interesting that, in the high tide of "postmodernist" writing, however, this peculiar Nietzschean "genealogy" has been suddenly revived with the even more shocking supposition that the whole of the Athenian theatrical "spectacle" can be understood afresh as a representational universe, or complex of significations, that are ultimately rooted in the archaic Dionysian experience.[2]

Derrida, in his inaugural essay for the seminal collection of essays on philosophical postmodernism, *The New Nietzsche*, speaks of Dionysus when he begins, "I speak of woman."[3] But he does one speak of both Dionysus and woman's body, other than in the

177

obvious way that the latter is the "god" of women in Greek religion and the incarnation of the "subversive" power of women's mysteries against the eristic rationality of Athenian civil society, as *The Bacchae* all too well lays bare? As the "Asiatic stranger," Dionysus stands in synecdochcal relationship to the entirety of Hellenic and, by extension, Occidental culture. As deity, he is the *sacred other*, and he particularly embodies a "divine" alterity in relationship to the familiar philosophical standpoint that valorizes the psychic as opposed to the somatic, the masculine as opposed to the feminine, pure discursivity a opposed to aesthetic symbolization. He is "woman's god," because he is the "dark" version of the transcendental signified at the end of the chain of phallic representation that codifies all cultural anxiety. In *The Bacchae*, Dionysus destroys Pentheus by mirroring the latter's fantasies and fears, spinning a web of confusion, self-doubt, and deception that leads to the king's demise.

This precisely "mimetic" character of Dionysus, as Froma Zeitlin argues, typifies the psychology of woman in the classical age.[4] Woman is the Greeks' "unknown self," and she becomes the seemingly accidental, yet essential, subject matter of tragedy. The "tragic space" of the feminine that interpenetrates with classic rationality is inhabited by bodies. It is both a space and a syntax that is "constantly under suspicion," that is "hypocritical" (from the Greek *hypokrites*, or "one who plays a role," who wears masks). "Woman is the mimetic creature par excellence,"[5] because she is the stuff of pure representation, as the body erotic must be in the last analysis. Her way of "seeing," as we discern in the figure of Cassandra, is toward the hidden warp of tragic events, in contradistinction to the mythic heroism of desire and action. Dionysus is the "altarity"—in Mark C. Taylor's sense—of the logic of signification, inasmuch as "he" is the ultimate desideratum about which that logic alludes and that it can never compass. Dionysus is indeed the "stranger" as a dangerous guest in the household of thought. He is the "unthought," but only because the body has not been thought—as woman has not be thought—in the West. He is not, of course, the "real signification" behind the complex of body-woman that is "naturally" thought as the "object" of desire, as the consummate representation of the patriarchal gaze. Just as Dionysus materializes and vanishes at will in the theater, so he evanesces from the circuit of signification. This vanishing act reflects the mimetic echoing back and forth between presence and representation. But it also points toward what may we really mean by *theological thinking*. Could theological thinking, in a word, be the thinking of the "divine drive" (*Dio-nisus*), the fathomlessness of desire? Could that not be what we really mean by a *batho-theology*, a thinking of and from the depths? Could it not be the thinking of the body in the most "transcendental" sense?

Just as the ancient theater of tragedy is foreshadowed by the "satyr play," the pure buffoonery and half-consciousness of phallic desire, so the theological thought of Dionysus carries us back to the "carnival," the procession of masks, the contradictory sensuality that remains simultaneously spoken and "scandalously" silent. "Everything profound loves masks," wrote Nietzsche.[6] We must remember that in Greek drama the mask, or disguise, is the "sacramental" element that renders the theatrical—that which is "envisioned"—*religious*. It is religious, because it is "mimetic" not of the things of the everyday world, but of the "beings of the other world," what are "holy" and "horrific."[7] Yet the greatest profundity is the body, a nudity interwound with clothing, which by its very concealment and suggestion becomes the very somatic signifier. The mask manifests the god because it conceals the face, just as the garment reveals the transcendence of the body through its covering and "dis-closure." One need only consider the mystical importance ascribed in pious quarters to Jesus' death shroud to understand the diacritical exchange in the religious imagination between clothing and the sacred.

Theological thought as somatology, as a strange kind of *sartorics* of the "flesh" (*sarx*), is but the true of effort of "theology" in its most traditional sense. If all "theology," as Hegel argued, is the thinking not simply of "God" in the most formal and abstract way, but the *thinking of the incarnation*, then the Johannine concept of the "word made flesh" (*sarx* brought within the full panoply of logos) is what we have in mind. Indeed, there honestly can be no higher task for "theology"—theology understood not as a "dogmatics" or a "system of exposition" based on some kind of kerygmatic encounter with Jesus, but as theological thinking that thinks deeply, thinks deeply into the flesh, anticipates and schematizes the secret and fullness of the "Christian faith," the *resurrection of the body*! In our Gallo-Germanic—let us say our *Aryan* or *Carolignian*—obsessions with the God of the skies, we have forgotten, as Nietzsche's exhorted us, to remain "faithful to the earth." This faithfulness has often been confused as a fetishism and a weird kind of "New Age" reconstructionism with respect to now forgotten and repressed archetypal projections. Goddess cults, eco-political parodies of the Third Internationale, the latest romantic rehash of "noble savage" sentimentality with a concentration on the aboriginal peoples of the planet—all abound. But this faithfulness is none other than that of the wanderer who returns to one's lover. Incarnation is indeed the "hierogamy," the "sacred marriage," of two worlds, of two conjugate orders in the universe of all signs, of "thought" (logos) and "flesh." It may, indeed, be that in the whole history of "Christian theology," the incarnational axis of faith has never been thought. It has never been thought because the "word" becoming "flesh" challenges, disrupts, and overturns the hidden premises of "logo-centric" and metaphysico-Platonist Christianity, which even in its Protestant forms has remained dominant for two millennia. If, as "biblical theologians" have told us, the ancient idea of the "body" is wrapped up with the formational concept of the redemption of the "flesh,"[8] then thinking the body is equivalent to thinking what "salvation" means in a most essential manner.

We confront here what is genuinely meant by the *eschatology of the instincts*. For, if *desire* in the Platonic sense is always the yearning for a transcendent fulfillment, the goal of *philo-sophia* and any constructive *theo-logia* is inherently beyond the limits of re-presentation; it is beyond the "forms" of truth; it is a longing for the "unveiling" of truth; it is eschatological! Theological thinking, therefore, as the thinking of the body, as the thinking through of the "incarnation," as the thinking of the "flesh" in its radical format as "carnality" and as "incarnality," as a thinking of the play of signs of the fullness of time and history and culture authentically attains the Hegelian thought of the thinking of the "depths of Spirit." For, if Spirit is the divine reflection into itself and for itself, then the "otherness" and alterity of what remains "unredeemed" is taken back into itself. Incarnational thinking becomes eschatological thinking, for such a thinking is required to think beyond the "tragic" consequences of the aim of the desires in their soaring toward self-transcendence toward a "fulfillment" from above. In the tragic myth of flight toward the sun, as Mark Taylor says, "Hegel"—*aigle* or "the eagle"—soars too high and plummets in a fiery wreckage.[9] The eagle flies, then burns. The burning is the catharsis, the dismembering, the "knowing," the aged solace of Oedipus. Taylor, although is an Hegelian by background, would have Hegel dismembered, "deconstructed" in the dark disquiet of the tragic aftermath of Western civilization. The question of postmodern religiosity is not "Athens or Jerusalem?" it is "Hegel or Oedipus?" But the Hegel of the "rose," the Hegel of the higher and erotic beauty, as opposed to the Hegel that burns in the fire, is the Hegel that points toward the eschatology of all signs, the Hegel of the unwritten last chapter of the *Phenomenol-ogy*, the Hegel of Easter morning, the Hegel in its angle toward the sun must ride atop the storm and be borne upon the "lightning flash," whose traces are left on the empty shroud of Jesus.

That, proleptically, is the importance of all "incarnational" theology. The eagle flies . . . and is transfigured! Oedipus dies. "Hegel" walks the road to Emmaeus.

The "unity" of the fire and the rose of which Eliot speaks poetically is the imaginal clue, however, to what we might call a *postmodern theological wisdom* that enfolds within itself at the same time the unity of Dionysus and Christ, of tragedy and resurrection, of "flesh" and "spirit," of truth. Theological thinking must embrace the thought of Dionysus, because only by struggling with the "dismembered" legacy of its signs and prophecies can it hope to receive the "parousiatic" flash of comprehension that comes in the "night when all cows are black." In the maenadic fire, the bones and limbs of dead cultural representations are consumed forever. Yet there is also a retrieval. After the fire, according to Eco's novel, when all representations have been burned up, there is still the act of "signification," and that signification is the "name" of the rose.

The name of the rose has "nothing to do with Dionysus," as the guardians of Athenian civil culture, the culture of the West, claimed "hypocritically" respecting their tragic drama. The rose is not a tragic signifier, because it is the sign of the eschaton. Its "name" is the unspeakable name. Yet it grows out of the Dionysian inferno. In that respect it might be thought in "dialectical" tension with the fire. The rose grows out of a chthonic past and toward the infinity of the stars. Its form, enclosing its beauty, is in both its flower and its thorns—like desire. The name of the rose is both *alpha* and *omega*, the protology of the flames and the eschatology of the sun, the body to be burned and the body to be raised. The "rose garden"—the garden of Gethsemane, which is transformed in symbolic space into the locus of the empty tomb of Easter—is where theological thinking must take origin. Thinking about the body must commence at the site where beauty and earth are conjoined, where the eagle alights for a time. The thought of incarnation is the thought of disjunctions, of ruptures, of tears, or thorns; but it is also of the instantaneous and fleeting "union" of the orgasmic ecstasy, of coupling, of joy, of roses.

The venture into Dionysus, of course, reminds us of the quest of Nietzsche. Nietzsche's Zarathustra is the "Christ figure" who has become Dionysiac, who has affirmed eternal recurrence,

who is able to "will" all that is and was. Zarathustra is the West-
ern philosopher who has "overcome" in thinking metaphysico-
Platonic Christianity, yet has not thought past it. First and foremost,
Zarathustra is a "dancer."

The dance of Zarathustra is what we mean by the *postmodern*.
The overcoming of metaphysics and the entry into the postmodern
is also the invitation to the dance, to the language of the body, to
the "chora," to the deconstruction of all the "postures" of philosophy and thought and the transformation of all texts and inscriptions of the past to be read into the "hypertext" of popular culture,
to the semiotic rhythms of the writhing and comingling global
civilization that is on its way to becoming the matrix of the
parousiac "flesh" that manifests when the music is over at the
"end," at the "flash." "Rhythm is a dancer," as the global hit
single by the rap-disco group Snap goes. Rhythm must dance. The
chora must become articulate. Desire must become signification.
The body must be transfigured.

Why do we, as well as Zarathustra, dance? Why is the now
forgotten cult of Dionysus hard to recover, but it was in essence
dancing? Although David danced before the Lord, why has theology remained a wallflower in the dance of the time? According to
Erick Hawkins, the dance "happens"; it is pure *mimesis*. The dancing body is a "clear place";[10] its beauty is in its effortlessness, its
movement of signification without "deconstructive" lesions, without dismemberment, without a tragic finale. The dance rises and
dies with its background rhythms; it is both their pure, visual
articulation and their effacement. Dance is not the artistic "representation" of the body. Like drama, it is "enactment" or *aisthesis*,
the making manifest of what is essentially and "epiphantically"
the semiotic procession and dim, evocations of desire that we call
bodily existence. Both dance and drama are *dromena*, "things done."
"What is the difference?" asks Snap in the lyrics of a song? "The
body, the motion." The dance is unceasing *differance*, but only in
the sense that the "differencing" of the different flashes of signification is what we mean ontologically by the body. The body is
desire pulsating, pushing forward, transcending itself, and achieving a shifting, temporal unity through language, memory, and
experience. But, at a primordial level, that is also true of the
dance. The body and the dance are, figuratively, one.

If the metanarrative of the history of philosophy centers on
the quest of epistemology, or the theories of "knowledge," the
motif of aesthetic culture is that of the body and its controlling
category "beauty." The connecting point between the philosophi-

cal order of discursive "truthfulness" and the aesthetic order is, of course, the category of beauty. But the beautiful as a form of intelligibility that regulates the act of *aistheses* can come from only a more "pretheoretical" level of semiosis and intentionality than the constitutive phenomenology of cognition. It must come from the body itself. The body, not the mind, is beautiful, because beauty requires movement. "Beautiful movement is true movement."[11] Even Plato understood this principle when in *The Symposium* he found that he could not separate the sense of the beautiful from the ascent of eros. The beautiful is not "formal," contrary to neo-classical or even modernist aesthetics, because the moment it is severed from the perturbations of desire, it becomes something else. The beautiful can never be, as Kant too understood, a type of "sense knowledge." The beautiful is the dramatics, the excessive self-signifying, of "sensuality." It is what Kristeva has termed a *hypersign*, the idealization of the full directionality of desire, that "never disappoints the libido."[12] It is most perfectly consummated in the sight of the body, which is why Greek art was long considered the "highest art." Greek art declined according to the canons of taste when the sense of the body changed, when the experience of the fourth dimension was added, when monumentality became movement, when Western culture was transformed into what Guy deBord has termed the *society of the spectacle,*[13] when the dance returned. If "dance is a metaphor for existence," it is because "the very ground of dance is the complete entity of body and mind, heightened in its doing, in time."[14] This grounding of dance, says Hawkins, betokens its "sacredness," its signifying completeness, a teleological ensemble, a realization of the intentionality of the senses.

The teleology of the senses and the eschatology of instincts can be understood in relation to the theological problem of incarnation itself and why it has not been thought. The Western effort to think through the "question" of the senses from the skeptics through the empiricists to the phenomenologists has always been couched in the terms set by Plato's *Theatetus;* that is, the elusiveness of "presence" and the reliability of predicative judgment. The integral connection between sense and signification, which is linked to the "psycho"-analytic of desire, however, can be viewed as the prius of aesthetic inquiry. Kristeva reminds us that life itself is "signification" and that semiotics as a "science" must take precedence over all other types of inferential endeavors, especially when it comes to the deciphering of "the unconscious meaning of humanity."[15] What the postmodern, aesthetic analytic of the body shows, however, is that the modernist dichotomy between the conscious and the unconscious may be misplaced. The resolution may be harbored within the somatological itself, the source of signs and therefore of both conscious and unconscious formations and representations. Such a view, indeed, was the objective of the later work of Merleau-Ponty, who developed what might be called a "somato-epistemology" along these lines.[16] The theory of the dance is also theory of the signifying body, and it may be the key to the "religious," which brings us back to Dionysus.

According to Simon Goldhill, the Dionysian is the "possibility of performance."[17] All performance "focuses the question of representation, of adequate realization, of determined meanings."[18] But it is as well the site of *sparagmos*, the "dismembering." The tragic text, as we have seen, is a kind of *sparagmos*. In its original enactment it served to disconnect the syntax of moral and cultural expectations, leading to cathartic rejuvenation. In its diachronic appropriation it requires a "violence of reading," a synthesis that is concomitantly an "effacement" of previous signs. We do not generally appreciate tragedy in the same way we extol "great literature" because of this effacement. Tragedy, if we are to benefit from it, requires that we become astounded and distraught like Oedipus. That is why tragedy can never truly be part of a "canon." The possibilities of "performance"—and "performance" is the postmodern principle—in the Dionysian "carnival" steer us toward both the rupture of all previous textual hermeneutics and the "stepping out" of the theological thinker into the living theater of popular culture.

Dionysus, like Jesus, was the deity of the *demos*, of the populace. The grounding of theology in popular culture is the celebration of the possibilities of performance. Can theology dance? To dance is to bring about the end of theology in the dance, in the enactment of desire, in manifestation of the "classic text" of the body. Theological thinking of and through the body is the only honest form of "liberation theology," because it does not assume the crypto-privilege of an interpretative stance, whether that stance by Marxism, feminism, environmentalism, or ethnicism. Thinking the body means to "identify" with the totality of the underside of all privileged, global communication, even that communication which claims to speak in the name of the "oppressed" and the disenfranchised while continuing to wear the robes and tiaras of its own elite discourse. Theology must become somatology, which means it must learn to "dance in the streets." It must dance as the rhythms of the street.

The history of Dionysus is only beginning to surface. There is no doubt that Dionysus is, and was, the "dark god." Dionysus' destructive power is all-to-well known and was portrayed ambivalently even by a literary radical such as Euripides. For theological thought to think the Dionysian does not mean some kind of libertinism and recrudescence of the ideology of the "pagan." A "new Dionysianism," coupled with the death of God movement, was attempted, and aborted, a generation ago.[19] It spoke of "love's body" and liberation, but meant little more than an antinomianism of the spirit. It did not understand what may be regarded as the somatic or "corporate" ecology of a new "Christian" faithfulness, if not an ethic, that derives from the incarnational dyadism of flesh and word.

Various current and dated scholarship has linked early Christian symbology to the broad type of Dionysian cult active in the Mediterranean basin.[20] The Johannine association of Jesus with the vine is probably reminiscent of the Dionysian cult. When Jesus referred to himself as the "true vine," he was most likely expropriating the Dionysian title—or at least making an association with certain Dionysian practices already present in Palestine—and interpolating with the Jewish complex of messianic associations, a move that accounts in part for the easy identification of early Gentile Christians, who had no appreciation of the Hebraic context of the "Master's teaching," with Jesus. This homology of popular religious forms, which explains the tremendous syncretistic capacity of what was originally the odd "Asiatic" gospel of the Nazarenes, can be detected in an incident described by Karl Kerenyi. Until the late seventh century A.D., wine-treaders still uttered the cry "Dionysus" while they worked, and the wine press itself was seen as a "ritual" agent of the god's dismemberment. The treaders also wore the masks of satyrs, a practice forbidden by the Second Council of Constantinople in 691 A.D., which required that they chant "Kyrie Eleison" instead.[21] The most convincing arguments demonstrating that early Christianity can be seen, in part, as a system of symbolical transforms that are anchored in a diffuse, agrarian Dionysianism come from the historian of religions Wilhem Bousset. Bousset maintains that there existed a pagan "kyrios cult," based on the worship of Dionysus, whose high holy day was January 6, the original Christmas, and that tremendously influenced Christianity in Roman times.[22] The archaeology of Christianity from the history of religious perspective, like the archaeology of sacrificial practices, reveals a deeper "logos" to the theological enterprise that has not been spoken yet within the "tradition."

The hostility of early Christian apology to the popular culture in which it was so intimately embedded, and from which it feared possible absorption, has had much to do with the formation of an "orthodoxy" of representation on which the "history of theology" and contemporary "constructive" or "systematic" theology ulti- mately rides. Because of the anxiety of ancient Graeco-Roman elites about the body and about woman, which by the Middle Ages had been codified as an unbiblical ethic of asceticism, was so strong from the beginning that the foundational writings of Western religious thought are thoroughly misogynistic as well as "metaphysical" in the contemporary philosophical meaning of the word. Women flocked to Christ in the same way they danced with Dionysus, a fact that most contemporary religious feminism in its romantic neo-paganism has ignored.

But theological thinking can go only so far with a historical revisionism that unravels the secrets behind its conceptual contra- dictions of the "tradition." Theological thinking is "historical" only to the extent that it seeks to recover the concreteness of the bodily context and the "en-gendering" of the primitive, cultural signs through which its ancestry first spoke. The problem with the "his- torical sources" for this kind of theological reflection is that, be- cause they were popular and hence nonliterate, they are mute today. But their analogues today have been discovered by the semiotic inventory and anatomizing that is coming to be loosely called *cultural studies*. Theological thinking must invest in these new forms of the "humanities" to the extent they are not borrow- ing the segment of the field that claims to be "critical" and de- scriptive but is so loaded with Marxist ideology that it has become laughable, ideological, and inconsequential. The thought of Dionysus is the thought of the beginnings of the popular culture hermeneutic that is signified in the phrase *Christ's body*. It is a thinking about the power of the dance, about the dynamics of signification, about desire, about the flesh, about "God" as the last postmodern metaphor.

Rhythm is a dancer. Rhythm is felt in the flesh; it dances in the lights of the electrified city at night. "You can feel it every- where," as the song goes. It is felt in the global movement of engendered, and engendering, bodies. It dances in the discourse. The discourse entwines; it is interrupted; it bend back upon itself. It is thought. It becomes thinking in its deepest sense, at its "theological depths." We do indeed, like David, "dance before the Lord."

The music never ends.
The fire blazes.
She is rhythm.
We are dancing.
The rose is in her hair.
The eagle takes flight.
Out of the darkness a flashing . . .
The sign of the "Son of Man" appears in the heavens . . .
Parousia . . .
The body is transfigured . . .
In a twinkling . . .

Notes

1. Eric Blondel, *Nietzsche: The Body and Culture* (Stanford, Calif.: Stanford University Press, 1991), p. 28.

2. See John J. Winkler and Fromai Zeitlin (eds.), *Nothing to Do with Dionysus: Athenian Drama in Its Social Context* (Princeton, N.J.: Princeton University Press, 1990).

3. Derrida, *The New Nietzsche*, ed. David B. Allison (New York: Dell Publishing Co., 1977).

4. See Froma I. Zeitlin, "Playing the Other," in *Nothing to Do with Dionysus*, pp. 63–96.

5. Ibid., p. 85.

6. Francisco R. Adrados, *Festival, Comedy, and Tragedy: The Greek Origins of Theatre* (Leiden: E. J. Brill, 1975), p. 256.

7. See John A. T. Robinson, *The Body* (London: SPCK, 1964).

9. See Mark Taylor, *Tears* (Albany, N.Y.: State University of New York Press, 1990).

10. See Erick Hawkins, *The Body Is a Clear Place and Other Statements on Dance* (Princeton, N.J.: Princeton Book Company, 1992), p. 64.

11. Ibid., p. 76.

12. Julia Kristeva, *Black Sun: Depression and Melancholia*, trans. Leon Roudiez (New York: Columbia University Press, 1989). p. 99.

13. Guy deBord, *Society of the Spectacle* (Detroit: Black and Red, 1983).

14. Hawkins, *The Body Is a Clear Place*, p. 119.

15. Julia Kristeva, *Language the Unknown: An Initiation into Linguistics* (New York: Columbia University Press, 1989), p. 287.

16. See Merleau-Ponty, *Signs and the Primacy of Perception*, p.

17. Ian McAuslan and Peter Walcol, eds., *Greek Tragedy* (New York: Oxford University Press, 1993).

18. Ibid., p. 284.

19. The term "new Dionysianism" was used in the 1960s to refer to the works, and influence on academic culture, of the writings of Norman O. Brown and Hebert Marcuse. Brown and Marcuse sought to show how the "Dionysian" liberation of the instincts would promote a transformation in the body politic of late industrial capitalism. See among other works Brown, Norman O. Brown, *Life Against Death: The Psychoanalytical Meaning of History* (New York: Random House, 1962); Norman O. Brown, *Love's Body* (New York: Random House, 1966); Hebert Marcuse, *Eros and Civilization: A Philosophical Inquiry into Freud* (Boston: Beacon Press, 1966).

20. See among other works Wiktor A. Daszewski, *Dionysus der Erlöser: Griesche Mythen im Spätantiken Antiken*. Cypern: Wiktor A. Daszewski, 1986; Peter Hay, "The Dionysus Connection," *Performing Arts* 26(May 1, 1992). I am also indebted for this analysis to the work of my former student Sharon Coggan of the University of Colorado at Denver for her doctoral research in this area.

21. Karl Kerenyi, p. 65.

22. See Wilhelm Bousset, *Kyrios Christos: A History of the Belief in Christ from the Beginning of Christianity to Irenaeus* (Nashville, Tenn.: Abingdon Press, 1970).

INDEX